ASSAULT RESPONSE AND PRISONER CONTROL TACTICS

Police Bujitsu Club, LLC

FOR LAW ENFORCEMENT AGENCIES Everywhere

Written By
GARY G. ALBRECHT

ASSAULT RESPONSE AND PRISONER CONTROL TACTICS

Police Bujitsu Club, LLC

FOR LAW ENFORCEMENT AGENCIES Everywhere

Written By

GARY G. ALBRECHT

Harrison House Publishing

PUBLISHER'S NOTE

The opinions expressed in this manuscript are solely the opinions of the author in addition, do not represent the opinions or thoughts of the Publisher. The author has represented and warranted full ownership and/or legal right to publish all the materials in this book.

The publisher does not have any control over and does not assume any responsibility for author or third party websites or their content.

Harrison House Publishing
www.theharrisonhousepublishing.com
info@theharrisonhousepublising.com
ISBN: 978-0-9861071-1-5
Library of Congress Control Number: 2015952721
Harrison House Publishing and the "HH" logo are trademarks belonging to
Harrison House Publishing.
PRINTED IN THE UNITED STATES OF AMERICA

INDEX

CHAPTER 1

CHAPTER 2

CHAPTER 3

CHAPTER 4

CHAPTER 5

ACKNOWLEDGEMENTS

This book was a long time coming from the original lesson plans drawn up more that twenty five years ago. In that thirty plus years, it has grown from just the original idea to being an incredible tool that hundreds of officers have been able to use on the streets. It has been handed down from the originator, Andries Cane, to the student. I am that honored student, Gary G. Albrecht. I was told " Here is forty years of my life, and the thousands of hours of learning what works best and easiest for officers on the street. Take this and let it grow with your knowledge." Well it has grown, with more study of Aikido and current police tactics, but the foundation is still the original.

I was able to produce this book through the help of my many friends and fellow officers. I want to thank them all.

Vera Mendoza

First my wonderful wife needs a special thanks for supporting me and has giving me the time it took away from us to work on this book, as well as the time to teach classes in between. Being an artist, and a student of martial arts, she has a great eye for arrangement and design in helping me put things together. She also edited this book, of which my writing skills have a lot to be desired. Thank you sweetheart.

Andries Cane

Thank you for all the years of guidance and training as my sensei, and as well as the friendship that you have given me. He also shot most of the pictures for this book and the next few books to come. Thank you for the encouragement you gave to me to write this book and to expand the original concepts to better instruct the officers on the street. You are one in a few.

David Morales

Thanks to David for being my "Uke" in the pictures. He was new to law enforcement at the time of these pictures and now has become a fine officer, still with eagerness to learn, not only in law enforcement, but in everything he does. He has a promising career as an officer and a student of Bujitsu, as well as being a wonderful individual. Thanks David for your help in this book.

Joseph Rodriguez

Again a special thanks to Joseph, for the multitude of computer problems he has solved for me. Thank you for all of your Tech support. He also steps in when I need something done. He has helped with taking photos and for the retakes that were necessary in a few cases. This young man has been a special friend to me and someone I can depend on anytime. Thanks for your confidence in me.

This course has evolved over the past years making it easier for the officers, BUT EFFECTIVE. What makes this course different from other courses out there is the Control. As police officers, control over an assailant during and after an attack is of vital importance.

These techniques have been taken from several different martial arts forms to make them more effective. This also gives the officers on the street a wider knowledge of martial arts. These techniques are taken from various martial arts styles to make the officers safe on the street. It is my hope that these techniques will give them the skills necessary to make it home to their families after every shift.

May GOD bless these officers, and I thank Him for all these wonderful family and friends that have given me the encouragement and help to write this book for police officers everywhere.

FOREWORD

As a young boy, I was always fascinated by feats of strength and our many super heroes of the time. I was never too fond of school work and was what I would call an average student. I guess you could call me more of a doer than a thinker. Not knowing what I may be good at, I tried many sports from grade school on. I was small boned and short in stature but was blessed in being an above average athlete. I first tried track and field and became a very good sprinter and competitive in the other field events.

While in junior high school, I excelled in physical fitness completing record times in sprints, rope climbing, push-ups, sit-ups, and anything physical I could find. It was here in junior high school that I found a teacher that was very special in my life, Mr. Ben Heron. He was a science teacher who also taught a special class of trampoline and tumbling early in the morning before school started. I took one look at this and knew that I wanted to learn to this skill. He welcomed me and taught me many things. After a few months, I was doing exhibitions of tumbling and trampoline work at the half-time of basketball games and at other events. I developed a great sense of balance and kinesthetic awareness from tumbling which was a solid basis for excelling in other sports. After a year of tumbling and trampoline training, I was lucky enough to meet the second teacher who had a lasting effect on my life, Mr. Beuler, who was the coach of the swimming and diving team. He had seen me do tumbling and trampoline work and asked me to dive for the swim team at the State meet. I told him I did not know how to dive, but he said he had seen me tumble and I would be able to learn diving and why not give it a try? After being instructed that afternoon on the fine points of diving, I was told the State meet was in two days, so I would have two days to learn how to dive. To my great surprise, I finished second in my first diving competition at State level. After swimming and diving for a few months, I thought I found my sport. I became a speed swimmer and broke multiple records in the 50 and 100 meter events in several different strokes.

When I got to high school, I found that physical educations was all but eliminated, so I tried out for the track and football teams and was good enough to set school and state records. I enjoyed sports but realized that I was not going to be able to make a career of sports so in my last two years of high school, I worked nights in a hospital and went to school during the day thinking this might be the path I needed to follow in life.

After high school, I went to Dickinson State University in North Dakota where I enrolled in their nursing program. I had received multiple scholarship offers to play college football but at only 150 pounds, I decided that might not be the path for me to follow but soon after my arrival in college that urge to compete was back. There was a great gymnastic program at the university, and my new roommate had been a gymnast for several years. Again I thought "Why not give it a try?". As a walk on without a scholarship, I made the team and became a gymnast and competed throughout the country and competed in international competitions. Gymnastics developed an even better physical awareness and balance in my life.

I graduated from college and worked only a short time as a nurse in a hospital in North Dakota before the urge to do something more physical as my life's work hit me and I knew I had to go. I joined the U.S. Air Force and volunteered for the elite Para Rescue Service. Para Rescue in the Air Force is the equivalent of the other services Special Forces (Army Delta Force, Navy Seal Teams) so needless to say this filled my need for something physical and I was also able to use my medical training to boot! I thought I had found my niche for life, but as fate would have it, this was not to be. I was injured in a diving accident which eliminated me from the Air Force. After I left the Air force, I was still looking for that physical training that I had been looking for since childhood. I found two things that peaked my interests, body building and martial arts.

I took a dare from a friend to compete in a body building contest and I found that I could compete and I made a go of it for a couple of years competing all over the country and won multiple amateur titles. In my last competition, I won *__Southwest Mr. America__*.

After several years of moving from state to state while competing in bodybuilding, I had the opportunity to study different styles of martial arts under several different sensei's. While never having the opportunity to really follow up and continue with one specific form, after settling in San Antonio, I was fortunate enough to meet Mr. Andries Cane. I became his student in the American Budo-kan style. Mr. Cane had been a worldwide competitor in Judo and through years of study in Europe , Japan, and Hawaii had studied Judo, Jujitsu, Bujitsu, and Aikido. He had received eleven black belts in these various martial arts. While studying under Mr. Cane, I joined the San Antonio. Police Department and quickly realized these martial art skills could be incorporated into police training tactics and work well for officers on the street.

During the years of developing the many martial arts skills, I studied the formal and informal styles. I took special interest in the informal training which was incorporated into training police officers. I had become an instructor with Mr. Cane and after many years of working with him, he retired and gave me the honor of taking over the forty years of his lifelong work. I have developed the Police Bujitsu Club, LLC. where his work is still honored, practiced and has been developed into training for police agencies all over the United States through hands-on training and the publishing of these training books.

POLICE BUJITSU CLUB

YOU CAN MAKE A DIFFERENCE

氣

ASSAULT RESPONSE
PRISONER CONTROL TACTICS

The Cane - Albrecht Method

Level 1

The Lawman's Martial Art

Techniques designed for law enforcement agencies and officers everywhere. These special techniques have been tried and proven to be most effective for more that thirty-five years.

You are about to learn martial arts skills designed specifically for law enforcement work, taken from traditional martial arts styles of Judo, Jujitsu, Aikido, and Bujitsu. Their design was specifically for the law enforcement officers in the field, by Andries Cane and lead instructor Gary Albrecht.

All courses taught are certified T.C.L.E.O.S.E. and now known as T.C.O.L.E. certified instructors also certified by Police Bujitsu Club, LLC.

AIKIDO

ai 合 (harmony, coming together, unification) *Ai* is the active principle of *ai-ki-do*.

ki 気 (vital energy) *Ki*, the life-stuff of the universe, has no English equivalent. An essential element of all aspects of oriental culture—philosophy, medicine, art, physical training—the full significance of *ki* only becomes clear through firsthand experience.

do 道 (Way) In Japan, any art that is practiced to develop both technical and spiritual maturity is considered a *do*, a "Way" to harmonize body and mind.

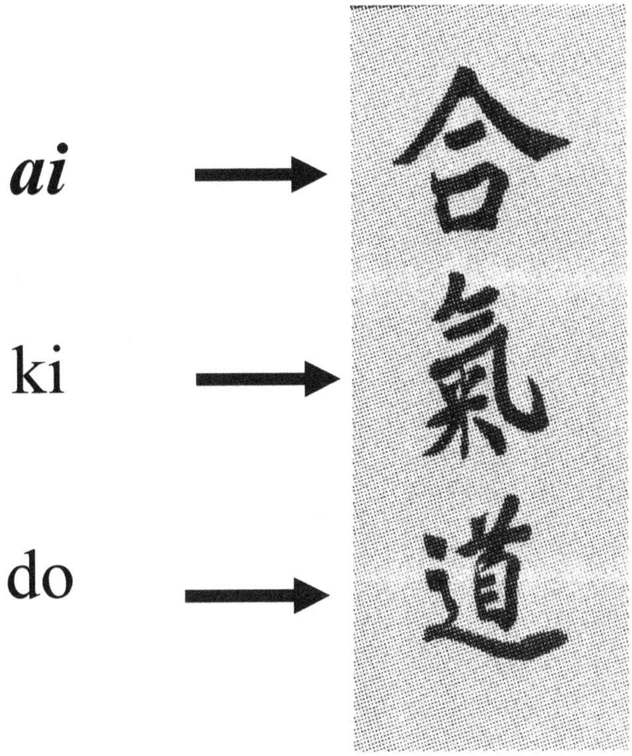

CHAPTER 1

Guidelines and Basic Moves

GOLDEN PRINCIPLES

OF DEFENSIVE TACTICS

1. ***Don't stop*** until you have won.
2. Assumption of Superiority — Never underestimate your opponent. Don't assume anything from appearance.
3. Danger Awareness — Listen to that inner voice that tells you something doesn't feel right. Call it intuition, call it instinct, but don't ignore it just because you can't explain it.
4. Flexibility — Be aware and flexible enough to adjust if a technique is not working, or if the situation has changed.
5. Minimum Confrontation Time — Do whatever you have to do, to end the incident within 5 to 10 seconds.
6. Moving Inside the Danger — Move inside a swinging blow to nullify the attack and get in close where your techniques work best.
7. Avoid the Armor — Attacking the parts of the body that are not protected by natural armor.
8. The Push/Pull Principle — When they pull, you push; when they push you pull.
9. The Secret of Moving Balance — Concentrate on your center and maintain perfect posture (hips under your shoulders and straight back).
10. High/Low Striking
11. Flanking Superior Numbers — Move to one end of the group and attack.
12. Distraction Principle — Take their mind off what they are doing.
13. Pain Breeds Control and Cooperation — You do not always have to severely disable a person. Techniques that can cause death should only be used in a life threatening situation. Measure your response to the danger perceived. In law enforcement, we are held to a little higher standard, of which we call the force continuum.

The Ten Cycle Method Of Control

To explain this method of control, I am going to relate a true story of which my Sensei, Andries Cane told me.

In his teen years, he was competing in judo and doing very well; however occasionally he would lose a match to a competitor that he knew he should have beaten. He asked his sensei what caused him to lose. He was told, "You got mad and lost control." was his simple reply. He asked " Well, how do I keep from getting mad?" His sensei smiled (because he knew he had him) and answered, " You don't know how to breath." His sensei smiled again and walked away. Not being able to wait for the Masters teaching for some other time, he hurried after him. Finally got his sensei's attention and pursued it further, " What do you mean, I don't know how to breathe? How am I suppose to breathe?" His sensei pointed to his naval and answered, "Breath down there and breath slow. That way, you'll always have control."

He followed his advice and for the next three years won the U.S. Army in Europe Black Belt Championships.

He found that by controlling your breathing, you could control yourself. Now this technique is taught to all who take the Cane/Albrecht courses, now through the Police Bujitsu Club. This technique is called the Ten Cycle Method. One cycle consists of one complete inhale and one complete exhale. Control your rate of breathing to ten or less breaths per minute and you will always maintain emotional control. Practice every day in everything you do until it becomes as automatic body response and you will no longer have to consciously direct it. Especially notice your rate of breathing when you become stressed and slow it down immediately. With practice, your normal breathing rate will stay below 10 breaths per minute.

The initial purpose of control is to enable you to use the powerful defense skills you are learning when you need them. The techniques taught in Bujitsu by the Cane/Albrecht Method are techniques that you will enable you to immediately hurt another person and even injure them badly. You need this to aid yourself against unprovoked attacks, but remember this, every time you embroil yourself in a physical fight, you are putting yourself in danger. Circumstances can change quickly— the unarmed man now has a knife or gun; the single man you thought you could wipe the floor with now has four very large friends who want to tear your limbs from your body. You must decide an appropriate response to aggressive people who want to goad you into a fight. By doing the **Ten Cycle Method**, you will be able to keep yourself in control. This does not mean swallow your anger, but using your breath to keep you from losing your temper and lashing out.

STEPPING INSIDE THE LINE OF DANGER

To explain this ***RULE,*** I will give you a scenario so you are able to draw a mental picture of what and when it is necessary for it to be applied.

Think of a fighter such as a boxer. When he is being struck with heavy blows to the body and head, where do you think the most damaging part of the punch is striking him ? At the beginning of the punch? Or at the full extension of the punch? Now let's think about it a little more. When the boxer is being struck hard and he needs to get away from the heavy damaging blows, where does he go? Well, he could step back and have his opponent come after him still swinging the heavy strikes, or he could come inside the strikes where the power is weaker and clinch until he is ready to do combat again. Now think about it. When a punch is thrown, at the beginning of the swing, there is little velocity and power. When the punch increases in speed so does the power. Consequently, at the end of the punch is the maximum danger zone. This is the point of the most speed and the most power. So, if that distance were to be cut in half or by some distance, the power will have been diminished some. Not saying that there is not any power, because by all means there is, but by diminishing some of the speed and power it will be a little easier to redirect and control.

In many of the techniques that are taught with the Cane-Albrecht Method, the use of stepping inside the line of danger is taught with that specific technique. Teaching you the technique is the easy part. The overcoming your automatic response is the hard part.

Take for instance, most people respond to a punch or someone trying to hit them with something, by covering up or leaning away from what they perceive as danger. Most of the time this results in still being struck and with the heavy part of the blow.

The object of this is again the "double edged sword" in doing this correctly. First, we have been talking about cutting the speed and power of the punch or strike. The second is to take you out of "line of fire" understanding that energy travels in straight lines. By stepping a little to the side and toward the swing, this will take you off target and cut the distance. Allowing you to make your move to redirect and control not only the outcome of the punch or strike, but control the actor. (Actor meaning assailant.) If you control the actor, you control the fight.

BASIC MOVEMENTS

Like all martial arts, there are basic movements to learn as a foundation. These moves are found over and over again in the techniques that you are about to learn. Of course, the better your foundation, the stronger your techniques will be, as well as faster and stronger the moves will be. Good technique is more important than strength, when it comes to the basic movements. Strength, muscle, and power can effect your moves by slowing them down, and may cause the move to be off in timing. Not to say that strength and power are a bad thing, but if the technique is performed correctly, strength and power can enhance the move and even make it to be devastating.

As the title says, these were movements designed hundreds of years ago by martial artists from China and Japan. Lets face it, a great move is a great move in any language or culture as long as the foundation of the move is correct. As you see, all good moves no matter what they are called all go back to their foundation, and if the foundation is solid the move will survive the test of time. Some of these moves are copied, some are readapted to a fit a specific task, or situation. Such moves create new moves or variations that due to there adaptation might be more effective in situations that they have been adapted for. For example, when the Japanese fought the Mongols, their techniques of fighting "man to man" had to be changed due to the Mongols fighting on horse back. The Japanese had to change the style to what was referred to as a long form, fighting from the ground to the man on horseback.

Getting back to the basic moves, as in anything we do, the more you practice the better that you become, and the stronger the foundation will become. Practicing on the basics will allow the building on the foundation an easier task, and a smoother transition to develop a more difficult move.

CENTERING CIRCLES

This a movement that is taught for the sole purpose of "Moving Balance". Learning to maintain your balance while moving in and out of the line of danger, will allow you to perform a technique to assist you, or keep you out of harms way. No greater emphasis can be made on a basic move than this one. The movement itself can not be done enough times, in other words, the more you do it, the more proficient you will become and the easier it will allow the other techniques to come to you.

1A

2A

3A

4A

Figure 1A. To start your centering circles place your feet about shoulder width apart, relaxing the knees, your head should be centered not tilted to one side or the other.

Figure 2A. Shift your weight to your left foot allowing the right foot to barely touch the floor which will allow you to move the right foot around to your left,

Figure 3A and 4A. Make one step with your right foot, keeping the body erect and in line for your balance, not bending at the waist and allowing your right foot to skim over the floor, stepping 180 degrees, so you face the opposite direction in one step. Moving in a smooth continuous motion in a half-circle will allow your body to be straighter and more erect than even shown in these pictures. This first step can be taken in either direction right or left. The object of this step is to move your center of balance in either direction and keeping your balance from being forward or backward, but still upright and under control. This is a circular motion of which can be used to redirect a straight attack.

5A

6A

7A

Figure 5A. You are now centered and completely reverse from where you had started. Your weight should be centered between your legs and your knees slightly bent.

6A and 7A. Now shifting your weight to your right leg allowing your left leg to come off the floor slightly as you bring your heel back behind you to continue your circle, now turning another 180 degrees back to a front position. Make your left foot just barely touch as you turn back around to the front. Remembering that the legs are never locked, and the foot should be barely off the floor, and your body should again stay erect and centered.

8A

8A. Arriving back facing forward completing a 360 degree circle still with your knees slightly bent.

NOTE

Centering circles should be done in both directions left and right. When doing these centering circles, you will find that they should be done with a continuous motion and with a little speed to allow your body to center. At first, you may feel a little awkward and off balance. After a few circles, they will start to smooth out. If you feel and look like a robot when doing your circles, you will find that your knees are locked. You need to relax a little so your body moves in a smooth movement. If you find that you are not able to stop your movement at the end, and continue to lean or lose your balance to the side that you turned toward, you will find bending your knees will bring your center down allowing you to stop at the end of your rotation.

9A

10A

11A

Figure 9A. Now to add a little speed to your turns, determine on the direction that you are going to turn and bring that hand to your center palm up.

Figure 10A and 11A. Extend your right hand out to your side with a little power at first, still allowing the body to be up erect and balanced.

12A

Figure 12A. This side picture is to show and remind you that you should not allow your arm to go behind you. As you swing your arm, allow your entire body to turn in unison, as one, as your arm starts to pull you in your circle.

Figure 13A. As your arm starts to pull you around, your weight will shift to the lead leg as your opposite leg will lift slightly as your body turns as one unit together.

13A

14A 15A 16A

Figure 14A. As your bodies continues to turn and being led by your arm, you will pivot on your lead foot as you turn.

Figure 15A. As you come to the 180 degree point, both feet will be on the floor again, but the motion continues following your extended arm. Your weight now changes to the foot you have just placed on the floor.

Figure 16A. Now lift the other foot and bring your heel around making a smooth transition now in a reverse movement.

17A

Figure 17A. When you return back to the forward position, your foot is planted on the ground and your knees are slightly bent as your weight centers over both feet. This is one complete centering circle. You will find that leading with your arm will make your circles much easier and smoother. The object of swinging your arm to the side is to build unity so the entire body moves in one unit as you turn. When your circles come together with practice, they will be smooth whether you do them slow or fast. You will never be able to do enough of these, and the better they become, the better you will be able to move inside and outside strikes and kicks that are directed toward you.

18A

19A

20A

Figure 18A. Now practice going the opposite direction, this time leading with your left hand. Extend your arm to the left with your palm up as you start to change your balance to the left leg.

Figure 19A. Notice as your arm starts to pull you back to your left, your body does not twist at the waist but the entire body moves together as a single unit.

Figure 21A. When your arm hits perpendicular to your body, you need to move with it. **Do Not** allow your arm to go past this point. Let the speed of your arm dictate the speed you will be turning. By the time your arm reaches this point, your weight should have shifted to your left leg, and the right foot should be just

21A

Figure 21A. When you hit the 180 degree point in your circle, notice that your left foot has pivoted forward prior to the weight change back to the right foot.

Figure 22A. The circle continues in the circular motion without stopping or hesitation during the weight change in your feet. The reverse step is at the same speed and smoothness as the first step . The left foot is again slightly off the floor as it comes back.

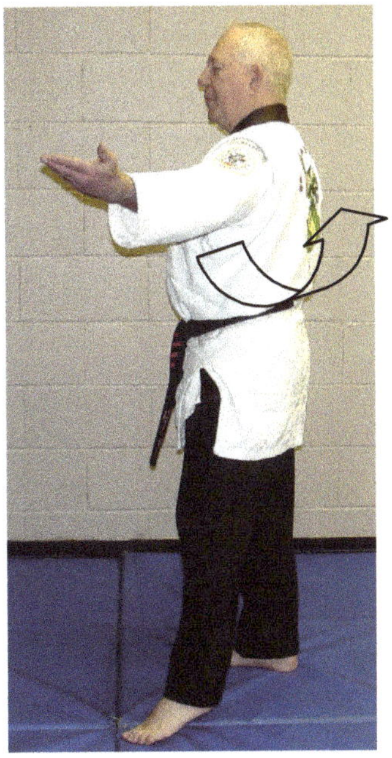

22A

23A

24A

Figure 23A. When returning back to the starting position, come to a stop. Do not allow your circular movement to pull you past center.

Figure 24A. Allowing your centering circle to stop may require you to bend the knees slightly lowering your center of balance to steady you. Bring your hands down toward your center.

This exercise should be done as many times as it may take to smooth them out as if it were a dance-type movement. This is one exercise that there can not be too many done in a lifetime. The object is to make this movement as smooth as possible and easy.

Now to add something on your own, try to shorten the distance in your step. It should be as smooth as one shoulder width apart. You know every situation is different. Sometimes you will have to turn faster and sometimes slower. But with the change in situation, you may have limited space and still need to turn to the inside or outside of a move coming at you.

Make this exercise easy and fun and at the beginning of every training session, you will notice that your balance will become more steady with the more you do. When you have your balance, you are stable and you are hard to take down.

FOLLOW FOOT
Demonstration

This technique of moving is designed to maintain stability as you move from position to position when controlling a suspect or prisoner. The stance is an erect stance keeping the back straight, and the knees slightly bent, and the feet about 8 to 10 inches wider than shoulder width apart. This wide base will allow for better stability. The main principle of this movement is that the feet never come any closer than shoulder width apart. The movement occurs when the foot on the side of the direction you are moving to will step 6 inches and the foot behind will pull 6 inches as if to drag it across the floor or surface you are standing on. This will keep the body in balance and not allow the body to move side to side as in a walking type movement. The body should stay centered between your legs and not bent over. By keeping the back straight, any pulling downward will pull through your entire body making your balance strong and stable, so you will not lose your balance, and fall forward. This will give you the ability to support a large amount

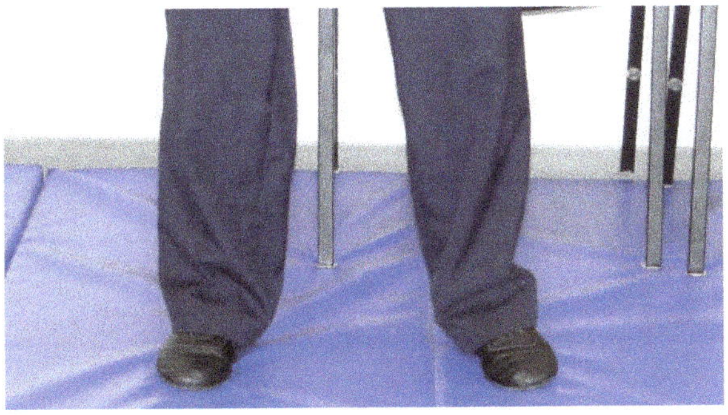

1B

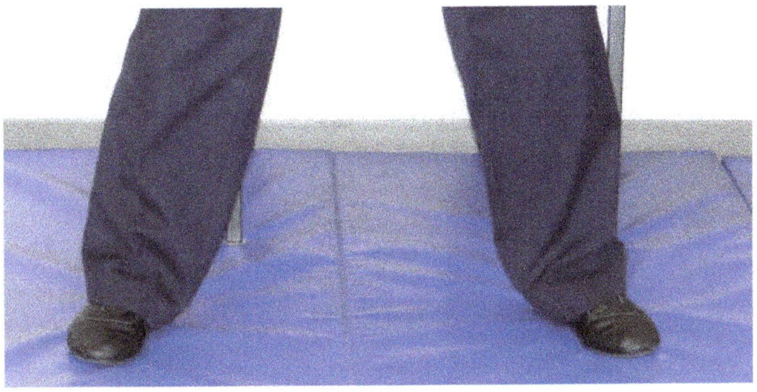

2B

Figure 1B. This stance is about shoulder width apart as a base stance, where the body is balanced. You should allow your knees to be slightly bent to absorb any shock or risk of hyperextension to the knees in case of a downward pull when handling a suspect on the ground.

Figure 2B. Step with the left foot going in the left direction, approximately 6 to 8 inches. This step will increase the width of your base stance lowering your center and will increase your stability. Still in this position, your back should be straight, your knees slightly bent, and your hips should be centered between your feet. All of these things will give you stability in your control when handling a suspect on the ground as you have to move him or her from their back to their stomach.

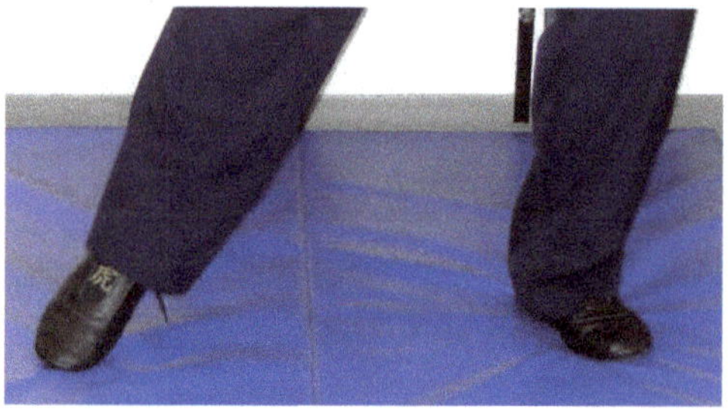

3B

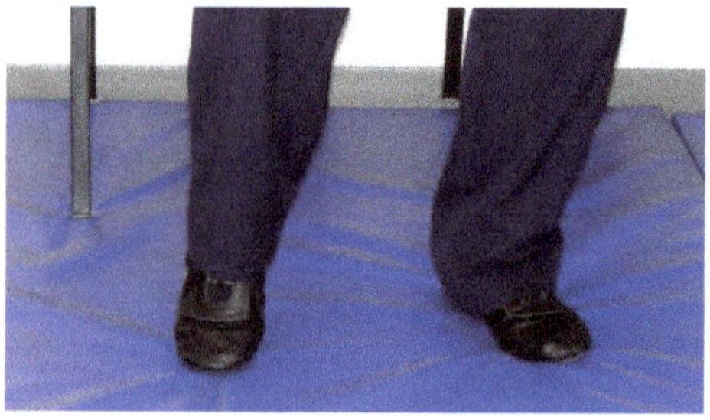

4B

Figures 3B and 4B. Show the right foot dragging back 6 or 8 inches that the left foot had stepped in figure 2B. Traveling the short distance to the left, but allowing the movement to be balanced and centered. Notice that when moving the feet that the foot that is moving is not picked up very high off the floor. It actually sweeps or even drags across the floor to its next position. This is allowing the body to be as close as it can to a balance point, even in between steps. This motion is called,

TRAINING EXERCISE

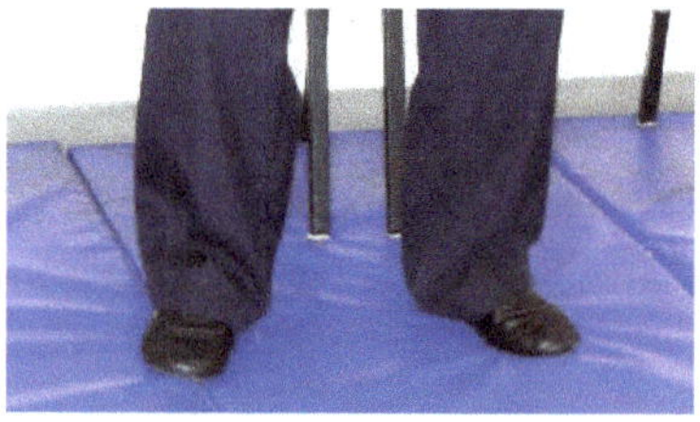

5B

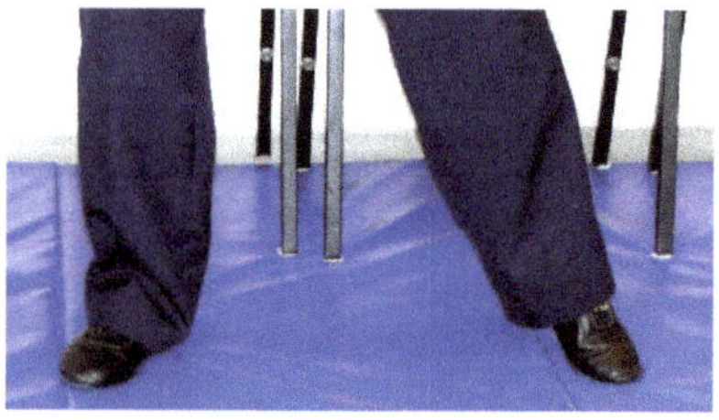

6B

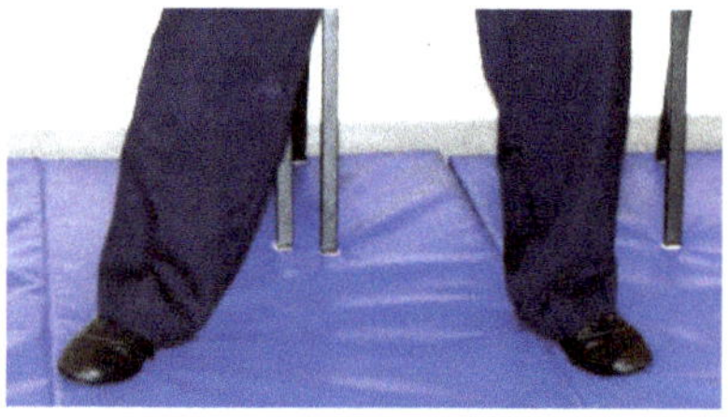

7B

Figure 5B. Stand with feet about shoulder width apart, back straight, head up looking straight ahead, and knees slightly bent.

Figure 6B. Step to the left with your left foot about 6 to 8 inches keeping centered.

Figure 7B. Shift your weight slightly to the left, allowing the right foot to barely touch the floor. Making sure that you are still upright and not bent over

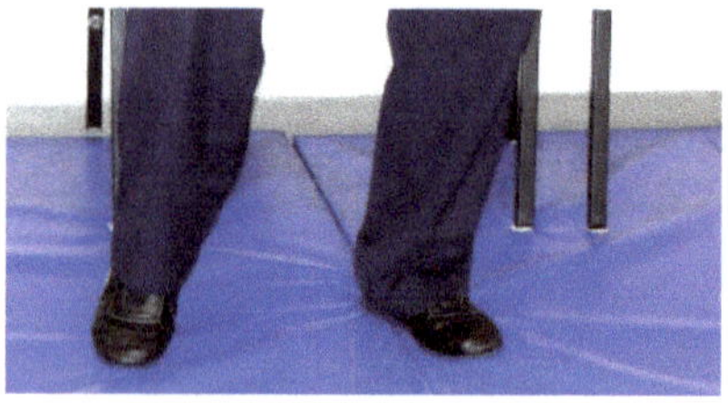

8B

Figure 8B. Pull your right foot in, as if you were dragging it lightly over the floor, back to the shoulder width position, and center your weight over both feet.

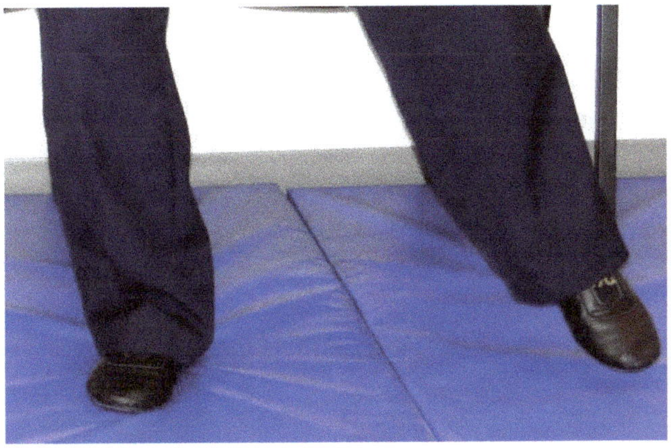

9B

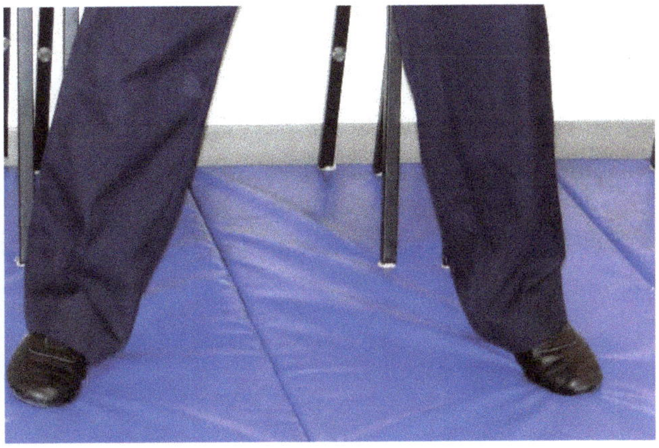

10B

Figure 9B. Again step to the left with your left foot about 6 to 8 inches.

Figure 10B. After you step, allow your weight to shift to a little past center to the left side. This balance movement is subtle so that your balance will not be too much to one side, causing you to be off balance but allowing the weight to transfer enough to move the right foot.

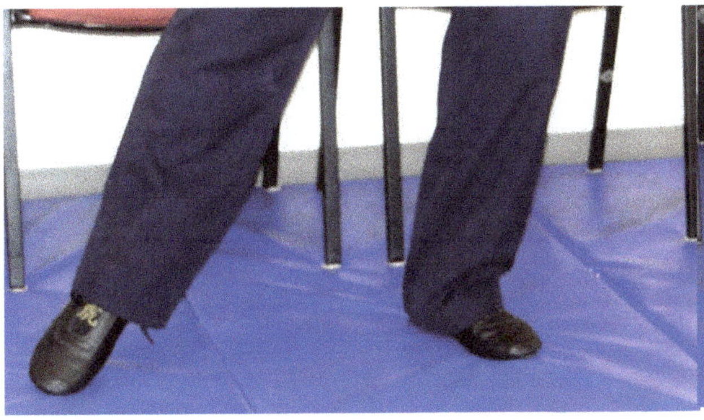

11B

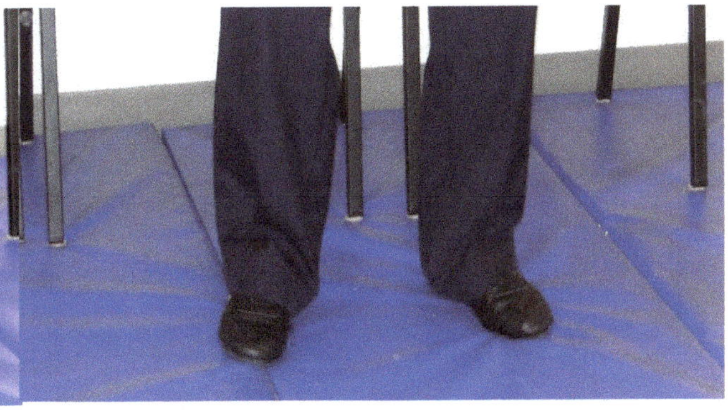

12B

Figure 11B. Now shifting you weight to your left side slightly, drag your right foot over the floor for the 6 to 8 inches you had just stepped with the other foot returning you again back to center as in Figure 12B.

This exercise is done in both directions. Now just repeat the steps in reverse, stepping with your right foot first, shifting you weight, then dragging your left foot across the floor, remembering the distance to step is about 6 to 8 inches. Keep in mind the back must be straight and the knees slightly bent.

When you are comfortable with this movement, move back and forth across the floor from left to right. This move is used to move suspects from their backs to their stomachs. This will allow you to maintain balance while moving, not to be pulled on by the suspect in a manner that you take the chance of losing your bal-

STANCES

NATURAL

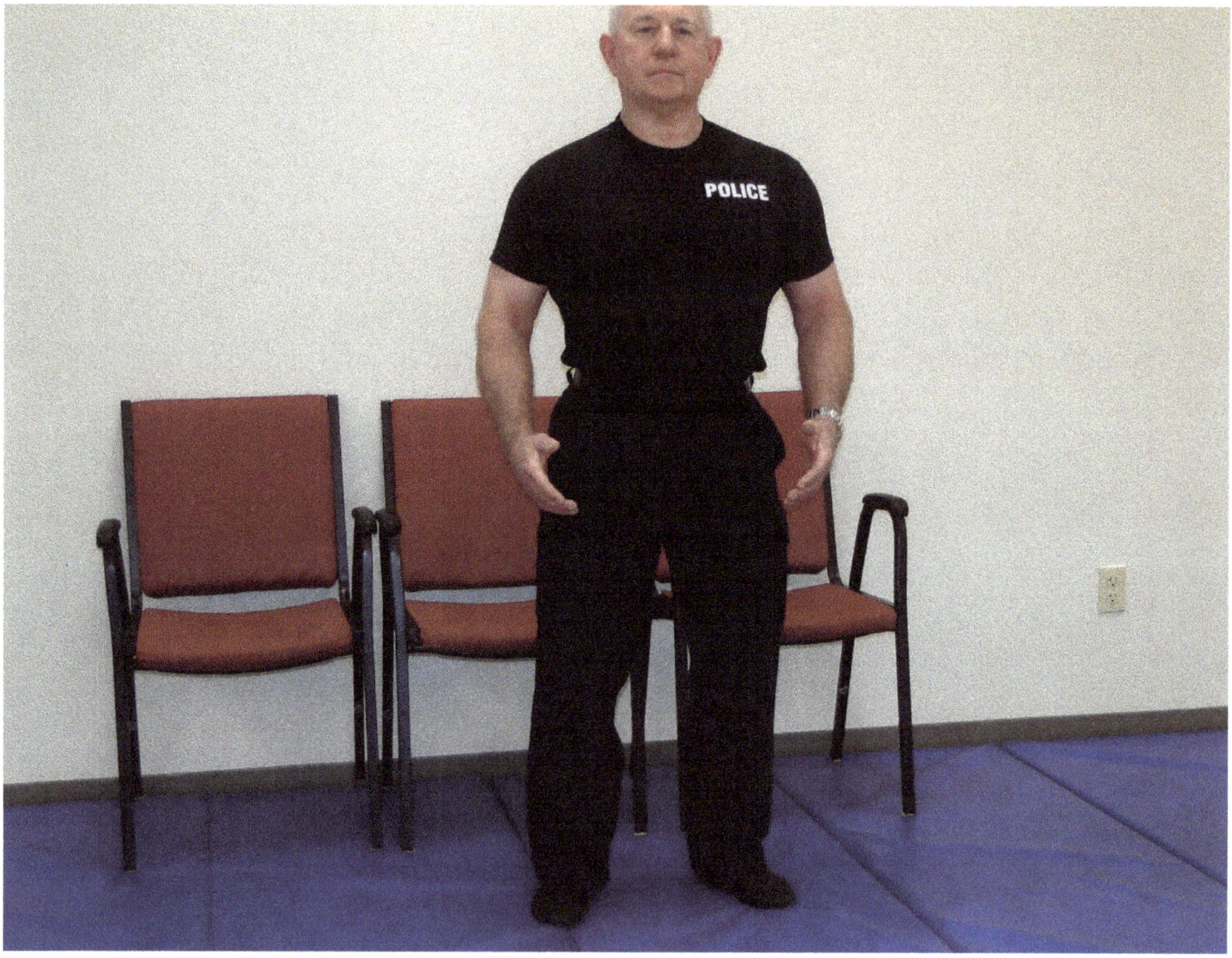

1C

Figure 1C. This stance is a normal relaxed stance that will allow your body to be balanced in the center of the stance. Your feet should be about shoulder width apart. The posture of your body is erect and shoulders back and head up and your arms to your sides slightly bent. The hands are open, but are relaxed, in other words, not in a fist and not open so that the fingers are extended straight and rigid. The thumb is relaxed as well, not pulled back and stiff.

RIGHT NATURAL STANCE

2C

Figure 2C. The right natural stance is what police officers refer to as an interview stance or a bladed stance. This stance would be for a left handed officer due to having his right leg forward which would place his weapon on his left hip away from the suspect. The right leg is forward about 12 to 18 inches still allowing the feet to be about shoulder distance apart. The officer's body is turned slightly back to the left side to match his stance, keeping his weapon side away from the suspect. This bladed stance allows the strong arm of a left handed officer to be away from the suspect. This stance is a ***ready*** or an ***alert*** stance not a defensive stance, but would allow the officer to get into a defensive stance very quickly if the occasion should arise.

LEFT NATURAL STANCE

3C

Figure 3C. The left natural stance is for the right handed officers to be in the interview or bladed stance . This will allow the right handed officer to keep his weapon side away from the suspect. The left leg is about 12 to 18 inches in front of the right leg but still standing with the feet about shoulder distance apart for balance.

This stance is a ***ready*** or ***alert*** stance as in the right natural not a defensive stance. This stance does allow the officer the ability to get into a defensive stance very quickly.

DEFENSIVE STANCE

This is a stance that is taken when a threat arises. Depending on the officer, whether he is right handed or left handed, will determine which foot he will place forward. As in the right and left natural stances, the officer, that is left handed officers, will put his right foot forward, and right handed officers will put his left leg forward. The knees will be bent slightly. The arms will be forward and bent with the hands up and open. The positioning of the body at this angle has a specific purpose other than less of a target. In aikido, the main goal is to take an opponent offline so you can redirect or control his movement. A simple explanation to get an understanding of the theory would be that energy travels in straight lines, and if you can redirect the energy, or combine with it by taking yourself out of the line of danger, you will be able to

LEFT DEFENSIVE STANCE

4C

Figure 4C. The left defensive stance is positioned with the left leg forward, as well as the left arm. The knees are bent for quick response and mobility. This is most used by right handed officers due to their weapon being on their right side.

RIGHT DEFENSIVE STANCE

5C

Figure 5C. The right defensive stance is positioned with the right leg and arm forward. The knees are bent for quick response and mobility. This position is most used by left handed officers due to the weapon being on the left side.

These positions are interchangeable and can be used by both right and left handed officers, depending on the type of attack. But as most humans do, we all have a dominate side. So the use of this stance on a weak side, is usually weak, as are the techniques done on that side. So "mirror image" techniques need to be practiced the same on both sides. However, there are techniques that are taught on the strong side that are not changed if the attacker attacks with the right or left side.

These techniques remain the same, it is the targets attacked that may change. This makes it easier for most officers when learning these techniques. The response is the same and no pre-thought has to decide on which way they may have to stand. All the officer has to do is automatically respond. The response will be correct, no matter if it was a right or left handed attack.

CHAPTER 2

Kicks

KICKS

The kicks used in this course are not fancy as some martial arts forms. The kicks taught are meant to be quick, effective, and used to be either as an effective kick or a distract. The use of fancy kicks may not be practical mainly because to accomplish high kicks, flexibility and speed are needed to be effective, along with a lot of practice. As police officers in general, most spend a greater percentage of there time on duty in a sedentary position. This causes the officer's muscles and joints to be stiff and inflexible. If needed as an immediate response, this may cause the officer to suffer a possible injury. Injuries such as muscle, tendon, ligament, and possibly even fractures can be occur due to quick responses on a cool or stiff body. Not allowing the officer time to stretch and warm up before a confrontation, high kicks, spin kicks, and fancy kicks, may be a detriment to the officer. The main reason for a kick would be for its effectiveness. It looks great in the movies, but lets be realistic. First you and I both know flexibility comes with a lot of stretching, and it is like anything else, it has to be worked on daily to maintain. Another realistic reason we all have to face is age. That's right, we can not be that youthful officer fresh from the academy that can try to take on any task. Most officers and people in general do not stretch to get good flexibility, let alone the ability to kick over their head or a good spin kick, at least without pulling a muscle or two. You possibly would be injured if it were done or attempted. Now, we get back to effectiveness, and why we do the kicks at all.

Kicks that we will use serve several purposes, are for specific targets, and are done so that the officer is not off balance or in need of beyond normal flexibility. Of course, kicks are used as a defense to attacks, but also in our case used as a distract. The use as a distract in many cases will allow the officer to start a specific technique by knocking the offender off balance, to break his focused attention, cause him to be distracted for that short period of time necessary for you to accomplish a specific task and to gain the control we are after.

FRONT KICK ANATOMY

The front kick is a quick movement kick, also known as a "front snap kick". This kick can be used as an effective defensive move, as well as, a distract.

This kick as a defensive move is meant to be a low quick kick no higher than the knee. The knee is the target when the front kick is used as a defensive move. This target does have different facets which has to do with the angle of which you are standing to your suspect or attacker. The knee being the target, but the angle you are striking the knee is the object of concern.

To get a little better understanding of why angles are important and what damages it may cause when the knee is struck at these different angles, a little look at the anatomy of the knee may give you a better understanding.

When the knee is struck from the front, you can see that the knee is actually in the strongest position it can be. In order for damage to occur the knee has to hyper extend backwards stretching the strongest and largest tendons.

In figures 1D and 2D. You are able to see the patella tendon is the main tendon to prevent the knee from going backwards. The attachments of these tendons to the lower head of the Femur, the largest bone of the leg, as well as the Patella or (knee cap) then attaches to the front top of the Tibia, the largest bone in the lower leg.

Knowing these attachments the most vulnerable place to strike the front of the leg with the front kick, as a defensive strike, would be at the attachment point of the Patella Tendon where it connects to the Tibia.

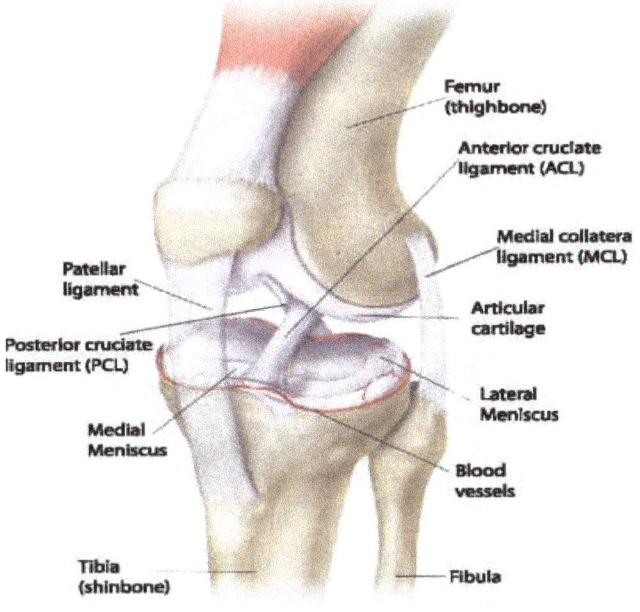

1D

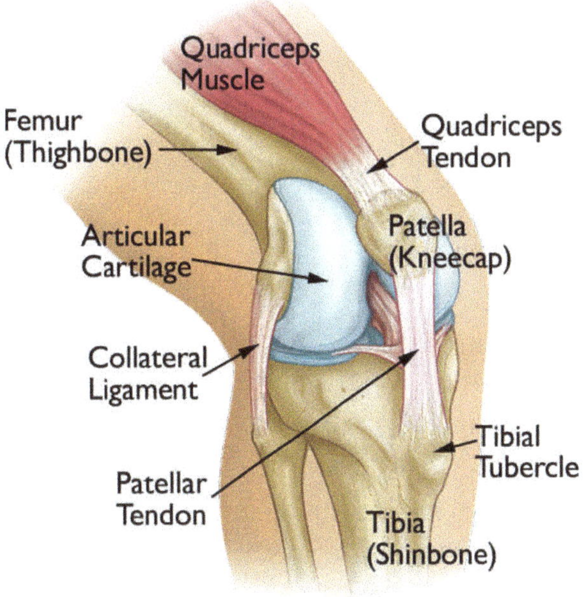

2D

One last look at the anatomy of the knee where the front kick would be involved. The frontal attack when facing the attacker, the target, was explained to be the attachment of the Patellar Tendon on the Tibia, marked with a red dot. You see that from the front when the area is struck, it causes the Tibia to shift backwards. When this happens, the meniscus is the first to tear, then the cruciate ligaments, depending on the amount of the shift of the Tibia, what other damages may occur.

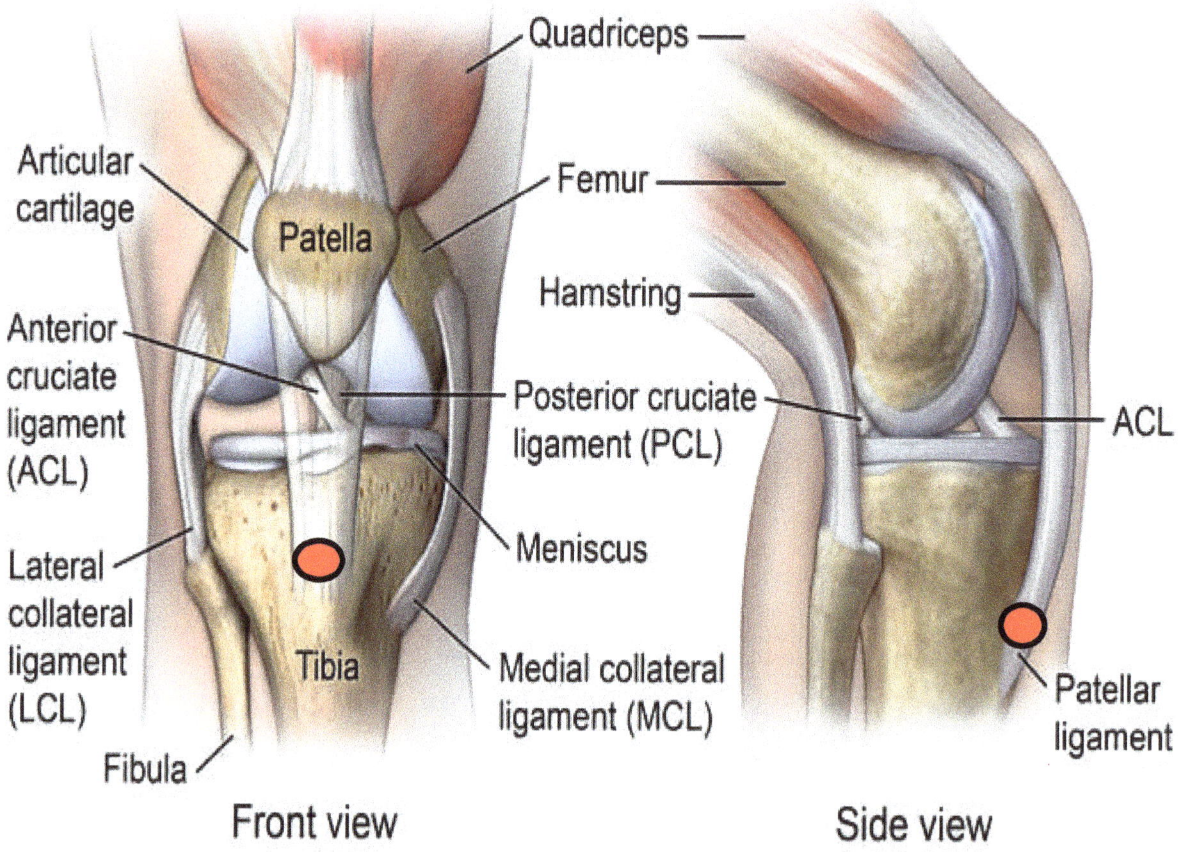

Knee anatomy

3D

Now the changing of the angle 90 degrees to either side of the attacker, with the front kick striking the side of the knee, you will find the weakest position of knee. Both sides of the knee have smaller ligaments for protection and will tear when the knee is struck at or right below the joint connection. If the knee is struck hard enough to tear either side of the ligaments, there will be a real possibility that the Medial Collateral or Lateral Meniscus will also tear.

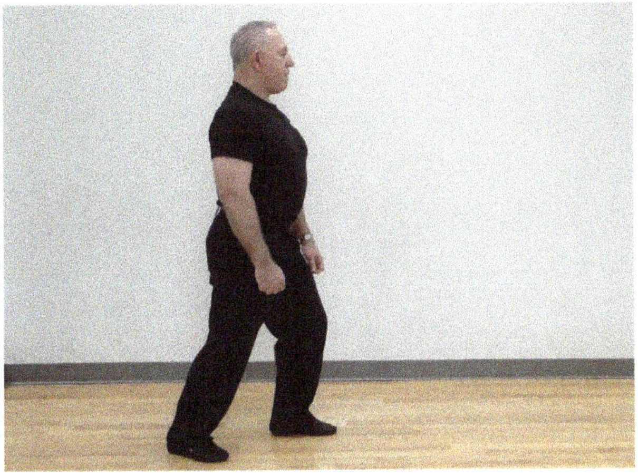

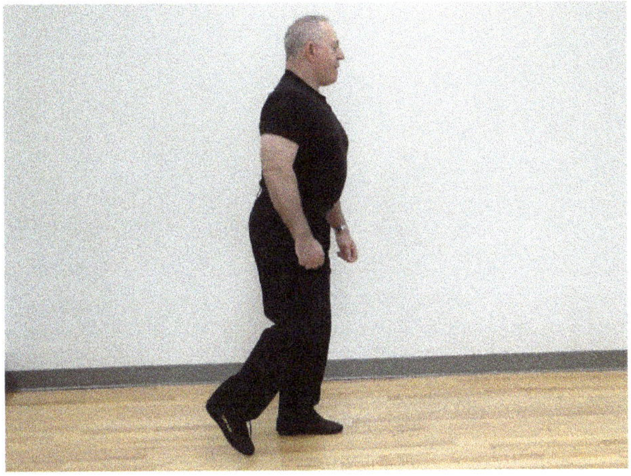

4D 5D

Figure 4D. This figure shows the left natural stance, or a natural stance of an officer being right handed. This is a ready stance for a right footed front kick. Observe the balance is centered between the legs and the posture is erect.

Figure 5D. In order to move the back foot, the weight is shifted slightly forward to the left foot, allowing the right foot to come away with the contact from the ground. This still allows the body to remain erect which gives little notice to the attacker or suspect that a change of balance has occurred.

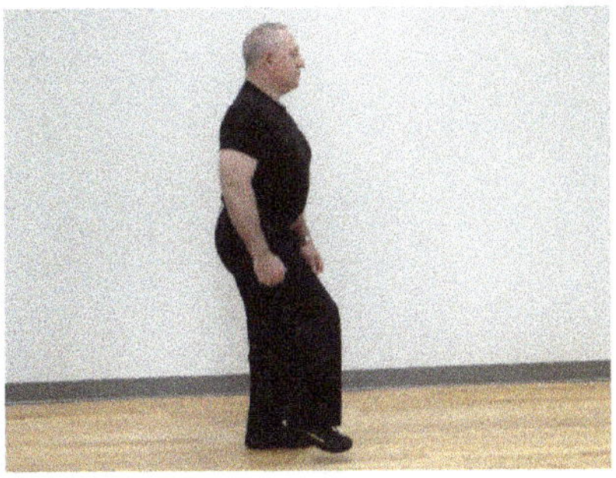

6D 7D 8D

Figure 6D. The weight has been shifted to the left leg, as the right foot stays very close to the ground, only bending the right knee enough for the foot to clear, as it passes by the other foot under your body.

Figure 7D. The knee remains partially bent as the foot starts to extend forward. ***NOTE: (A full bend in the knee at this point would take a little bit longer, as well as telegraphing your movement to the attacker. So allow your foot to sweep forward from the back position all the way through.)*** Also, at this point the toes of the right foot begin to be drawn back.

Figure 8D. With the right leg fully extended, the foot should strike with the ball of the foot, the body still remains erect and not leaning forward to maintain balance. The entire movement is to be a smooth quick sweeping movement from back to front allowing very little body shift in weight.

9D 10D

Figure 9D and 10D. After the foot has been extended to strike it's target, it is withdrawn at the same speed and smoothness as it was extended. Still keeping the body straight and erect.

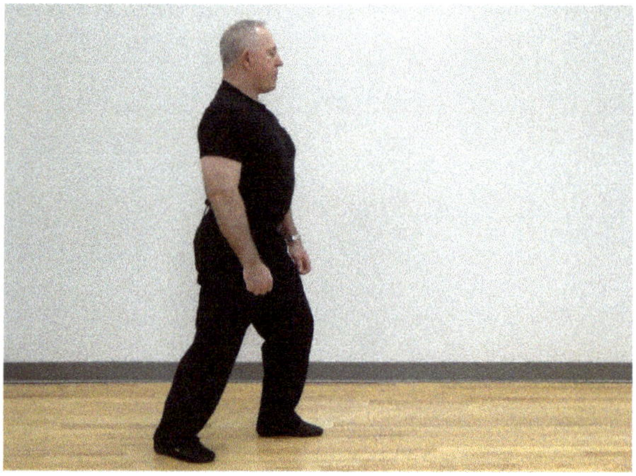

11D

Figure 11D. Returning the front kick to its original starting position, and maintaining your posture in the event the kick needs to be repeated. This also places yourself back in balance preparing you to perform the technique that is needed to take care of whatever situation you have encountered.

NOTE: ***(The front kick as we spoke of previously can be used as a defensive technique, which as explained, may damage the attacker's knee. Now the second use for this front kick is as a distract. The use of this kick is more frequently used as a distract in the Cane-Albrecht Method.)***

When this kick is used as a distract, it is not necessary to have a specific target, as long as the kick strike hits the attacker. The kick does not have to cause injury, or even pain, the object is to distract. Just take the attacker's mind off whatever he is doingat that specific time, so you are able to start your technique easier.

CROSS KICK

The "cross kick" is a defensive kick that is used to cause injury to an attacker if used. This kick is used to cause injury to the knee, and to specific parts of the knee. Figures 12D thru 17D will be showing a solo exercise.

12D

13D

Figure 12D. First observe that the stance is similar to a left natural stance, but the right foot is farther back and that most of the weight is distributed forward on the left foot to keep the balance forward.

Figure 13D. The weight is shifted entirely onto the left foot, allowing your right foot to come free from the floor.

14D

15D

Figure 14D. When the weight is brought forward onto the left foot, the knee bends as the body starts to turn back towards the left. Start bringing your right shoulder and hip around to your left side as well.

Figure 15D. When the body turns back to the left side, the right knee will pick up speed to allow your body to pivot on the left foot. The toes of the right foot are pulling back so the strike will be done with the heel of the foot, not the front.

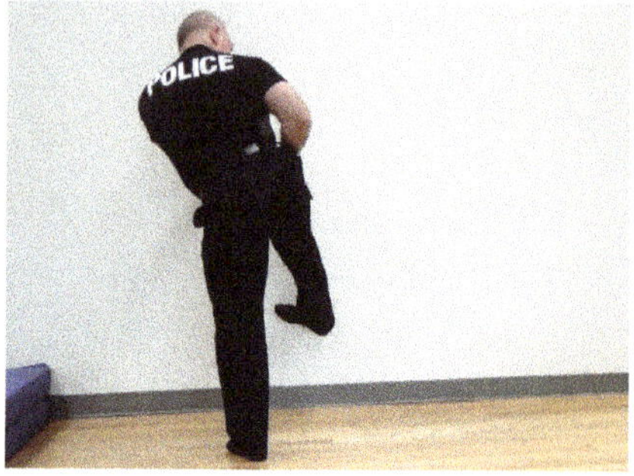

16D 17D 18D

Figure 16D. When the right foot comes to the front of you, the knee will keep extending and the toes continue to pull back.

Figure 17D. When the right foot is almost in front of you, the right hip is starting to rotate, allowing the foot to turn sideways. This also allows the heel of the foot to lead in the strike. The left foot is now pivoting more allowing your body to accommodate the swinging of the right leg to prevent any injury to your left knee.

Figure 18D. Extending your right leg allowing the left foot to pivot, as the right leg follows through. Do not stop the kick, not allowing the follow through. The follow through allows the energy to continue and not be withdrawn.

The Cross Kick with an Attacker

18D 19D 20D

Figure 18D. When an attacker or anyone approaches, first observe their body language and the way they stand. This tells you a lot about their balance and possible intent. Knowing the distance that is needed in a technique takes a little practice so you know when and how to respond.

Figure 19D. If your intent is doing the cross kick, you need to change your stance. The stepping back with your right leg first will lower your center and will change your distance from the attacker, giving you just a little more response time to change to another defensive technique if needed. This is also allowing your balance to be centered in preparation for this kick.

Figure 20D. Shift your weight forward to the left leg keeping your body erect and preparing your hands in case they are needed.

21D

22D

23D

Figure 21D. Shift your weight to the left, bend the knee and bring the knee and hip forward on a quick smooth circular path.

Figure 22D. When the right hip comes around in front, there is a pivoting started on the left foot. The knee is extending outward with speed and the toes of the right foot are pulling back to allow the target to be struck with the heel and **<u>not</u>** the top of the foot.

Figure 23D. When contact is made with the attacker's knee, the heel of your foot should be to the inside of the attacker's knee driving it out to the side.

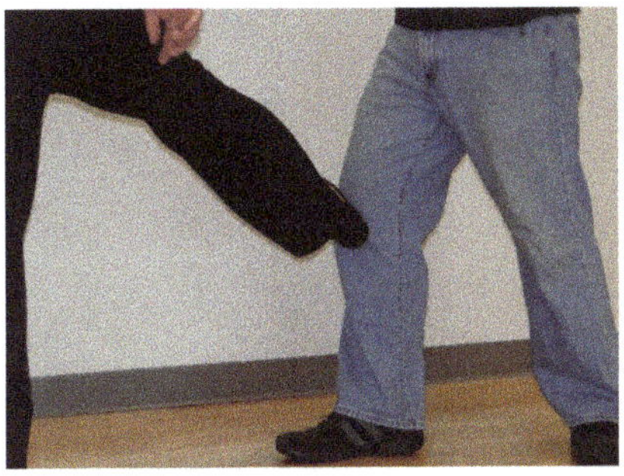

24D

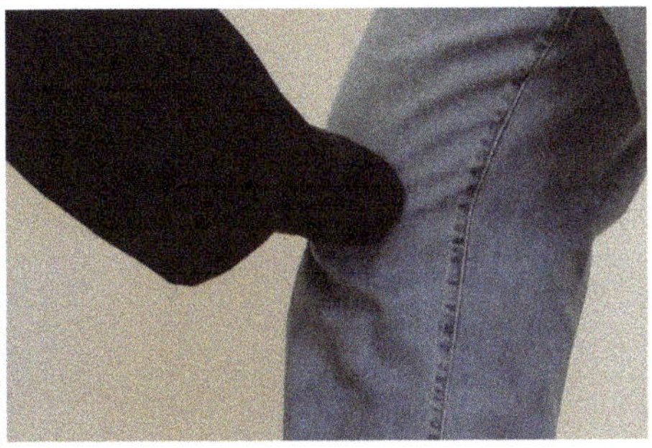

25D

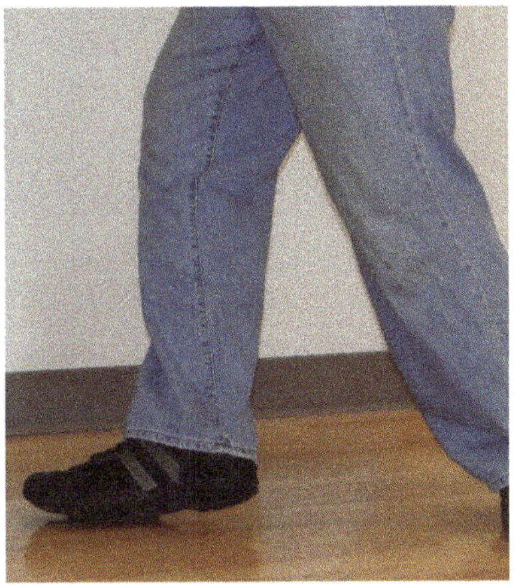

26D

Figure 24D. The strike to the inside of the attackers knee is only made with heel of your foot, as it follows

Figure 25D. This is a close up of the contact point. Striking to the front of the attacker's knee assures your strike to go through, maintaining your balance, as it causes damage. The strike connecting to the front of the attacker's knee causes a twisting of the knee. If you have a large heel on your boot or shoe, this will cause a large amount of damage to the Patellar Tendon. This tendon may even stretch to the point of turning the Patella or (knee cap) completely upside down on the knee.

Figure 26. This figure shows how the leg has to turn when the strike is followed through. The balance of the attacker will shift to his right side, and his weight will be placed on the foot that is rotating. This shift of weight also causes damage to the knee, and possibly even to the ankle. The attacker will fall almost at a right angle to where he is facing.

BACK KICK

The back kick is used in the event you are aware of someone coming from behind you or actually grabbing you from behind. This kick is also done no higher than the attackers knees. These pictures are taken as a solo exercise.

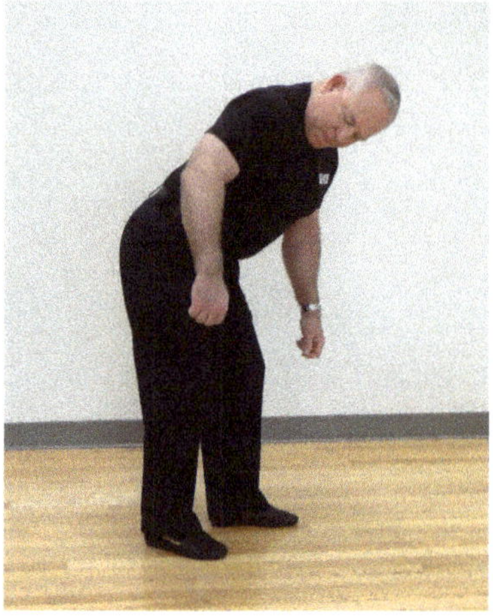

1E

2E

3E

Figure 1E. Starting this kick requires you to see your target that you are about to kick. An accurate kick is worth the time it takes to get a target acquisition. You accomplish this by leaning forward and looking under your arm.

Figure 2E. Shift your weight to the opposite leg that you are kicking with and bend the knee slightly. Still bending over looking for your target.

Figure 3E. While your balance is now shifted, push your foot backwards, **not** drawing your knee forward and bending it. This movement at this point is like pushing straight back dragging your foot lightly across the ground.

4E

5E

Figure 4E. Pushing your foot backwards will cause your foot to lift off the floor. Still watching your target under your arm.

Figure 5E. Remain watching your target throughout the kick from under the arm. At the end of the kick, you should pull your toes forward and extend through your heel, until you have made contact with your target.

CHAPTER 3
KI and Handcuffing

氣 *"KI"* 氣

Body and Mind Coordination

Every traditional martial art in existence has an origin that one would find the theories and principles of "Ki". Through the years, the theories and understanding of exactly what "Ki" power really is may be somewhat forgotten. Some like to market "Ki" as some mystical power that only they or the few that study that style may possess. "Ki" is no secret. The word itself translates to "vital force, internal energy, life-force, spirit, or breath". In the scientific communities, it is the phenomena of physics. It is also referred to by Christians as God's Holy Spirit.

"Ki" is the energy that all objects in the universe create, and it can be focused through the human body. First, we need to be aware what Ki is, then we can channel it through our bodies. There is an unlimited amount of Ki in the universe; all you have to do is learn how to focus it. A good way to describe Ki to the average person is to explain that is like electricity. First off, you can not see Ki. For this reason, it is very much like electricity. In electricity, you can not see the power of it, but you can see the effect. Ki is the same way, you can not see the power but can see the effect. Once you are aware of Ki you can feel it flow through you, like electricity through a wire, but the flow is unseen.

Who Has Ki?

The answer to this question is simple. Everyone has Ki. There are many examples of people using Ki and not even knowing what they are using. Many examples are explained as adrenaline or simply fear and panic.

We can draw on Ki at any time we need it. Many times, we don't even know we are doing it. You have heard of many instances of people doing super human feats like picking up a car off of someone who is trapped under it or deflecting a moving object as it is endangering a person's life. All of these examples are Ki flow. Some describe their unusual amount of strength, as a force that came over them when it was needed. This is not far from the truth on how it really works.

However, the force was not actually coming over them, but through them. Others have said, it was like the strength came from everywhere and focused through them to give them the strength to do these impossible tasks. Again, this is not far from what happens. A person that has experienced Ki flow, often, because they are unaware of Ki, do not know how to describe it. Once you become aware of Ki, you can tap into it at anytime you need it. Everyone has access to Ki, and everyone can use it.

Many do not use Ki because they are not aware of it. Hopefully, this book will give you some insight and enlighten you to its presence. This will give you an advantage over many others in physical appearance. If it is used correctly, it will give you control over your environment, plus help the way others perceive you and interact with you. You will find that persons that have good Ki flow are more confident. This is because with the right Ki flow, a person is in charge of his or

How Much Ki Do I Have ?

There are many different ways to measure Ki; all of which are not accurate. The limit of the amount of Ki you have is in your own mind. This is kind of explained in a statement that almost everyone has heard before. The only limits you have are those you place on yourself.

The imagination of your own mind is the limits to how much Ki you have. If you can only imagine your universe as being your home or your work place, your universe is very, very small. If you can only imagine your universe as being the town you live in, or even the state you are in, your universe is still small. Now imagine your universe is the size of the country you live in, you guessed it, your universe is still small. Believe it or not even the size of the earth itself is still small. That's why I ask you to imagine the "**UNIVERSE**". One must think beyond all known objects to be able to have a good-sized universe. The size of your universe is the area that you can draw Ki from. So if you limit your imagination, you limit the amount of Ki flow. To increase your universe, you must open your mind to the entire universe. The more you are aware of, the more you can use. You have possibly heard the statement, " ***Open your mind and everything is possible***." Ki comes from all moving objects; think of everything you know that moves. Now think how vast it can be; think of your home and work place, now a little bigger such as the earth that moves around the sun, then our galaxy, then many galaxies, all moving around out there. All of which you can draw your Ki.

Remember the person that allows his Ki to flow to the end of the universe as his focus, will be a powerful force with no limits. This is all possible if you use your mind to it's fullest abilities.

How Is Ki Important To Me?

This question has many, many answers. It is not just the physical abilities to do impossible tasks. There are many uses for Ki in your life. The simplest is it helps to make you more aware of your surroundings.

There are many types of examples in everyday life such as when you walk into a room and you are flooded with Ki (energy). It may a room where people are happy from a joke or from being together. When you enter the room, you feel good and happy, but you don't know why. On the same token, if you enter a room where something bad has happened, you get this feeling that something is not right. Why do we feel these changes that come over us? The reason is that energy flow in an area or room is filled with that type of energy (positive or negative), and you pick it up by having a high amount of Ki which allows you to be more receptive to everything around you.

If you can feel the Ki flow from others, this will allow you to avoid bad situations, or as an officer, this will give you the edge you may need in a bad situation either to prevent a physical altercation or to be able to counter this action before you are injured.

There is another way that this may be helpful in your encounters with people that may be violent or aggressive. If your are able to reverse the flow of negative or aggressive behavior by allowing another person to feel your energy by projecting your Ki toward that person, this could allow you to control the situation. The stronger your Ki flow is, the greater your ability to control your environment - "your universe".

Another way to use Ki in your every day life is to use it internally. If you are aware of your Ki flow as it goes through your body, you can control or fix problems that you may have.

Ki can be used for slowing your heart and breathing, allowing you to become more calm in a stressful situation or after a situation has occurred. It has also been used not only for stress but also in slowing bleeding if an injury may have happened.

One of the ways that Ki is very useful is what we call scanning. This is a technique that Ki is projected through your body and out the palm of your hand. Your hand is placed along the surface of another person. The hand is passed over a subject who may be having physical problems. As you project your Ki toward them, you will receive your Ki back into your hand. If there are no problems, your Ki flows back without feeling. But if it returns back to you as a rough or distorted feeling, you know that there is something wrong. The more you use your Ki in this manner, the more sensitive you will become and will be able to distinguish the differences between problems.

How To Practice Ki !

The first way to practice and improve your Ki would be simple meditation. You can do this as a simple exercise. Focus on your stomach as an intake valve for water. Allow Ki to flow into you. Then you must channel the water or your Ki out through your hands, feet and the top of your head. You will find the slower you do this exercise, the more the Ki will flow. Allow your mind to control the movement of the imaginary water to be pushed out through you limbs to the farthest you can imagine to the ends of your universe. This will give you incredible Ki-flow. The Breathing is also an important part of these exercises. When you are concentrating on pushing the water or Ki out of your body, breathe out to assist the flow.

Another way to practice Ki-flow is to use it while you are punching a heavyweight bag. Focus your water flow "Ki-flow" into your hands, fist, and your feet. With practice, you will find that you hit with more impact without using more physical force. Remember to focus your energy as far as you can think or imagine. You'll find that it has more power behind it.

Ki is the power which enables you to move objects, strike harder, move faster, and even break things that are stronger than your hands. You see different martial arts that break boards, bricks, ice, concrete and just about anything you can imagine. When they break objects, the Ki flow is through the part of the body that will be striking the object they intend to break. This is called focusing your Ki.

A DEMONSTRATION OF KI
The UNBENDABLE ARM

1F

Figure 1F. To start, place your arm upon the shoulder of the person working with you, palm up, so there will be no chance of injury. Have the person working with you place his or her hands above your elbow so he will be able to pull down.

2F

Figure 2F. Here is where you need to think a little different that you may be used to thinking. I want to extend your fingers, and think of yourself as a large tree trunk of which your arm is a large branch of that tree extending over his shoulder. Now think that this tree branch does not stop at your fingers tips, but extends way beyond his shoulder through your fingers and the sap of the tree is flowing strongly through this branch out to the leaves at the very end, and beyond like a fountain. When you visualize this thought, tell your assistant to bend your arm by pulling down at your elbow. Remember, to continue the thought and the feeling of the sap running through and out the other end, as he pulls down.

3F

4F

Figures 3F and 4F. These figures show my assistant pulling as hard as he can to bend my arm at the elbow, but due to Ki the arm does not bend. Even if your assistant is twice your size and much stronger, they will not be able to bend your arm. The object of this little exercise is to get you to think in a little different way to show you how important Ki is and how it can give you power and strength that you never new you possessed, and that this power can be tapped into upon your will, when you know how.

TAPPING FOR SAFETY

The "Tapping for Safety" when working with an "Uke - person receiving the technique" or a fellow officer is an understanding that is a must in training. Tapping is used when a technique or position becomes uncomfortable and to prevent pain and injury to the person you are working with when doing a hold or technique. When tapping for safety, use a hand to pat or tap against your body creating a universal signal for the person doing the technique to stop the pressure that is being exerted. The object is to learn the technique or hold, **NOT** to show how strong you are or how well or fast you can do the technique.

REMEMBER: Your partner in training is allowing you to do these techniques on him or her. First, so you can learn what is being taught. Second, so he or she also can learn

1G

2G

3G

Figure 1G. An example of tapping - a figure four arm lock is being placed on the uke as a demonstration. The wrap under his left arm with the left arm just above the elbow, to prevent the bending of the uke's arm.

Figure 2G and 3G. The right arm comes up and the right hand is places on the uke's left shoulder pushing back to get him to extend his right arm that is locked under your left arm. Your left hand comes over the top of your right arm forming

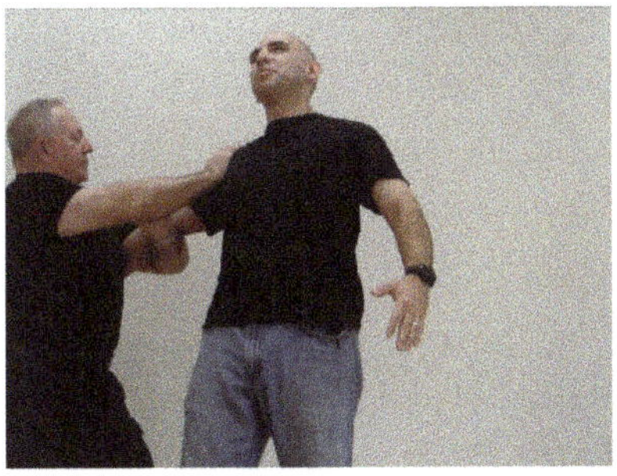

4G

5G

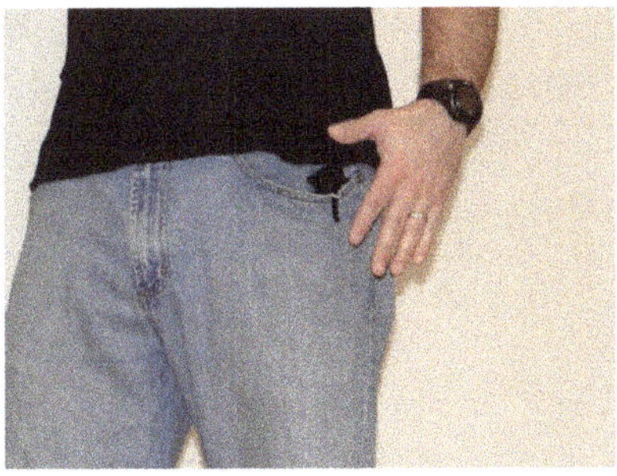

6G

Figure 4G. Pressure is applied in two ways in this position. First, raising your left wrist by pushing down with your hand against your arm. Second is to apply pressure by arching your back, and leaning backwards to hyper extend his arm.

Figures 4G,5G and 6G. Observe when pressure is applied, the left hand of the uke slaps his left hip. This tells you that the pressure is too great and to let up before any injury can occur. By the way this is a figure 4 elbow hyperextension lock.

HANDCUFFING POSITION
USING FOLLOW FOOT

This and parts of this technique will be used over and over again throughout your training and the rest of your career in law enforcement. This technique of cuffing a prisoner is unique because it is a method of handcuffing that allows the officer to maintain control over his prisoner. This control starts as soon as the pris-

1H

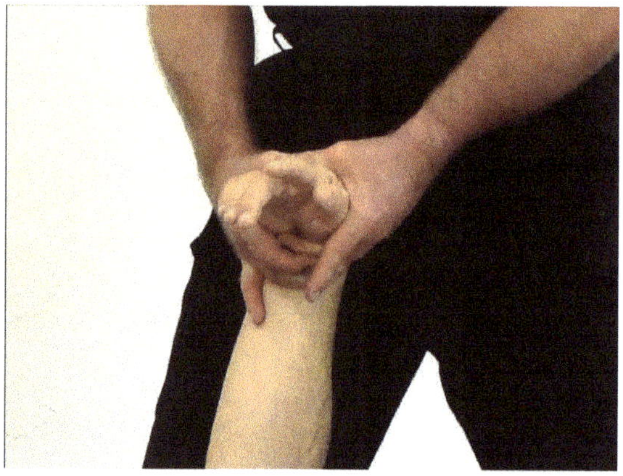

2H

Figure 1H. When the suspect is laying on his back, the suspects arm is pulled upward to keep it from bending. In most cases, if his arm is bent that means that you have bent over, and that would place you in an off balance position. If you are off balance, your control over the suspect may be cut short, due to a push or pull, and in this case, a pull from the suspect.

Figure 2H. Special attention should be observed in the hand positions. Both your right and left are placed around the hand of the suspect so the wrist of the suspect is bent at a right angle bending his fingers toward his body. Your hands are placed around the suspect's hand so that your fingers are at the bottom around the palm of the suspect's hand, and your thumbs are placed on the back of the sus-

3H

Figure 3H. Next to the grip, the stance and posture are the next in important step. A wide stance of about 8 to 10 inches wider than shoulder width will give you a good base for your balance. Keep your back straight so you don't bend over. If the suspect pulls down, with your back straight, he will have to pull through your entire body which is now balanced, stable, and strong.

4H

5H

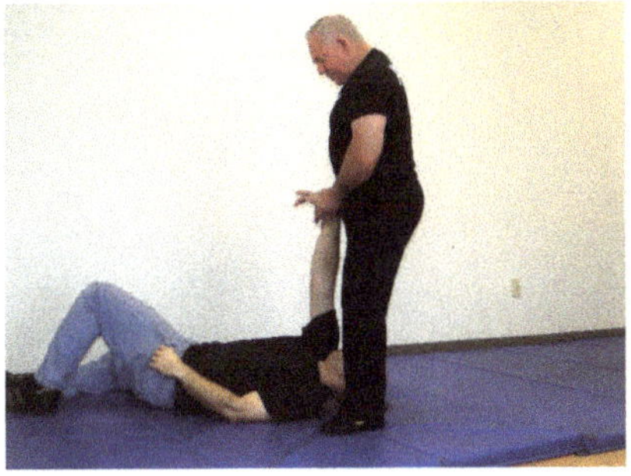

6H

Figure 4H. Now is the time to start to turn the suspect over to his stomach. The technique of "Follow Foot" is now applied. You have to work your way around the suspect to the opposite side but remaining close to the suspect keeping his arm straight up and close to your waist. Notice that the suspect's hand is kept in front of you at a 90 degree angle. Take a six inch step close to the suspects head with your left foot.

Figure 5H. Keep your back straight, and the suspect's hand at 90 degrees at your waistline. Shift your weight slightly onto the left foot and slide your right foot along the floor for the same amount of six inches.

Figure 6H. Stepping again with your left foot around the head of the suspect. The moving around the suspect needs to be a movement that stays close. If by chance, you would stray away from the suspect's body as you move around it, you would find that the suspect's arm would become at an angle. If this angle is created, it would allow the suspect to us more muscles to pull down with. This would give the suspect a chance to get up or possibly pull you off balance.

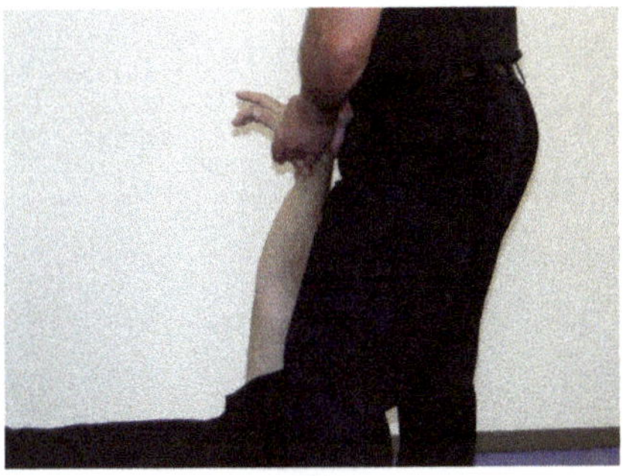

7H

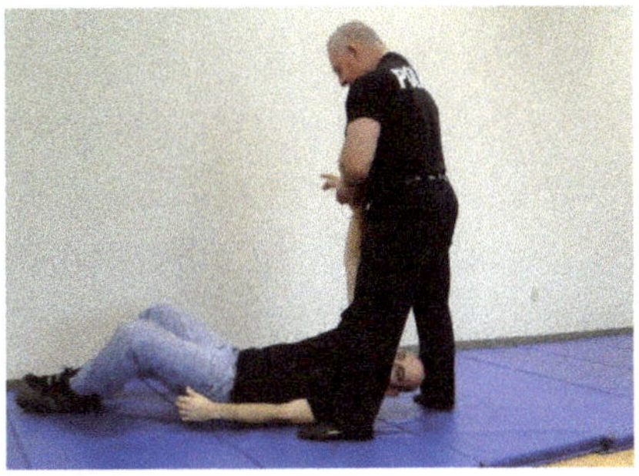

8H

9H

Figure 7H. Observe as you step around the suspect's head, and as he starts to turn over, he will role onto his shoulder which will extend this arm. The extra length in the arm needs to be adjusted for by continually pulling up on his arm as you step around the suspect's body.

Figure 8H and 9H. Continuing the follow foot technique, stepping six inches and pulling six inches as you move around the suspect, keeping the suspect's arm straight in front of you, with the suspect's hand at the 90 degree angle also in front of you.

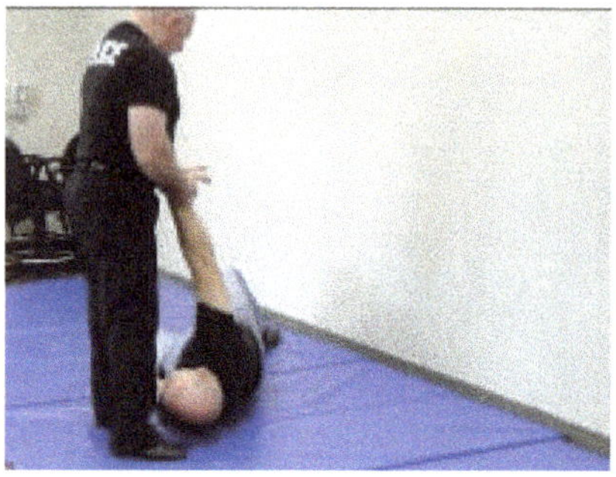

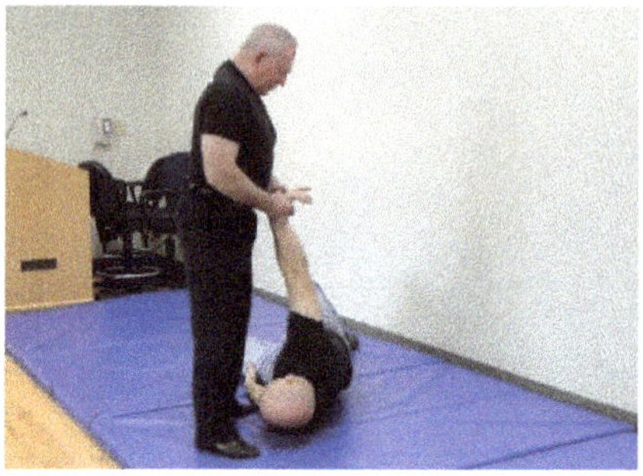

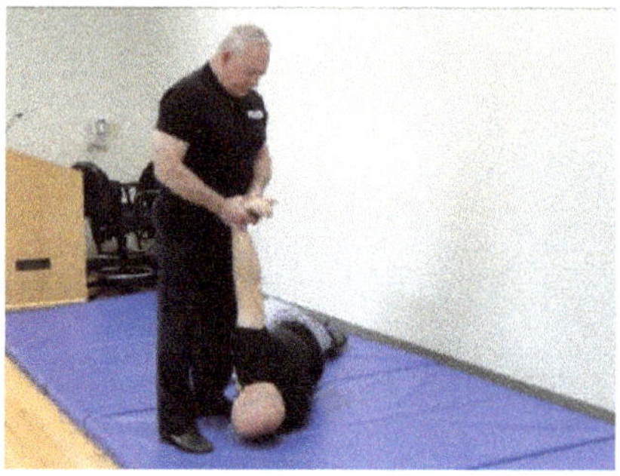

10H 11H 12H

Figures 10H,11H,and12H. These figures show as you step around the head of the suspect and come alongside of him, the suspect's hand remains at a 90 degree angle in front of you. The right shoulder of the suspect rotates as the officer comes around to the right side. This is a control factor for the officer.

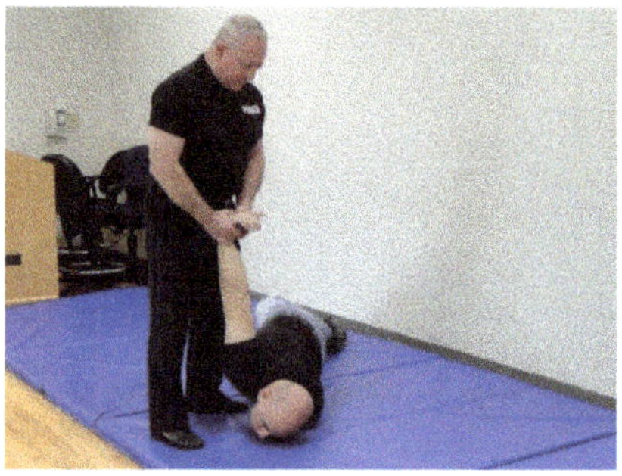

13H 14H 15H

Figure 13H. When you come perpendicular to the suspect's body, you can see that the suspect's shoulder is not flat on the ground. This may happen if the suspect has good flexibility in his shoulders.

Figure 14H. By overcoming the shoulder problem of the suspect not being flat on the ground, the wrist of the suspect is turned slightly toward the head of the suspect. This will rotate the shoulder in the socket and cause pain which will cause the suspect to place his shoulder forward onto the ground.

Figure 15H. After the suspect's shoulder is flat on the ground, shift your weight

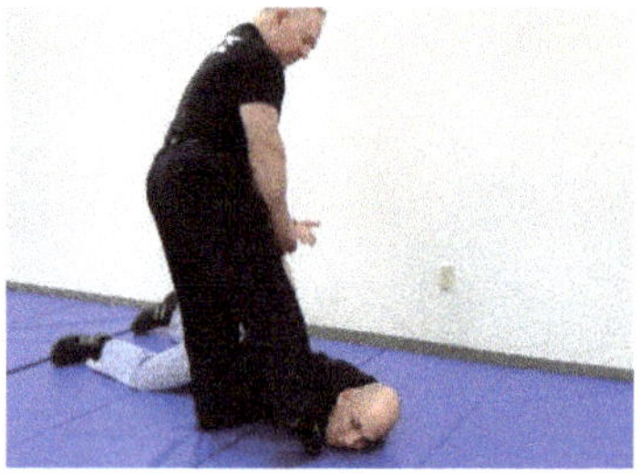

16H

17H

Figures 16H and 17H. The right foot is placed close to the face, under the shoulder and clavicle of the suspect, with the toes pointing back toward his body.

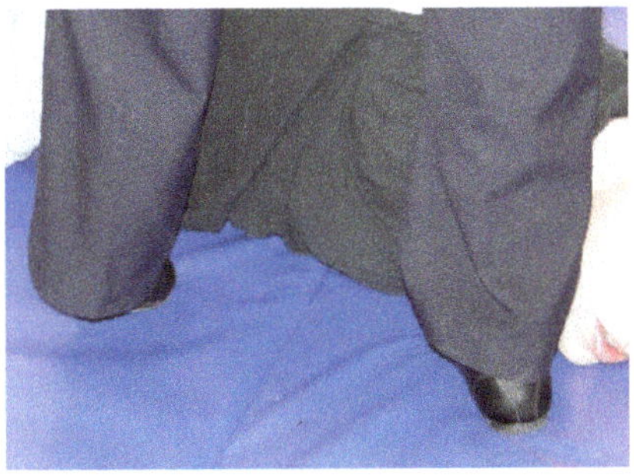

18H

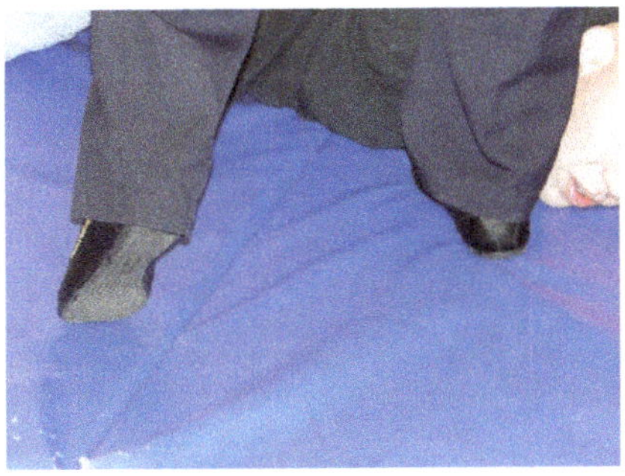

19H

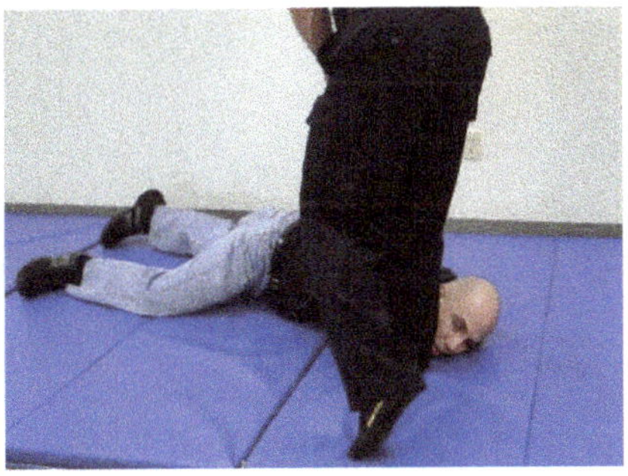

20H

Figures 18H,19H, and 20H. The weight now shifts to the right foot and the left foot is brought back to your left side in a smooth one step motion.

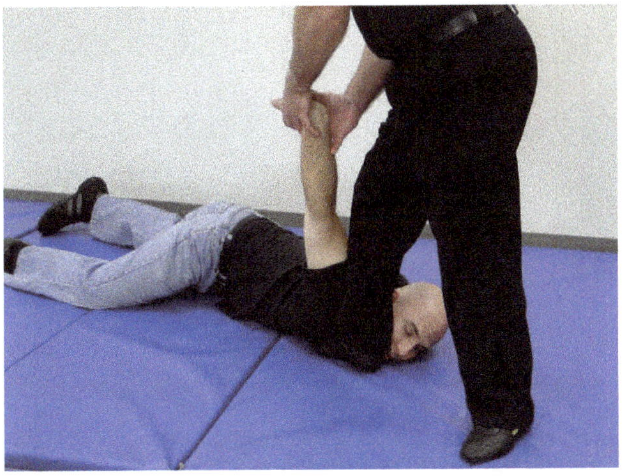

21H

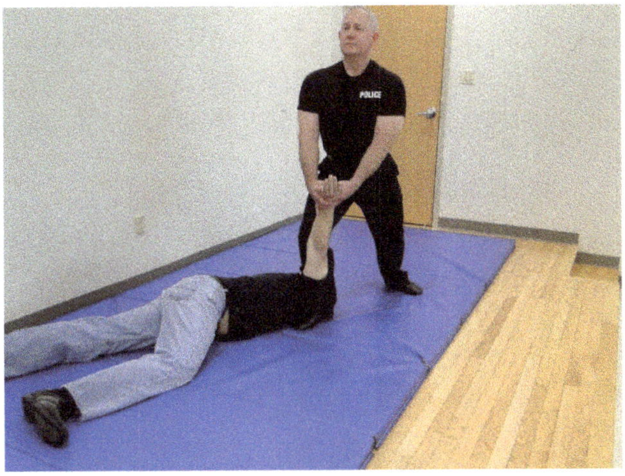

22H

Figure 21H. The right foot should step back behind you, allowing the suspect's arm to come away from your body as little as possible. The suspect's arm is in a position now that is locked and tension is being placed on the shoulder as well as the elbow.

Figure 22H. Keeping the suspect's wrist bent down, and forward, the arm kept pulled back toward the shin of your leg will keep him locked in a position. He will not be able to pull out of it. This is also the point that you need to stop and reevaluate the situation. What I mean by this is that while the suspect is under control take a short time to bring yourself down from this major amount of focus that you have on the suspect. Look up and make sure there are no partners to the suspect that may be a danger to you or that would atleast try to interfere with the arrest that you are about to make. If no persons are coming at you to interfere, now you need to take an even better look around you. Take at least three long deep breaths. This will bring you back to focus from a possible tunnel vision you may have on your suspect and allow your heart rate to go down. This will ease that adrenalin flow that would be racing through your body at this time and allow you to catch your breath and allow you think more clearly.

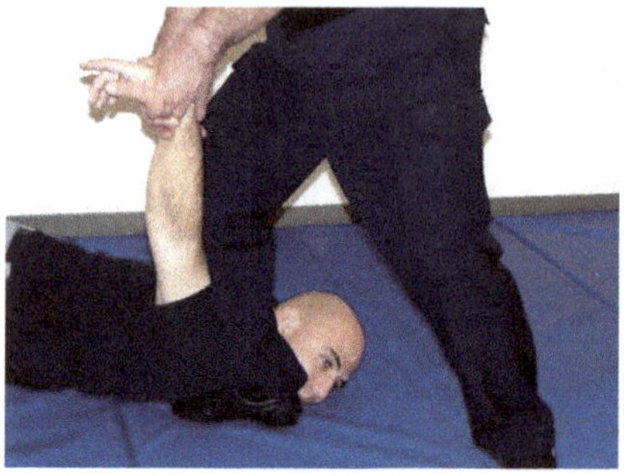

23H

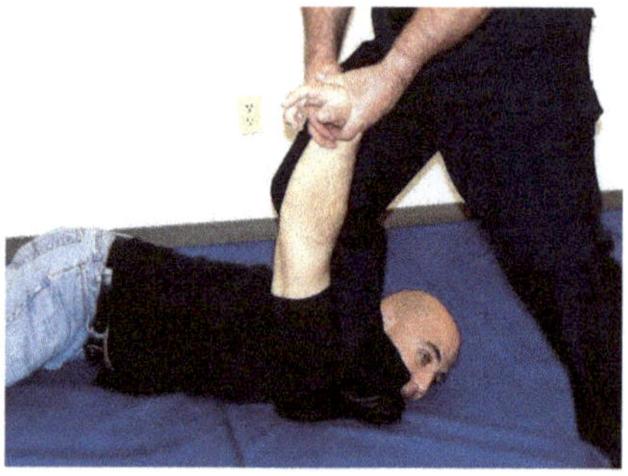

24H

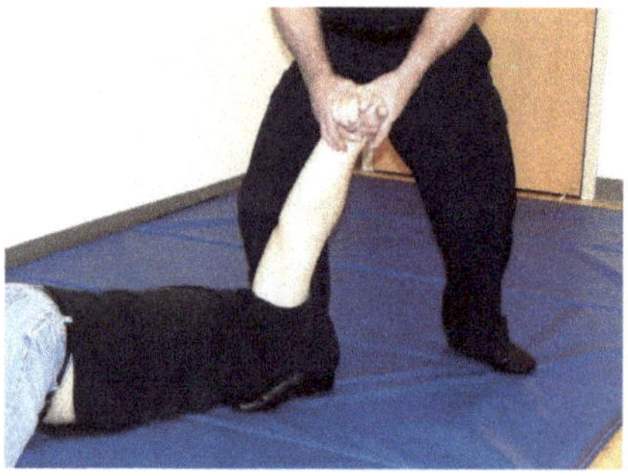

25H

Figures 23H and 24H. Locking out of the suspect's arm is more than just stepping behind the shoulder. Pressure is needed across the triceps and inside the elbow to increase the pressure for pain and compliance. Bending your right knee forward as you pull back on the suspect's arm will assure that the arm is locked out.

Figure 25H. There is a danger of breaking the elbow of the suspect if the pull

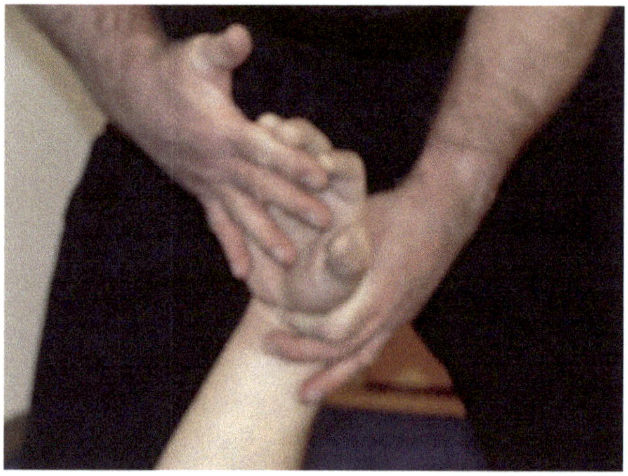

26H

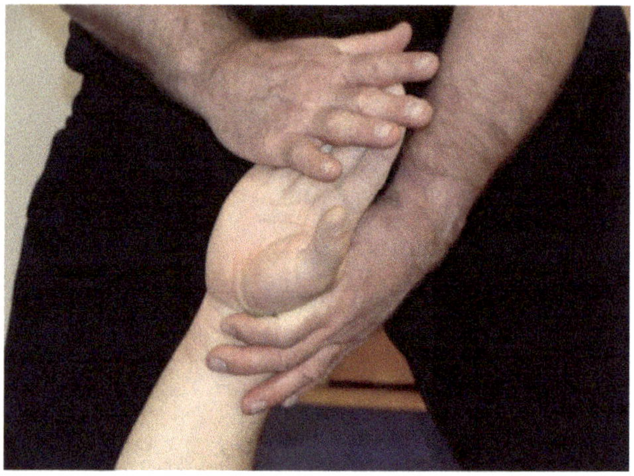

27H

Figure 26H. From the shoulder lock out position, the suspect's hand has to be opened and turned to place him in the handcuffing position. The right hand is released from the suspect's wrist, while a firm grip on his wrist remains with your left hand. The left hand opens the suspect's hand to extend the fingers back toward you. To open the suspect's hand will not be difficult from this position. Place your fingers under his fingers and extend them back.

Figure 27H. As the fingers of the suspect extend back, pressure is applied to the finger area to continue the extension and to start the rotation of the wrist toward the outside of the suspect's body. If the rotation of the suspects wrist goes toward the body side, you will experience problems with the flexibility and will not be able to take his arm down to the handcuffing position. You should be able to see this problem right away when the next step of grabbing the hand will not be in the correct position.

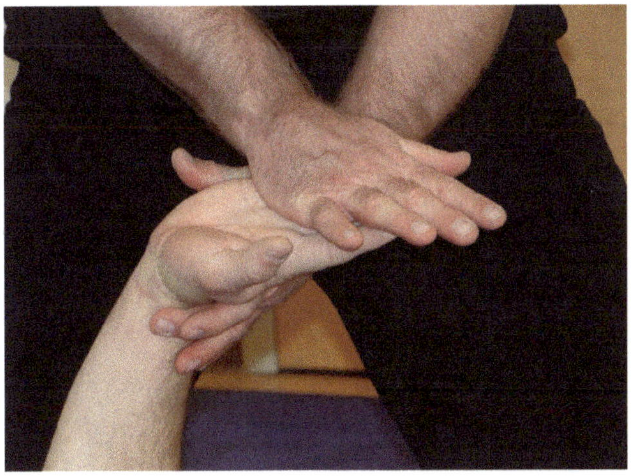

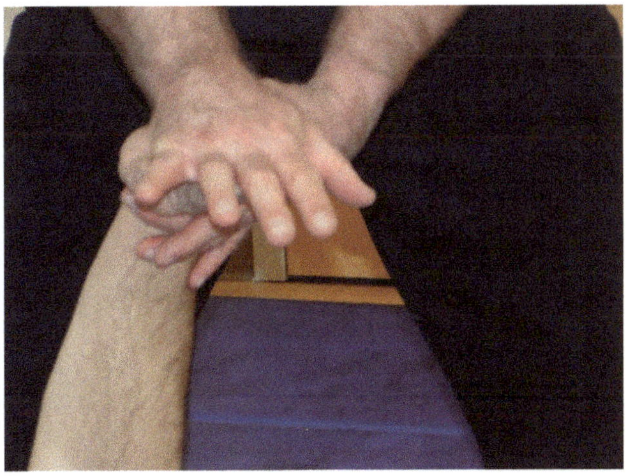

28H 29H

Figure 28H. Rotating the hand of the suspect back toward his feet, your palm remains down on top of his palm which is facing up. Your left hand remains at the suspect's wrist to control the arm an keeping it straight. Your right hand keeps the suspect's hand flat and bent back at the wrist as it rotates the hand back to the left.

Figure 29H. The suspect's hand is now rotated as far as it should go Fingers are pointed toward the suspect's feet. Your palm is on top of the suspect's palm opposite each other. Your right hand is still putting pressure down on the suspect's

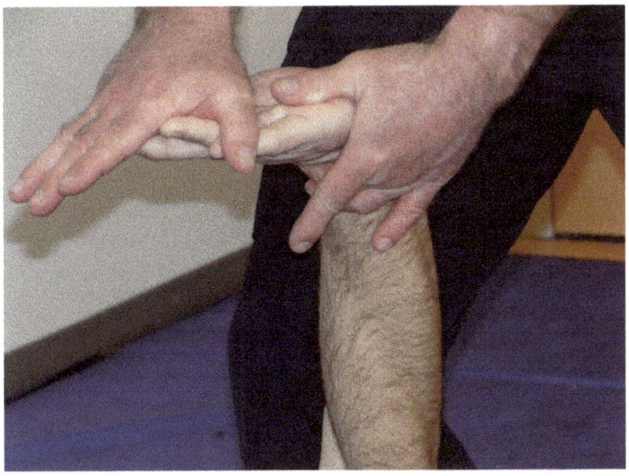

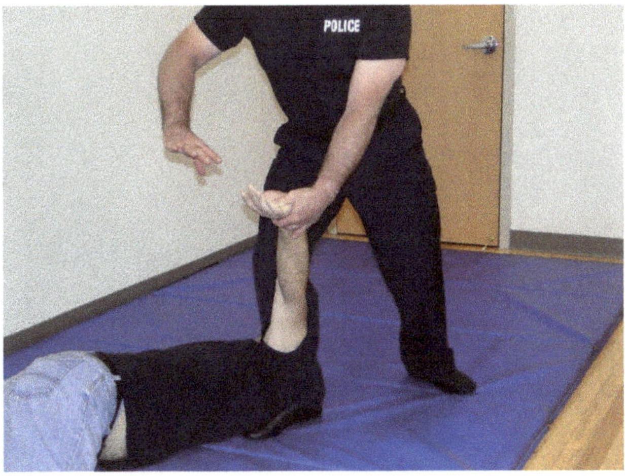

30H 31H

Figure 30H. Demonstrates the release of the suspect's hand just prior to the re-positioning for the takedown of the arm. The right hand pushes to the tips of the suspect's fingers, and the left hand makes sure the suspect's hand stays bent at the wrist and flat. To release the right hand, and secure this position, the thumb of your left hand is placed on the palm of the suspect's hand.

Figure 31H. When your right hand is released and away from the suspect's hand, it is tilted inward as if in a handshaking position.

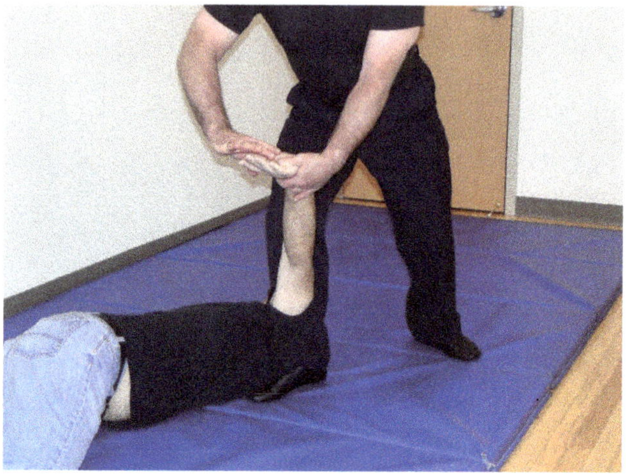

32H

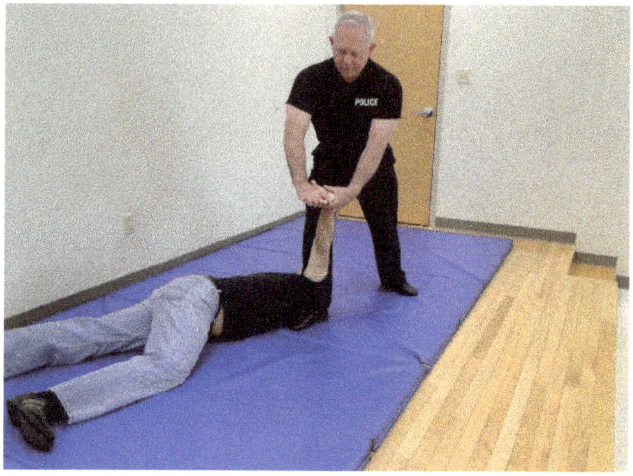

33H

Figure 32H. Reach in "palm to palm" in the handshaking position. Keeping the suspect's arm straight and pressure against the elbow with your right knee by keeping the knee bent enough to keep the suspect under control. Your shin should be across the triceps of the extended arm, pulling back on the suspect's arm to keep it tight.

Figure 33H. Once the hands meet, secure your grip deep into the hand, pushing the web portion of your hand between your thumb and index finger tight against the web portion of the suspect's hand. Grip down with your fingers into a tight grip, still keeping the suspect's wrist bent back.

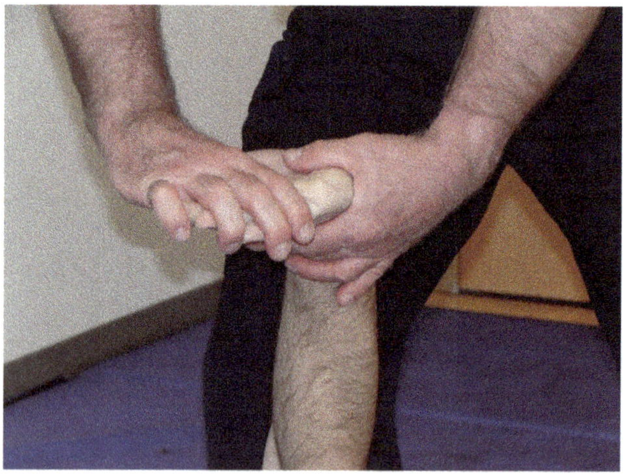

34H

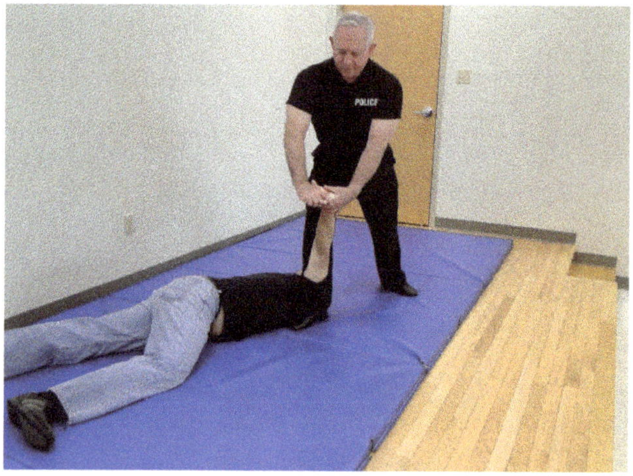

35H

Figure 34H. This close up shows how the suspect's hand is placed in a tilted back position as your right hand grips deep. The left hand fingers are under the suspect's wrist and the thumb is on top of the palm.

Figure 35H. This is the position that you should be in right before the take-down to handcuffing the suspect. The right foot is under the suspect's shoulder and the right foot is back almost 180 degrees from him.

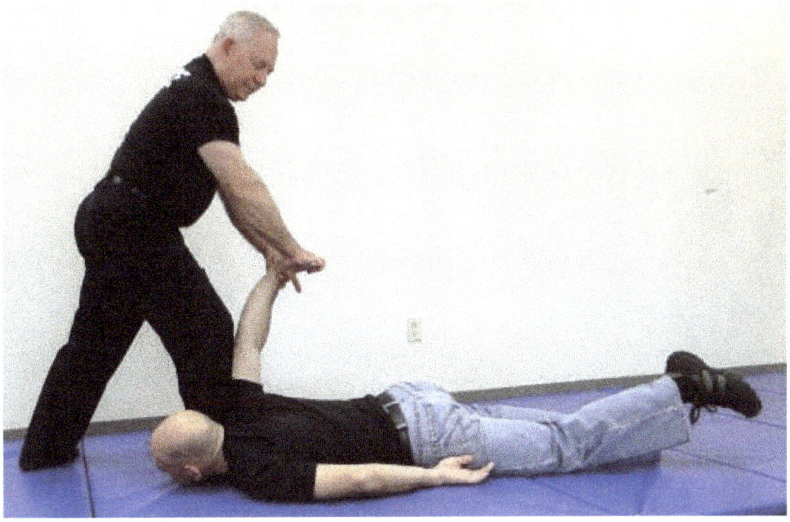

36H

Figure 36H. The takedown of the suspect's arm to his back starts as you start the turning of the suspect's right hand back toward the suspect's body. Please remember when practicing to do this slowly. It will prevent injury to the elbow and shoulder of the uke or partner you are working with.

NOTE: When this torque is applied to the suspect's wrist, there is an automatic response from the suspect, to let you know that your hand position is correct. The response is a movement of the suspect's feet. The feet will turn or come off the floor as in the picture.

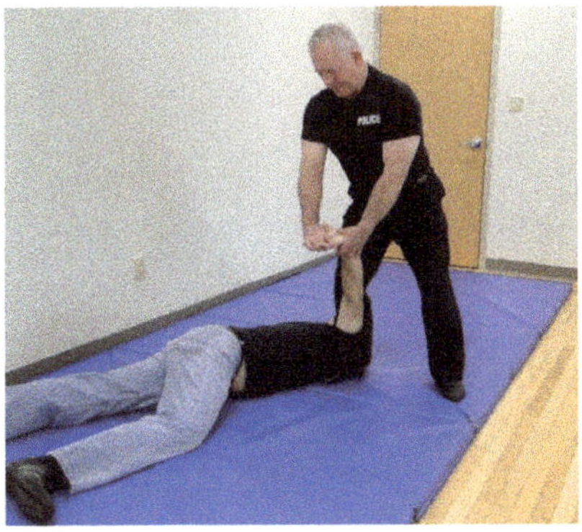

37H

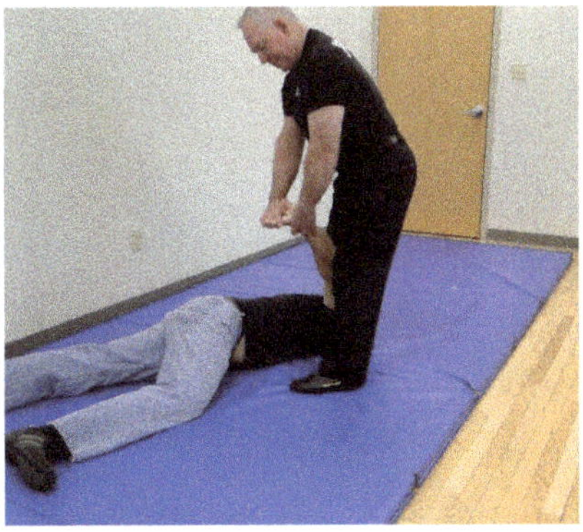

38H

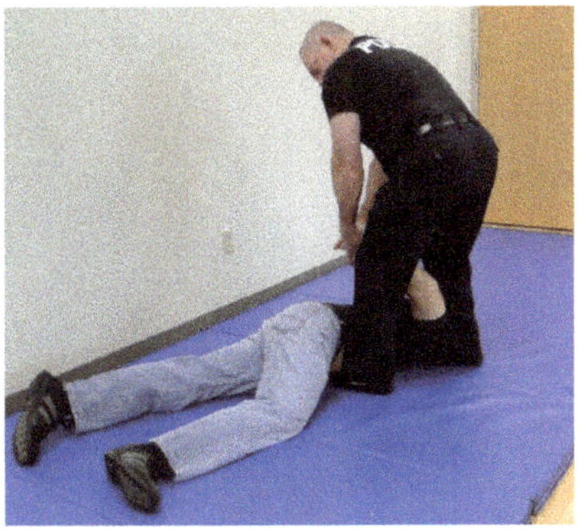

39H

Figures 37H,38H, and 39H. The movement of your left foot should be done in one smooth step from the back position to the suspect's waist. As the step is being performed, the suspect's wrist is turned back to a 90 degree angle of the suspect's body and the arm is allowed to be brought down to the small of the back.

NOTE: This is a crucial point in bringing the arm to the back. Remember in practice this is a person that is allowing you to do this technique on him or her. The arm should be lowered with care.

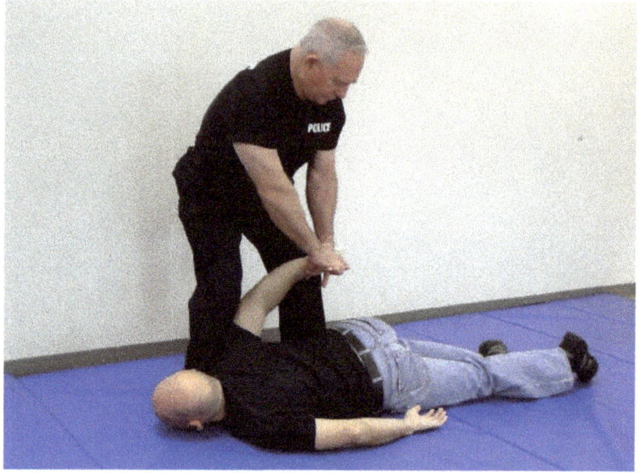

40H

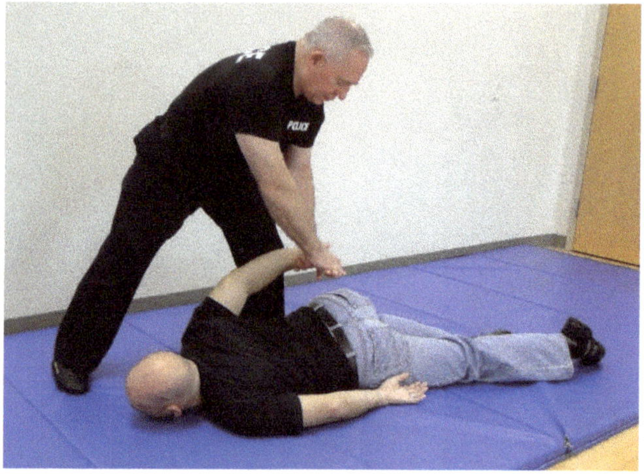

41H

Figures 40H and 41H. When stepping to the suspect's waist with your left foot, your right foot will pivot. When the step is completed, the right foot is brought back as you start to kneel down and place the suspect's hand on his back.

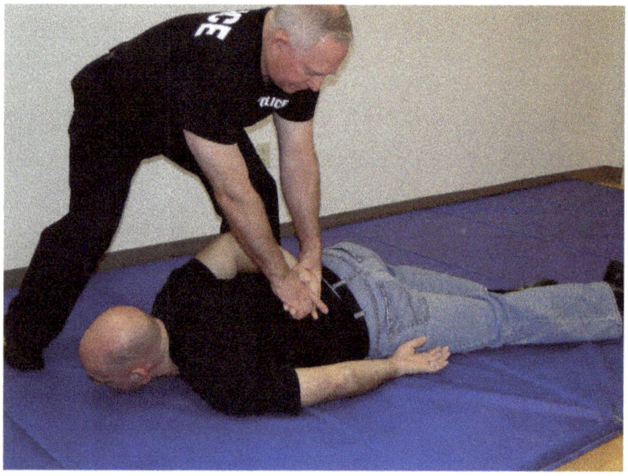

42H

43H

Figure 42H. When the suspect's hand comes in contact with his back, both of your hands are still in contact with his wrist and hand. Your left foot is still moving back behind you. You are now at a 90 degree angle to the suspect's body.

Figure 43H. Your right foot is back three to four feet from the suspect, and your weight is forward on your left foot. Your hands will secure the arm of the suspect. Observe that the right elbow of the suspect is bent, but it is above your left leg which is positioned at his waist. This is one of the more secure positions that has to be performed to prevent the suspect from pushing down with his arm in the attempt to get away or to begin rolling. Also, remember you are still applying pressure to the suspect's wrist on his back. This also assists you in your balance when bending down with his arm.

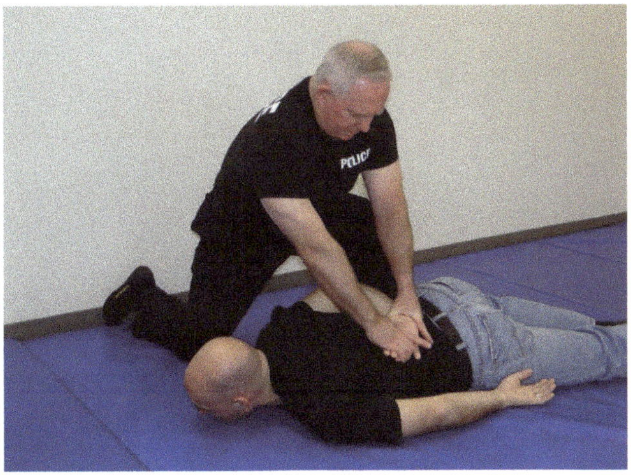

44H

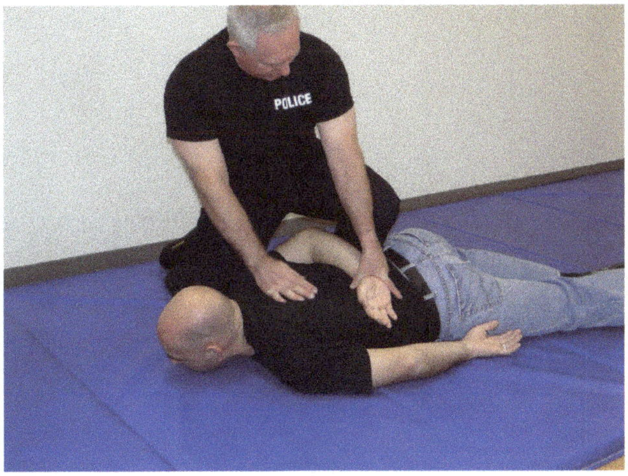

45H

Figure 44H. Your right knee is now bent behind you and your left foot is tight against the waist of the suspect.

Figure 45H. With your right knee bent, push your weight forward allowing your left knee to bend forward across the back of the suspect but still behind his arm securing it in its position.

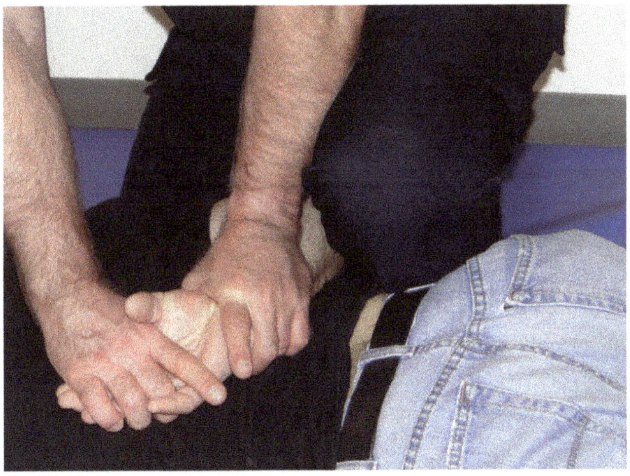

46H

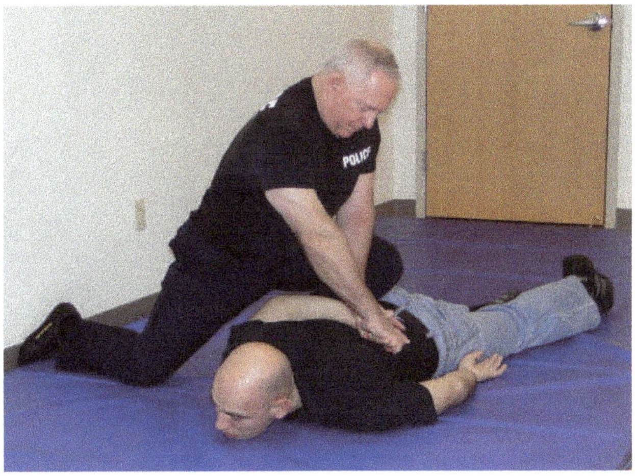

47H

Figures 46H and 47H. These pictures show how the left knee is now pushed forward onto the small of the suspect's back and behind the suspect's arm

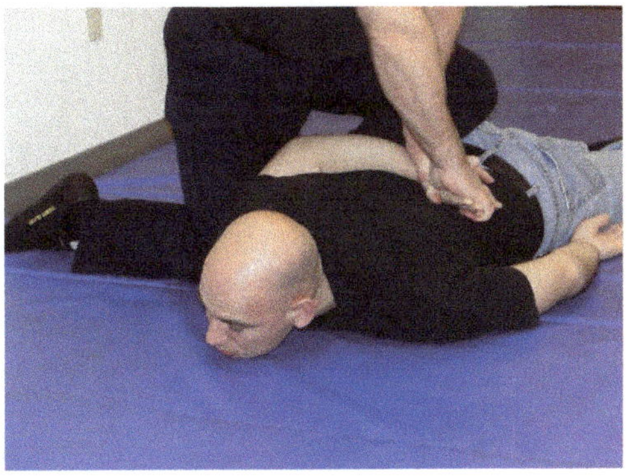

48H

Figure 48H. The next step is locking the suspect's arm by bringing your right knee forward against his elbow. This movement has two purposes. The first is to lock the arm from coming back at the elbow. The second is to push the right arm of the suspect over allowing you to have more room across the back for handcuffing the second hand when it is brought back.

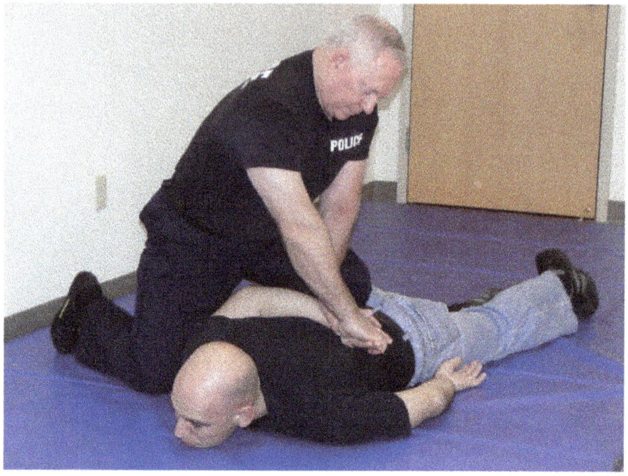

49H

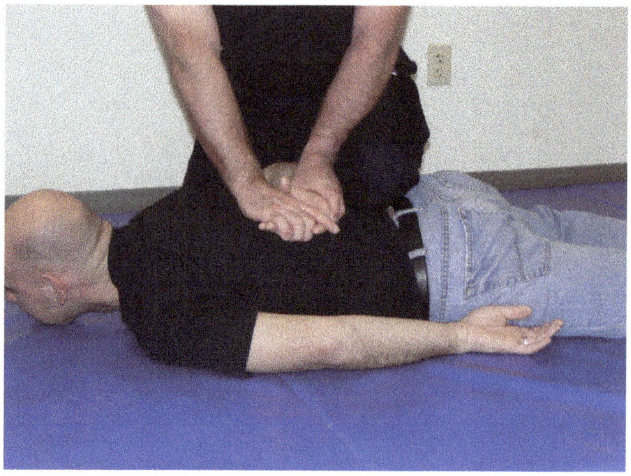

50H

Figures 49H and 50H. These two figures show the suspect's arm locked out by the use of both the right and left knee. Being locked out with both knees, prevents the suspect from rolling or being able to push his arm down.

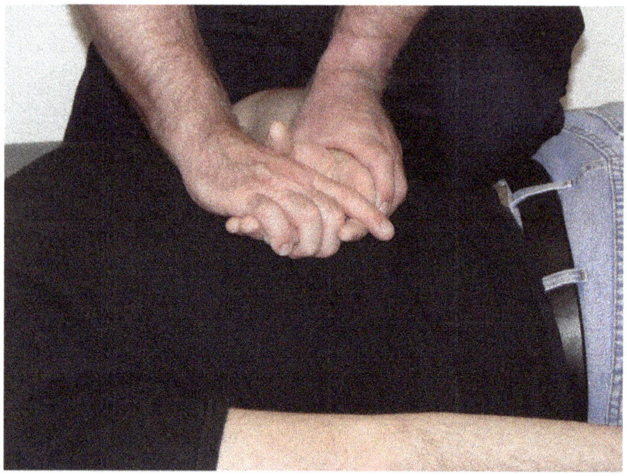

51H

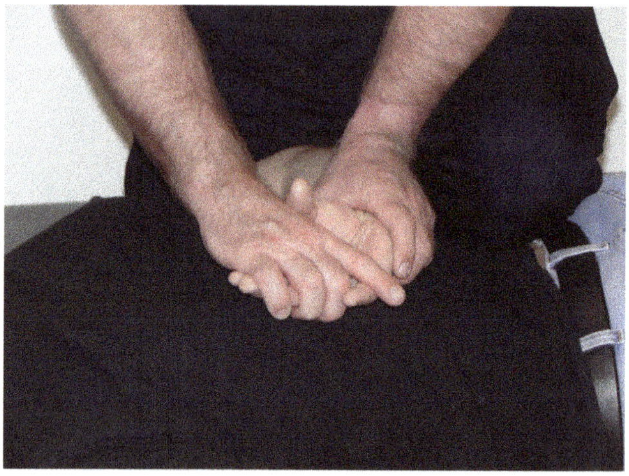

52H

Figures 51H and 52H. After the arm is locked out, it is important to make sure the suspect's hand and wrist stay flat for the best control. Keeping the hand and wrist from bending back will be done by supporting the wrist with the left hand and still in the handshaking position with the right. Having the hand and wrist flat, allows you to apply pain by twisting the hand sideways. The joints of the wrist are not made to have pressure applied in this manner. If the wrist were to bend back instead of sideways, it would be less effective. The pain compliance is important in bringing the left hand of the suspect to his back to be in the handcuff position which is necessary. The suspect would be given commands by you to put his hand behind him, before pain compliance would be used. Even if the suspect would be laying on the hand, with the pain compliance applied, this will cause the suspect to bring his hand out from under him and placed on his back.

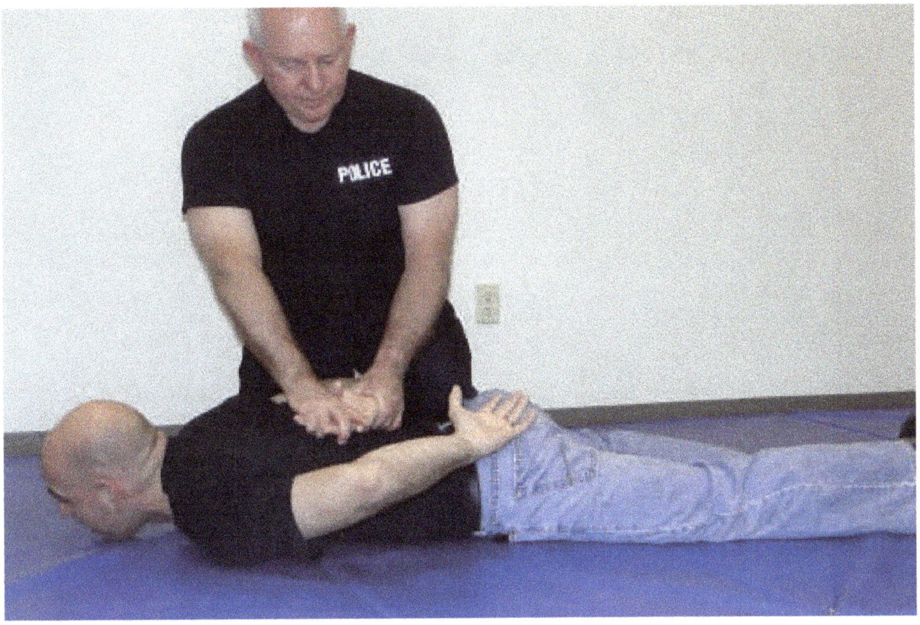

53H

Figure 53H. When the arm and hand of the suspect is secured, and the wrist and hand are flat, the command for the suspect to place his other hand on his back is given. When the lock is correct and a small amount of pressure is applied on the suspect's hand, he will give the other hand willingly.

54H

Figure 54H. When the unsecured hand is placed on his back upon your command, the suspect is ready to be handcuffed.

CHAPTER 4

Hitchhiker I

HITCHHIKER I

The "Hitchhiker" is the first of basic moves that are the foundation of the Cane-Albrecht method. Like all great moves in martial arts, a good technique is priceless. Any technique used in martial arts should be effective, not difficult to learn, and can be performed easily by officers of different sizes and statures. What makes a good technique a great technique is the ability to teach it to all police agencies and for it to be the most effective.

A technique may have same similarities in different martial arts and may be named due to what action the move creates. The Hitchhiker move was named in English so as to be easier to remember for the positioning of the hand in order to do this move. This move in the traditional Japanese language would be called Te-nage, meaning hand throw and in Aikido it is known as kotegaeshi.

HITCHHIKER POSITION
SOLO EXERCISE

Learning the Hitchhiker position will be better understood if we first do this in a solo exercise. The solo position will break it down for you one step at a time. You will be able to feel how the pressure is applied and understand how it becomes so effective as a technique.

1I

2I

Figure 1I. Extend your hands out in front of you with your palms down and bent at the elbow.

Figure 2I. Reach under your left hand with your right hand now turning both palms upward. Reach toward the thumb side of your left hand.

3I

4I

Figure 3I and 4I. Place your fingers of your right hand around the "meaty portion" of the thumb or heel of the left hand. The thumb of your right hand is placed on the back of your left hand between the middle finger and the ring finger at the base of the knuckles. Now, apply pressure to the back of your left hand with your thumb bending your left wrist forward until it can no longer bend.

5I

Figure 5I. After the wrist is locked back to a stopped position, it is then turned to the outside, also, to the stopped position. After you feel it stop, you will see that the next movement that will occur is the elbow will turn in and the shoulder will drop. These movements are all movements that occur in order as the body breaks down from a standing position.

HITCHHIKER PARTNER EXERCISE

The partner exercise will allow you to get the feel of your hand placement on another person. The identification of the feel of someone's hand in yours in this position will assure you to develop a mental image. Being able to develop a mental image will give you the ability to recognize the feeling of this position in your hand so it can be an instinctive response when it happens.

1J

2J

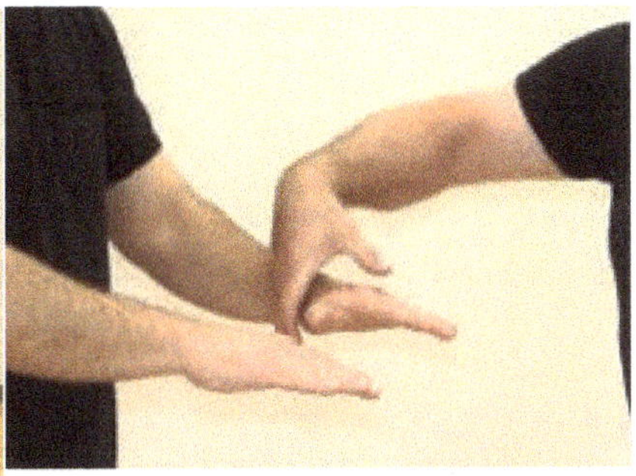

3J

Figure 1J. Have your partner extend his hands in front of him slightly bent at the elbow. You need to stand in front of your partner and reach over the top of his hand. Either hand will work since both hands will be used in this exercise.

Figure 2J. Reach over the top of your partner's hand allowing your fingers to reach inside the thumb side of the hand directly in front of you.

Figure 3J. Extend your fingers around the thumb side of your partner's hand to grab the meaty part of the thumb.

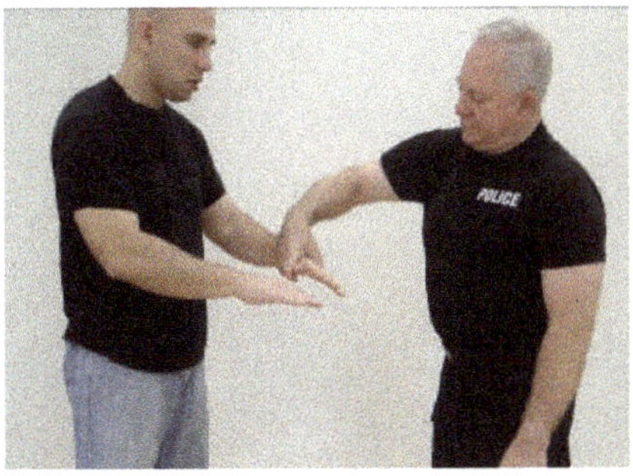

4J

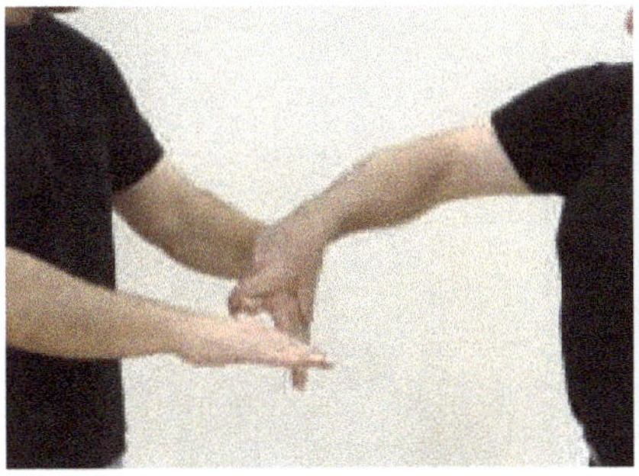

5J

6J

Figure 4J. After reaching inside over the top of your partner's hand, your fingers will grab the meaty portion of his hand and your thumb should be placed on the top of your partner's hand. Your thumb is placed on the back of the hand on the knuckle area between the middle finger and the ring finger.

Figure. 5J. When your grip is secured bend your partner's wrist down until you can feel it stop. This is a locking position which will change from person to person due to peoples varying flexibility.

Figure 6J. Now, turn the fingers inward and upward keeping the wrist in a locked down position.

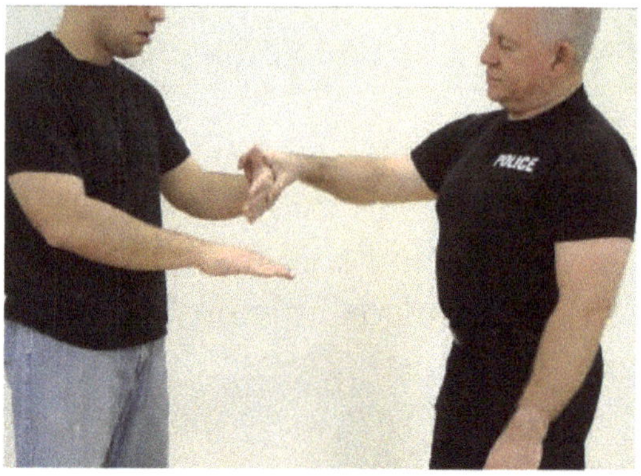

7J

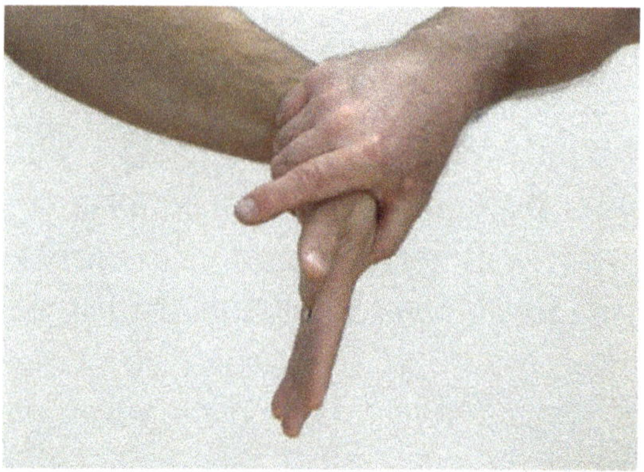

8J

Figures 7J and 8J. Keep the fingers in the correct position and your partner's hand pressed down to a locked out position while keeping your grip tight.

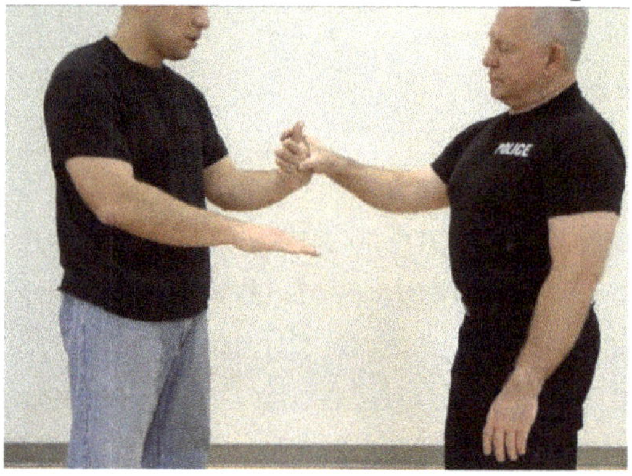

9J

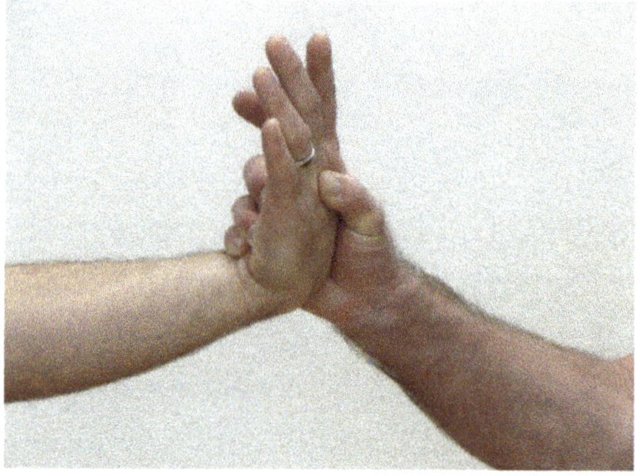

10J

Figures 9J and 10J. When the wrist is locked down and back, it is turned inward and upward so the fingers of your partner are pointed up.

11J

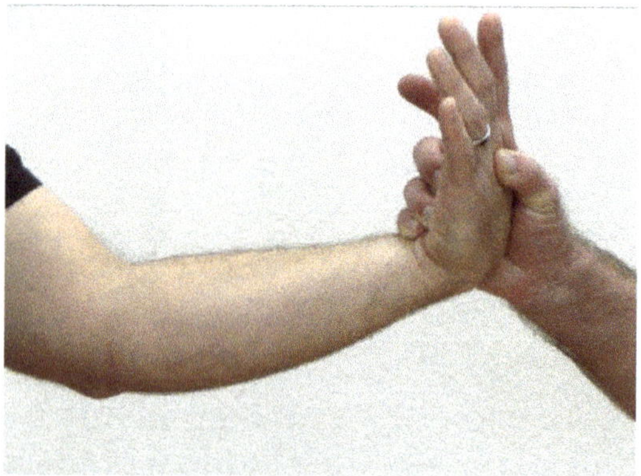

12J

Figures 11J and 12J. When turning the wrist up, the wrist will again come to a stopping point to another locked position, again which will vary from person to person according to the amount of flexibility. Still, your grip is tight, keeping your partner's wrist now locked back and locked to the side position.

 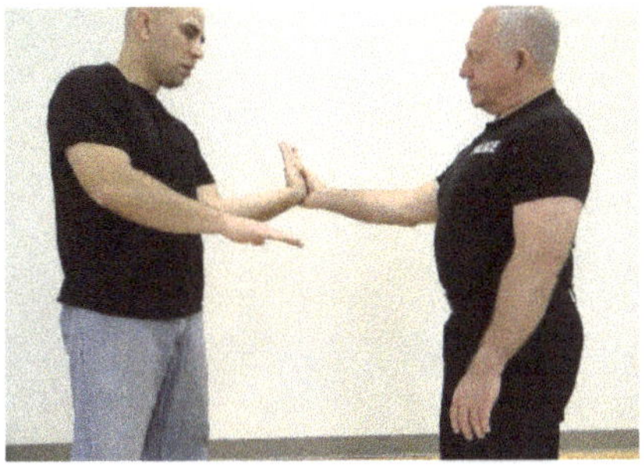 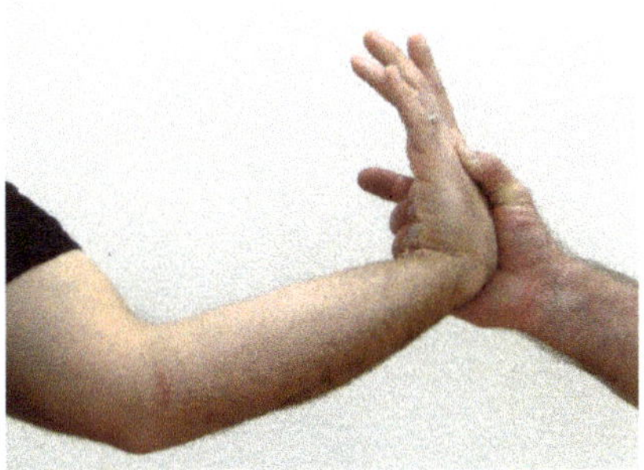

13J 14J 15J

Figures 13J, 14J, and 15J. When your partner's hand stops at the stopping point, and switch hands and do the same movement with your left hand. Become familiar with this motion on both the right and left hand. Switch back and forth for several repetitions to allow both of you to feel where the hand stops in the down posi-

ADDING HAND PRESSURE

To Secure Your Grip and Increase Your Power

 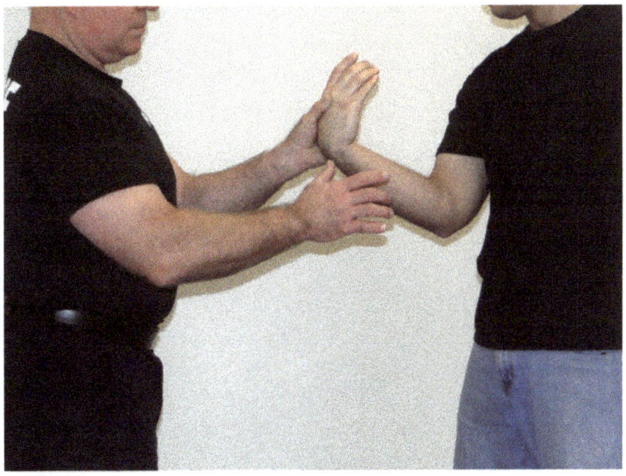

16J 17J

Figure 16J. And 17J. When your grip starts the motion of the hitchhiker with either hand, you will take the chance of a possible strength or weight difference or even you, or your suspect's hand become sweaty and you may lose your grip. Using your second hand to support your grip will increase your power and secure your grip. From whatever position the suspect may have you in, you need a secure powerful grip to prevent his getting away so that your technique will be strong when preformed. Once your technique is started in motion, the second hand should be brought up as you are starting to place pressure on the back of the suspect's hand in the first locking position.

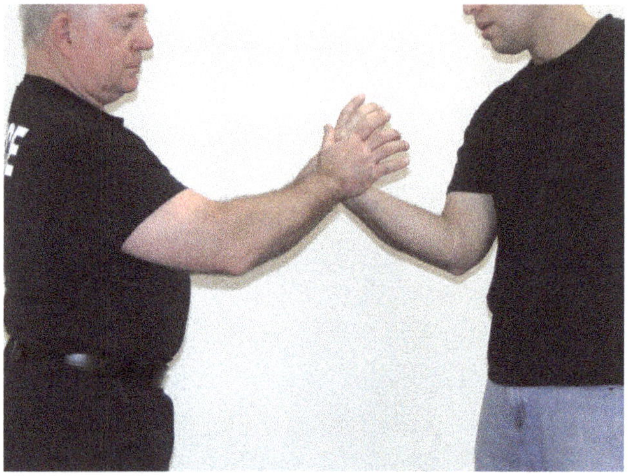

18J

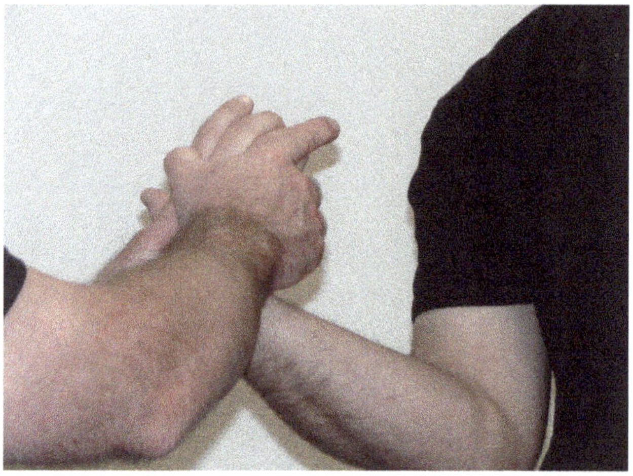

19J

Figure 18J. When your second hand comes across and meets your suspect's hand, your hand should stay open until the palm and heel of your hand makes contact with the side of suspect's hand.

Figure 19J. When your hand makes contact, you grip so that your thumb will be on the back of his hand and at least three fingers should be placed in his palm.

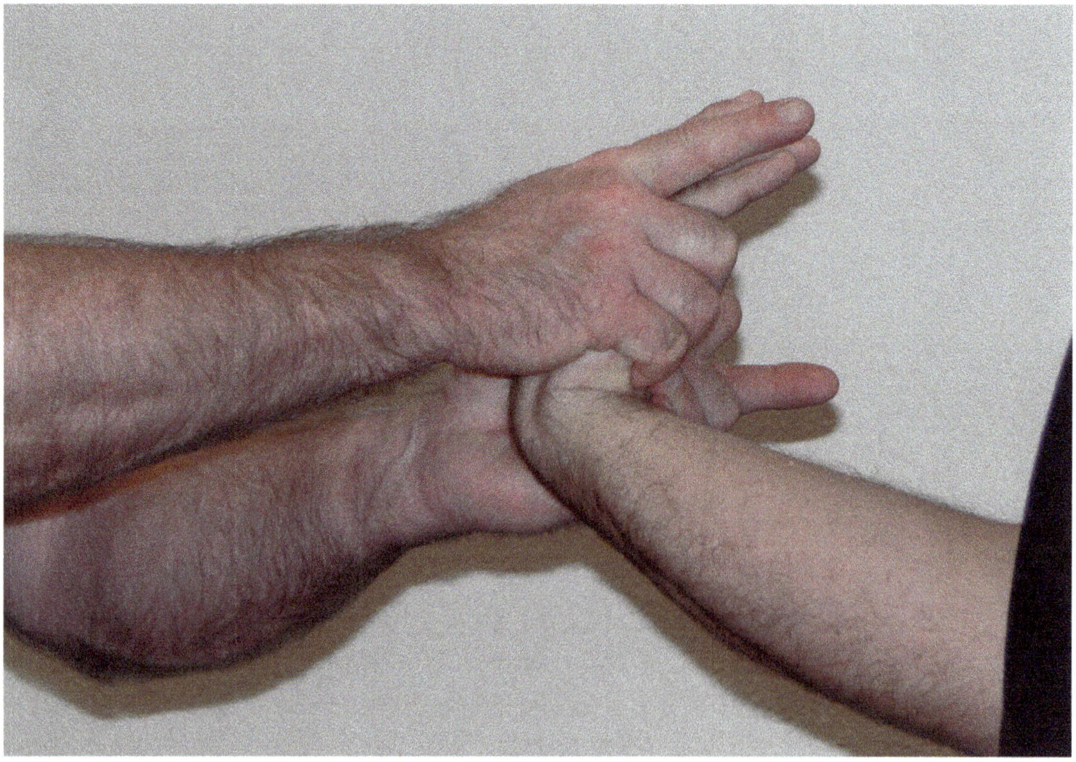

20J

Figure 20J. This close up shows how the grip clamps around the suspect's hand to secure the grip and assist in locking it back and to the side to do the technique.

THE HITCHHIKER
BODY BREAKDOWN

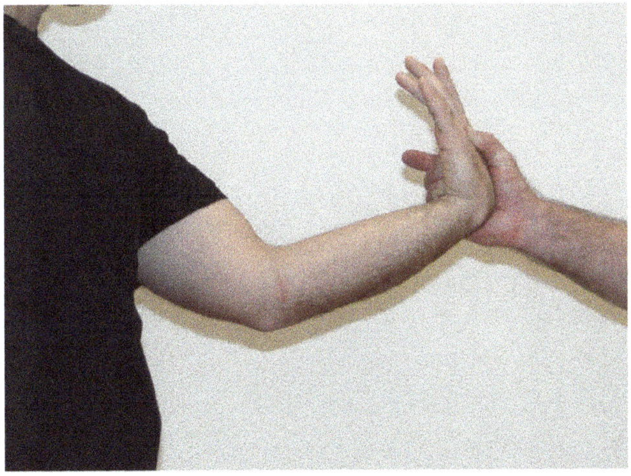

21J

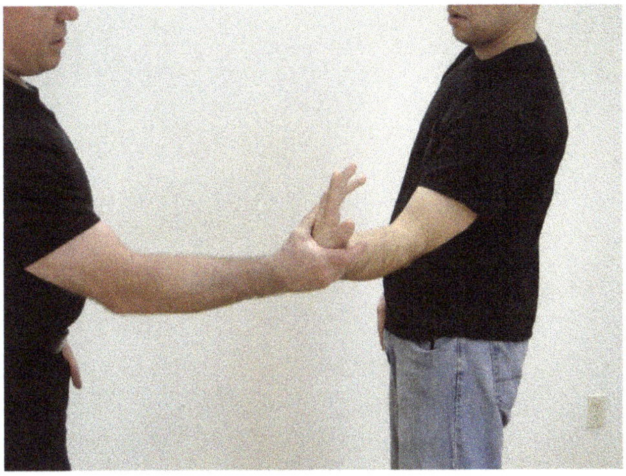

22J

Figure 21J and 22J. When the wrist can go no further and the hand starts to go beyond the stopping point, you will see the breakdown of the suspect's body start with the elbow turning in toward the body.

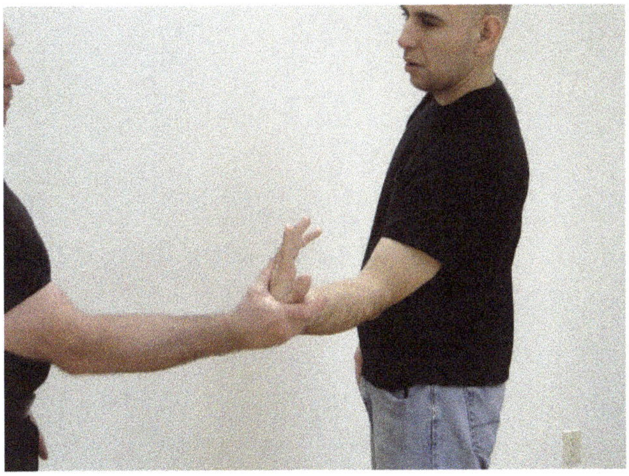

23J

24J

Figures 23J and 24J. Once the elbow turns in, the body starts a major breakdown causing the suspect's posture and balance to come off center. When the elbow reaches its stopping point, the shoulder will dip to that side and the body will lean to that side bending sideways over that hip. The "off centering of the body" and "each joint reaching it's stopping point" are all causes of a controlled movement that is in your control. The objective of the hitchhiker is to breakdown the body, part by part, until you have the suspect on the ground.

25J

26J

27J

Figure 25J, 26J and 27J. When the elbow turns in as far as it can, the "Shoulder Drop" will occur. When the shoulder drop happens, it will shift his weight to the left side, and by doing so, will cause his left hip to lock. This will not allow him to step to that side so he can regain his balance. Further breakdown of the body's posture will occur. The body's weight will continue to shift to that side and the left knee will bend forward slightly.

28J

29J

Figures 28J and 29J. At this point, the body's posture is completely broken down and his balance is gone. There is no chance that he will be able to regain his balance due to the continual pull of the suspect's hand. The pulling of the suspect's hand will cause him to break balance in two directions now. After the knee bends forward, the pressure is still being placed on the hand and wrist, pulling him to his left side, but also forward. He will not be able to bend the knee forward and go to his knees because the pulling forward of his arm now causes his left shoulder to come forward. Instead of falling just to his side, he has to fall to his left hip. When the weight of his torso has passed over the left hip and foot, and the weight has shifted all to his left foot, his ankle is locked. As he continues to fall to his left hip, the slight tension to the front, and you staying upright and not going down with the suspect, will roll his left shoulder forward keeping it out of play when he makes contact with the ground.

TAKEDOWN

WHEN USING A PARTNER

30J

31J

32J

Figure 30J, 31J, and 32J. Have your partner in the hitchhiker hand position and simultaneously, make sure he is in a kneeling position. Apply the locking of his hand back and to his right side. When the elbow turns in and his torso weight passes over his hip, he will lose his balance and lay to his right side. His right shoulder will turn toward you and he will lay over to his right hip.

33J

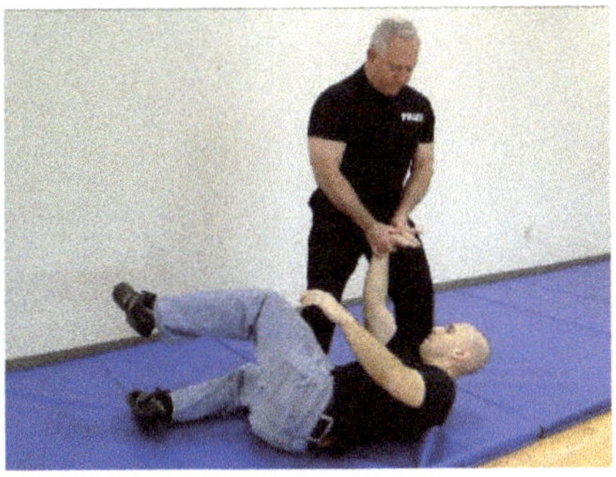

34J

35J

Figures 33J, 34J, and 35J. These figures will show that as your partner's hip touches the ground, your hands pull back to your center close to your body. This pulls the shoulder forward and lifts it out of the natural falling path so that he continues to turn on to his back. In this position, his weight will settle onto the ground, and his body will stop turning. You need to make sure that your feet are spread apart so you are able to develop a good base and your back is straight. Pull up on your partner's arm to make sure that it stays straight. With your body straight and not bent at the waist, if you are pulled on by your partner or a suspect, it will assure you to maintain your balance. This position will make it impossible for him to pull you down or over because he would have to pull through your entire body.

CHAPTER 5

Hitchhiker I, Distract and Takedown

DISTRACT PRINCIPLES

Understanding the distract and its principles is fairly simple. During any grab, choke, or holding of you, or any part of your body, the attacker is focused on one thing, keeping his hold on you. His mind is in the mode of dominating you by whatever hold he has over you. If you fight directly against this hold, it either gets tighter or he moves in a way that he will be able to secure his hold over you. Imagine you should have something in your hand. The second that someone touches your hand to take it away, what happens? Your grip gets tighter and you become focused directly on this point, so as not to lose whatever is in your hand.

Which brings us to the first words of wisdom - ***DO NOT FIGHT THE HOLD, BUT FIGHT THE PERSON.*** Fighting the person and not the hold is somewhat of a distraction in itself. Think about it. A person can not think of protecting his entire body at the same time he is thinking of keeping a hold of you. So there are many targets that are open for you to strike.

The second words of wisdom are - ***A DISTRACT DOES NOT HAVE TO BE PAINFUL.*** I know that you may be fighting with a person who has the intent of hurting, injuring, or even trying to kill you. The object is ***DISTRACT.*** This will take the assailant's mind off of what he is doing for that split second. ***Yes***, that split second is all you need as long as you have a plan or in our case a good technique. The distract will not mean anything if you are not able to do something in that precise moment the distract takes place. So you will have to be ready and in reality, timing is everything. In that split second, your response, your distract, and how you respond once the distract is being applied is vital. As I had just mentioned, the distract does not have to be painful. Again think what happens when someone touches you anywhere on your person. Just for that second, your mind tells you that there is something or someone touching you whether or not you see them. Keep in mind that may be because you don't have anything else going on at that moment. You may even think that you may be watching something, and all of a sudden, something flies by and you flinch, duck, or just take your eyes off the thing you were watching, again for that ***SPLIT SECOND.*** Understand that as long as the mind has to focus on something, no matter how simple, painful or not, the focal point for that short period of time is not you. Now is when you, as they say, "**DO YOUR STUFF!**" This is the time you do the technique that you will know so well by the time you have finished this book and have been able to practice with a partner. Remember the distracts used in this book are not set in stone, but just the ones I chose to use. There are an infinite number and only limited by your imagination. The distracts that you use are ones that come easy to you and will become second nature to you.

COVER AND DISTRACT

To "Cover and Distract" is a procedure you will become very familiar with. This procedure is very important to learn in this order. Like many things that we do, it also has more than one purpose. Lets look at the first part, **The Cover.** When you place your hand over the top of the offender's hand, you are creating a focal point for the offender. He will think one of two things. One, he may think you are grabbing his hand to pull it off of whatever he has his grip on. In this case, he will tighten his grip to prevent you from pulling his hand off. This has created a focal point in his mind that will demand all of his attention for a short period of time. It is now necessary for a distract to be done to move his mind for that precious "***split second"*** you will need to remove his hand. Second, he may think something is going on that he may not want any part of, so he will attempt to pull his hand away. If your cover is fast and strong, you now have his hand. This also creates that focal point for your assailant to again place his attention on this hand. Again, it is very important to take the focus of this hand onto another part of his body, so that you will be able to start your technique.

The purpose of the cover is to prevent his hand from pulling away and to place your hand in a position that will be functional in the technique you are about to perform. The placement of your hand will determine the direction the suspect's hand will come off and the technique you are about to use.

Now, we are back to the distract of your assailant. As we said, there are an infinite number of distracts you will be able to use. The object is to change his focal point for that ***Split Second*** to allow you to start the technique that will give you control of the assailant and where he will end up. The distract in this case is a kick to his shin. With a little practice, the timing of the cover, distract, and the removal of the assailant's hand all come together.

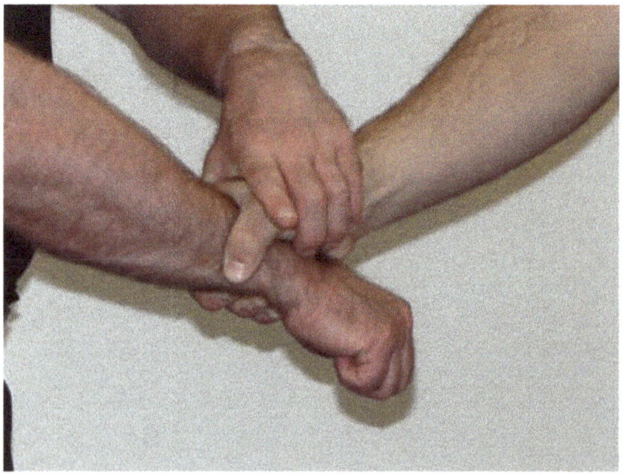

COVER

DISTRACT

HITCHHIKER I - ATTACKS
From Cross-Wrist Grab Right Hand

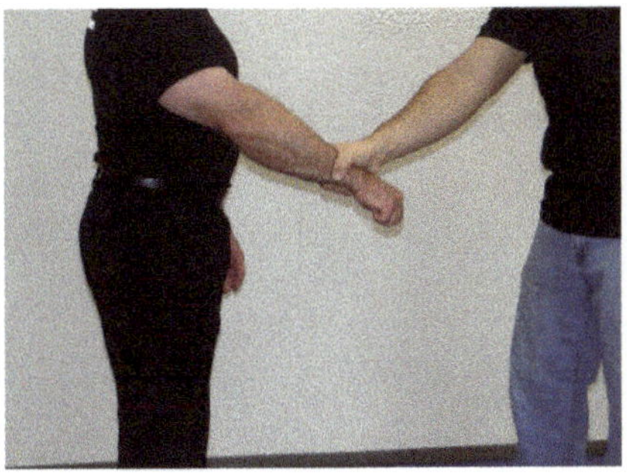
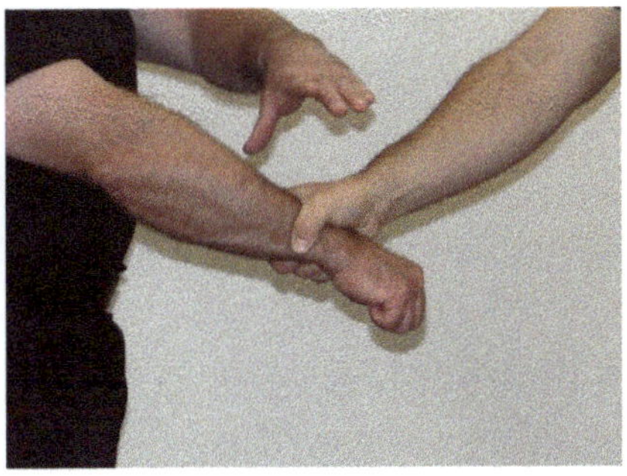
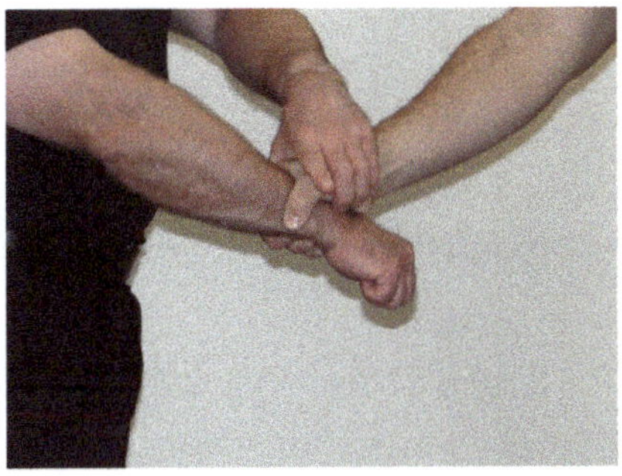

1K 2K 3K

Figure 1K. The move starts from a grab from the opposite side called a cross-wrist grab using his right hand to grab your right wrist.

Figure 2K. As soon as you are grabbed, you need to reach over the top of the hand that grabbed you with your opposite hand; this is your cover. Your grip will be with your left hand and should be aimed to place your fingers over the lower portion of the thumb.

Figure 3K. When your left hand makes contact with the hand that has grabbed you, you must first press down on his hand, to assure the hand is not pulled away. Your grip is placed over the top of the hand so your fingers wrap around the meaty portion of the thumb, and your thumb is placed on the back of his hand between the knuckles of the middle finger and the ring finger.

NOTE: When grabbed, only two scenarios will play out. The first is that the person that grabbed you will try to let go, and prevent you from grabbing him. The second will be, when your "cover hand" contacts his hand he will tighten his grip to prevent you from pulling his hand away from your wrist.

4K 5K 6K

Figures 4K, 5K, and 6K. After the covering of your partner's hand, you are ready to place the hand in the hitchhiker position as soon as the hand is taken off your wrist. The distract is performed, in this case, the distract is a front snap kick to the suspect's shin using the right foot. This distract is done only as a distract. **Remember that a distract does not have to be painful.**

7K

8K

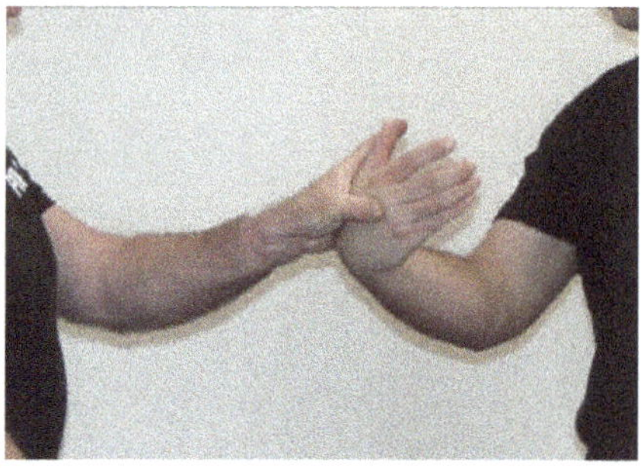

9K

Figure 7K. As soon as the distract has been done, there is a “***split second***” period of time that the suspect’s attention will be taken off his grip on your wrist. In that “split second” time, there will be that opportunity to start the hitchhiker technique and remove the suspect’s hand from your wrist.

Figure 8K. The suspect’s hand is pulled back to your left side as the right arm is pulled back to the right side so there is no attempt for the suspect to grab your arm again.

Figure 9K. Push the suspect’s wrist back to the first locking position.

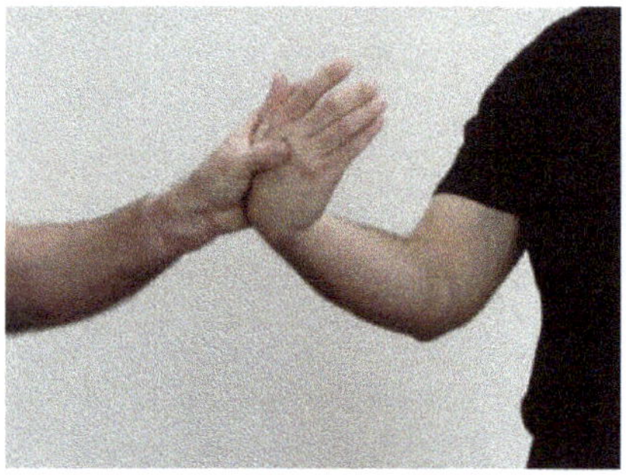

10K

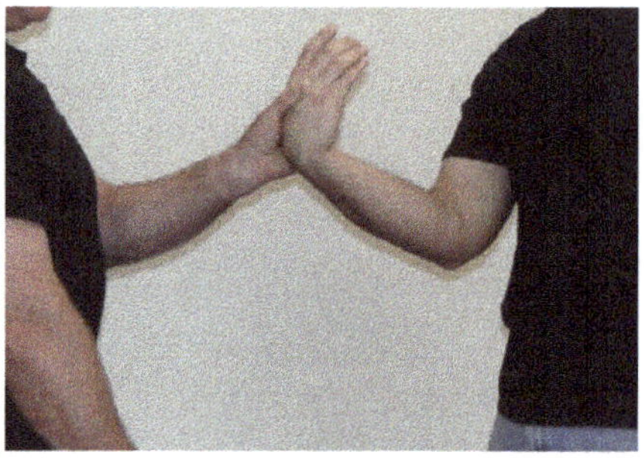

11K

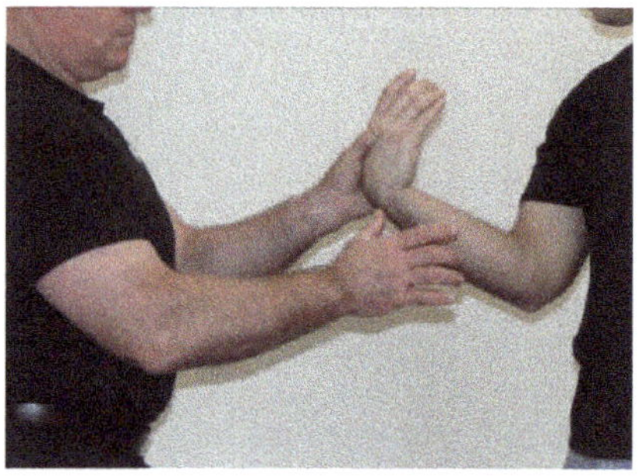

12K

Figure 10k and 11K. When the wrist of the suspect is locked back, it is now taken in a small circular movement back to your left, keeping the wrist locked back.

Figure 12K. While the hand is being taken in this small circle, your right hand comes up to assist.

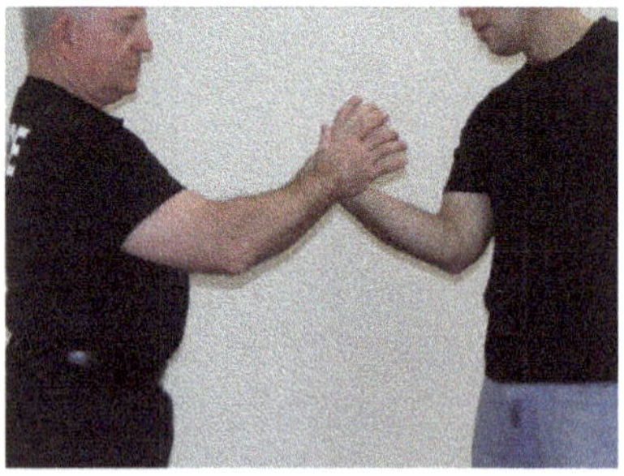

13K

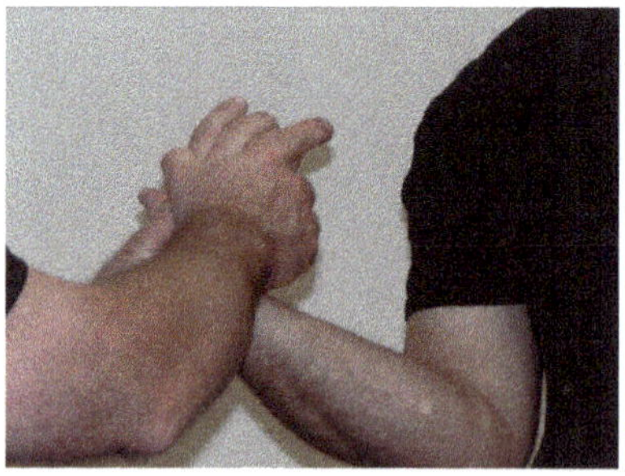

14K

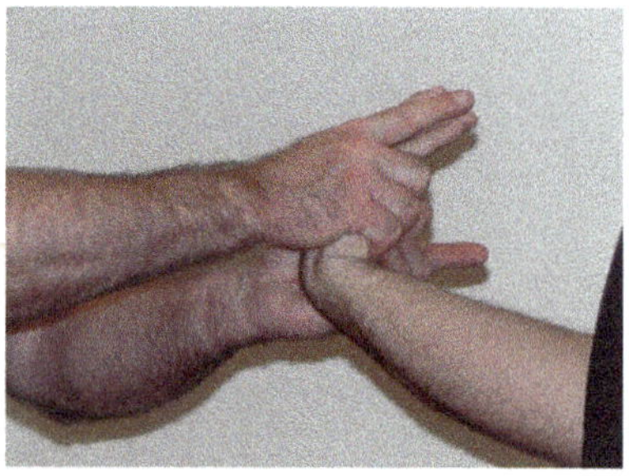

15K

Figures 13K, 14K, and 15K. Your left hand is placed on the heel of the suspect’s hand with your thumb on top pushing the hand into the second locking position.

16K 17K 18K

Figure 16k. The second locking position is where the suspect's hand is kept locked back and turned back toward the thumb side of the suspect, until it stops.

Figure 17K and 18K. When the suspect's hand goes past the locking point, this will start the breaking down of the posture. The elbow will turn in toward his stomach and the shoulder will drop as his weight will shift from the centered position to his right side. His torso will be over the top of his right hip.

19K 20K 21K

Figure 19K. Continuing your circular motion with both hands, the suspect's body starts to break down. When the elbow of the suspect turns in, the shoulder drops, and his weight shifts to his right side. When his torso leans over his right hip, his hip will be locked out, and his right foot can no longer move to catch his balance.

Figure 20K. You continue to push with both of your hands to continue the break - down of the suspect's body. Further shift of his body will cause the left leg to come off the ground and all the weight will be placed on his right leg for a short period of time due to his "over balance" of the torso weight.

Figure 21K. At this point, the suspect has no alternative but to fall to his right side since the shift of his weight past the right hip. Keeping your grip tight at this time is very important to prevent him from yanking his hand loose to catch himself as he falls to the ground. You also should notice that while he is falling, since you have control of his right arm, that his body will not fall straight back but in a curved body position with his right shoulder forward. The suspect's hips will push back as his feet come off the ground as his weight shifts to the outside of his right ankle.

22k

23K

24K

Figure 22K. At the point that the suspect's body comes in contact with the ground, it will be on the right hip. Your arms will be fully extended forward and down allowing his hip to touch.

Figure 23K. After the touchdown of the suspect's hip, you need to pull your hands back to your waist. This will pull the suspect's shoulder back under him making him turn over on his back.

Figure 24K. Pulling your hands up to your center will make the suspect straighten his arm, preventing him the ability to use the strength in his arms and shoulders to pull you down. You have to make sure that you are not bent at the waist and that your back and shoulders are back and straight. Your feet need to be wide to give you the best base possible.

25K

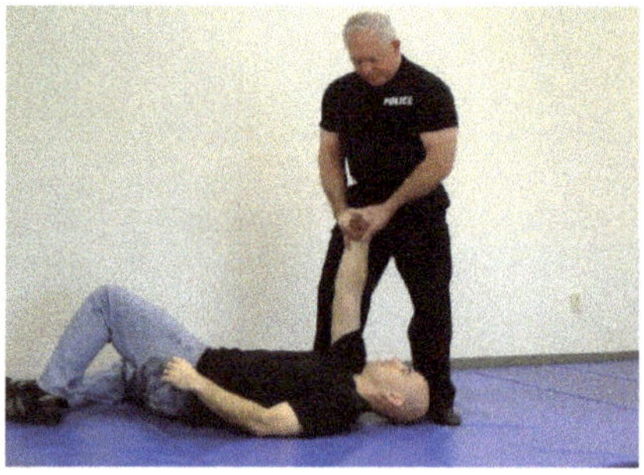

26K

27K

Figure 25K. After your base is established, you are ready to start your movement around the suspect to turn him over. First, step six inches with your left foot which is the lead foot keeping it close to the suspect. As you move, you need to keep tension on the suspect's arm.

Figure 26K. When the first step was made by the left foot, you now need to pull six inches with the right.

Figure 27K. Step another six inches with the left foot around the top of the suspect's head. Understand that as you start to go around the top of the suspect's head, you will be over the top of the suspect's face. The suspect's arm needs to remain straight, because as you start to go around the head, the suspect's body will turn onto the shoulder which will make the arm longer, and the arm needs to be kept straight at all times.

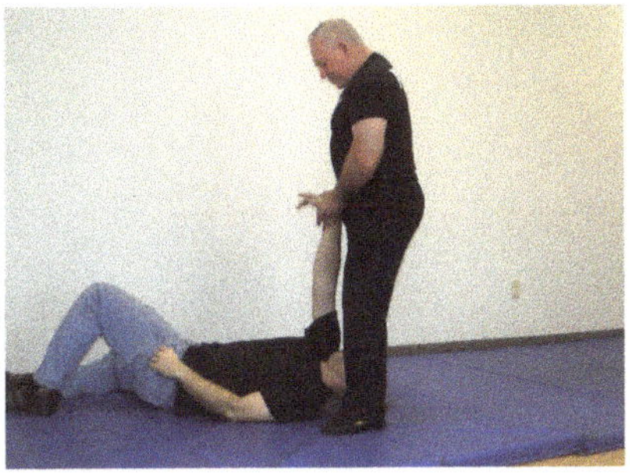
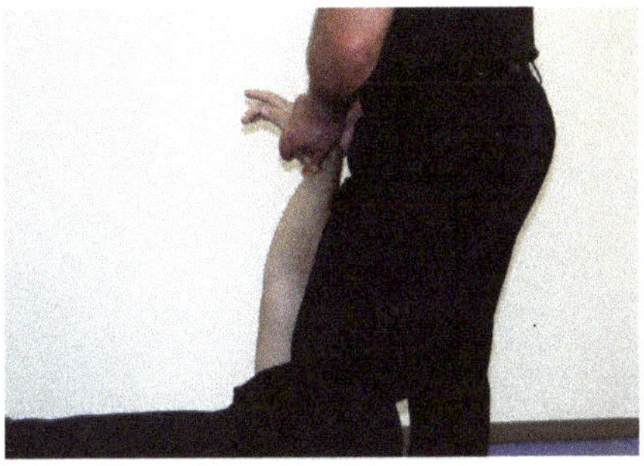

28K 29K 30K

Figure 28k, 29K, and 30K. These figures show the suspect's arm being pulled up and kept tight to your waist. The suspect's right hand is kept at a 90 degree angle from your waist, and the wrist remains bent down and forward. When moving around the head, stay as close to the suspect's body as possible. Still stepping six inches with the lead foot and following it by pulling six inches with the back foot.

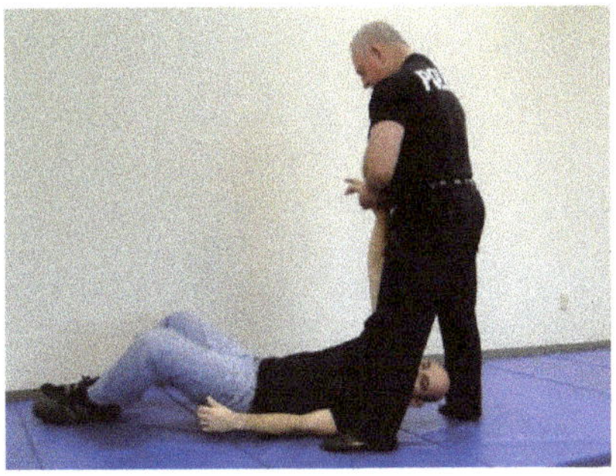
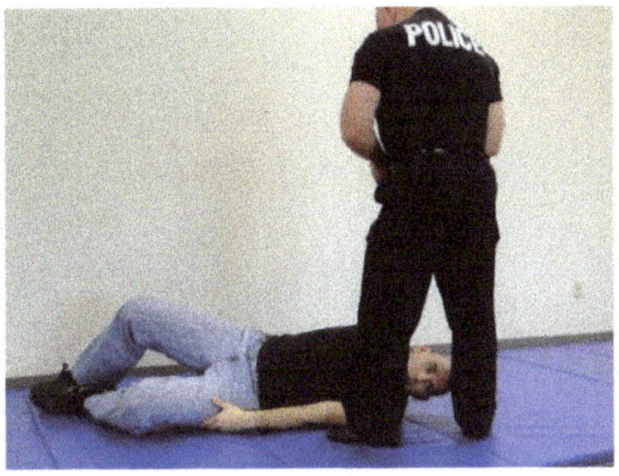
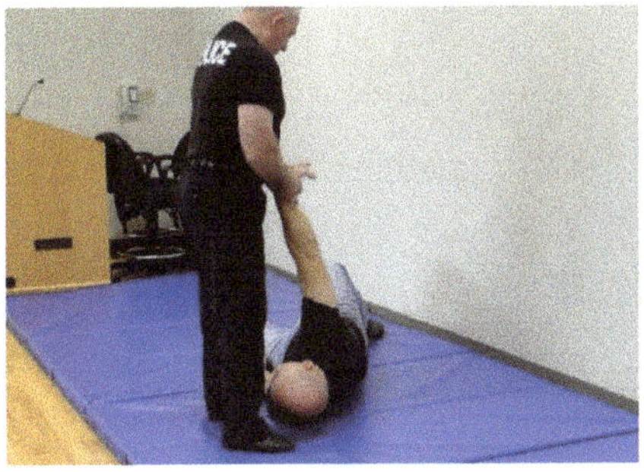

31K 32K 33K

Figure 31K, 32K, and 33K. Move around the head still using "follow foot" and be aware of when the suspect turns over to his stomach that he turns onto his shoulder first. While on his shoulder, the arm will become longer, and the length needs to be taken up in order to keep the suspect's arm straight. The suspect's hand stays tight at your waist. Also, be aware that the arm is also twisting around

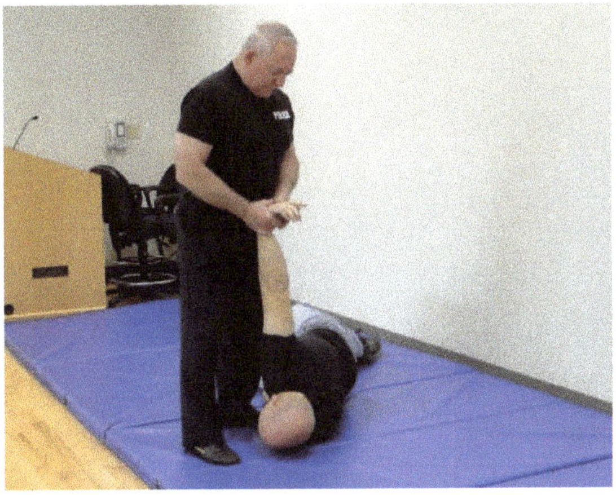

34K

Figure 34K. Once you have moved to the right side of the suspect and established your base, his shoulder may still be up in the air. This means that the suspect is not laying flat on his stomach, and the shoulder is not touching the floor. This position may vary due to the amount of flexibility of the suspect's shoulder. If you are in the correct position with the suspect's hand in front of you, and the shoulder is not down, a small amount of torque is needed to drop it into place.

35K

36K

Figures 35K and 36K. When the shoulder does not touch the ground, the suspect's hand needs to be turned slightly to your left. By turning his hand toward his head and pushing down on the arm, this will lock the shoulder joint and cause the suspect to push his shoulder into the ground. Once the shoulder is down, now is the time to move back to the front of the suspect.

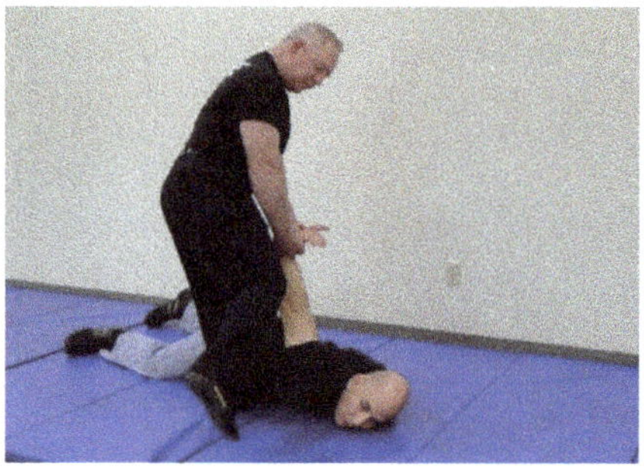

37K

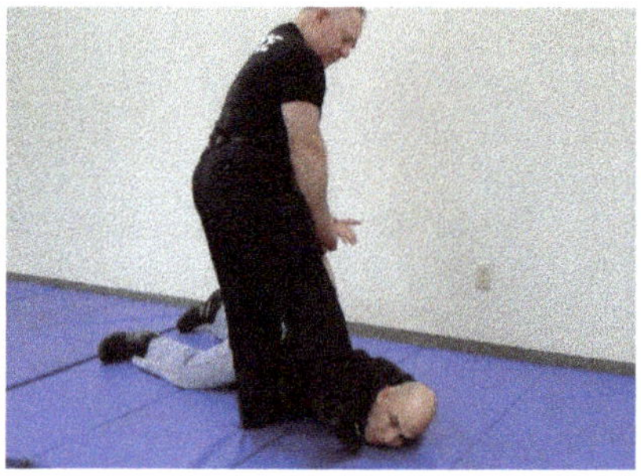

38K

39K

Figure 37K. When moving to the front of the suspect, the right leg is brought back and brought around to the front.

Figure 38K. The right foot is turned back toward the body of the suspect as you make one step completely in front of the shoulder.

Figure 39K. When your right foot is in front of the suspect's shoulder, the toes of your foot are placed close to the neck under the chest side, but across the top of

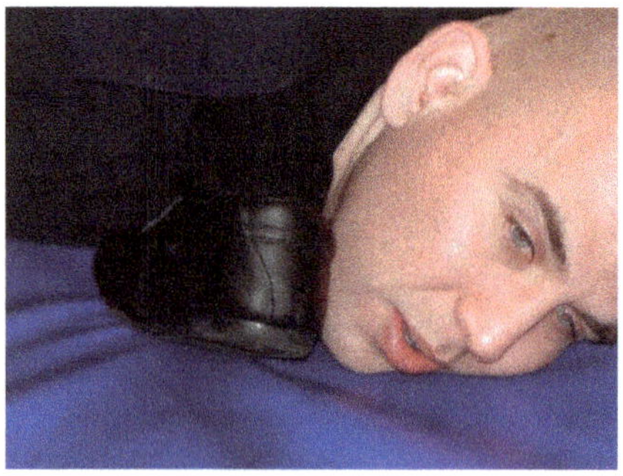

40K

Figure 40K. This is a close up showing how the toes of your right foot are tucked under the shoulder area as close as you can next to the face of the suspect. The foot is pressed under the shoulder as tight as you can make it while changing your weight to this foot, and still maintaining control over the suspect's arm when moving the left foot back.

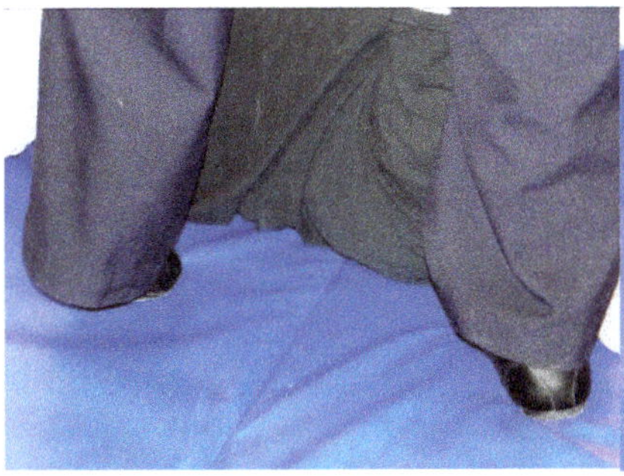
41K

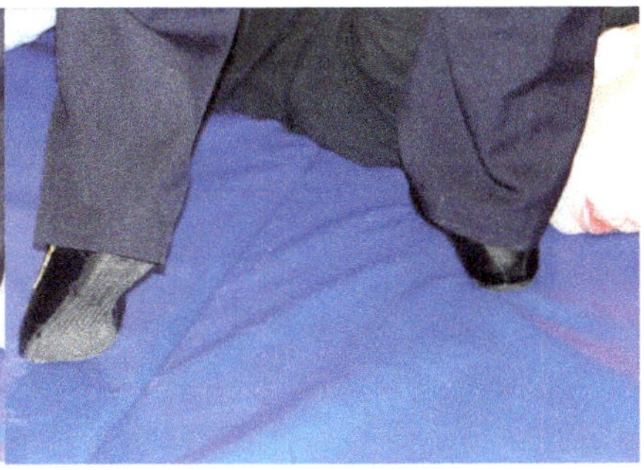
42K

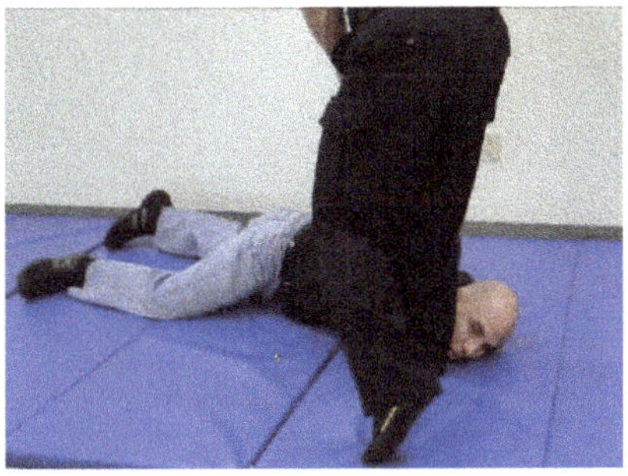
43K

Figure 41K. When your right foot has been tucked under the shoulder of the suspect, your weight shifts to the right foot and the left foot leaves and prepares to move.

Figures 42K. Your left leg swings back behind you in one step.

Figure 43K. When stepping back, the suspect's shoulder will pivot in place and remain against the ground. Only a small amount of pressure will be needed to keep the shoulder on the ground as your body will be turning 90 degrees back to the right.

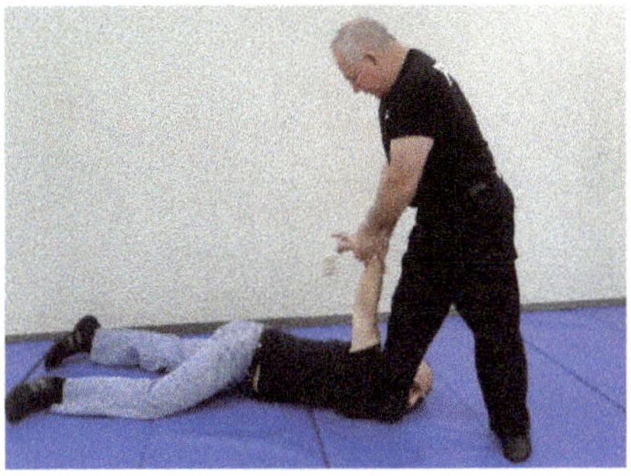
44K

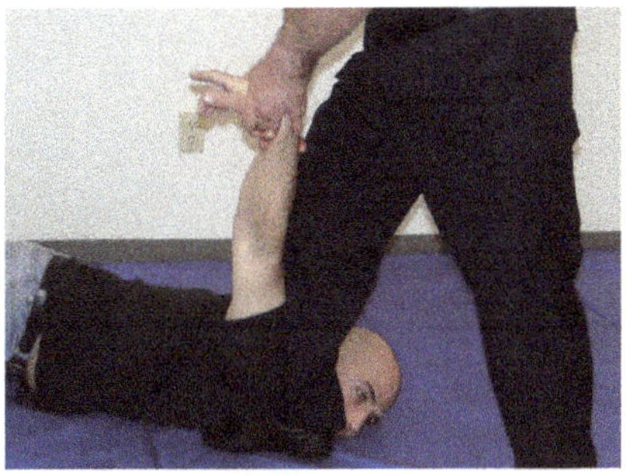
45K

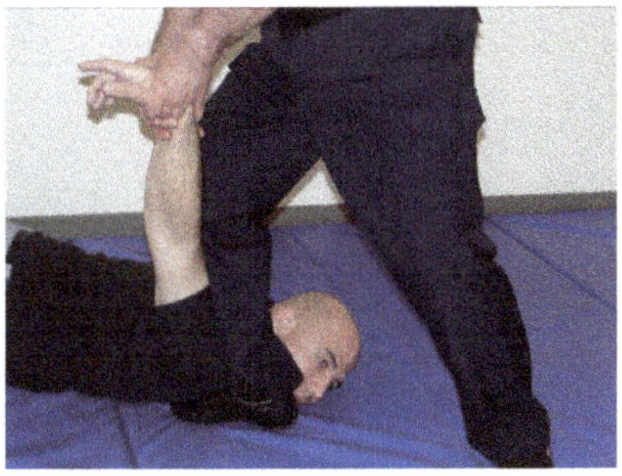
46K

Figure 44K. The left foot has now stepped back from the suspect's waist 90 degrees behind you. You are now facing toward the suspect's feet. The suspect's hand is still bent palm down and his fingers are also pointed toward his feet.

Figure 45K and 46K. These two figures show once the step behind you has been taken, your stance is wide for balance. Now, the suspect's shoulder and arm have to be locked. By pressing your right knee forward to the inside of the suspect's elbow and keeping his arm straight, you will lock the shoulder. If by chance the suspect is uncooperative and resists, more pressure is placed on the suspect's arm by bending your knee forward and pulling back on his wrist. If by chance, there is another assailant that may be involved and putting your life in jeopardy or even coming at you, and there is an urgent need to have you hands free, the suspect's arm may be broken to take this suspect out of the equation, by bending your knee forward and pulling the suspect's arm back hard and fast.

This is also a stopping point where you slow down and evaluate what is going on around you before continuing, slowing your breathing, and becoming aware.

47K

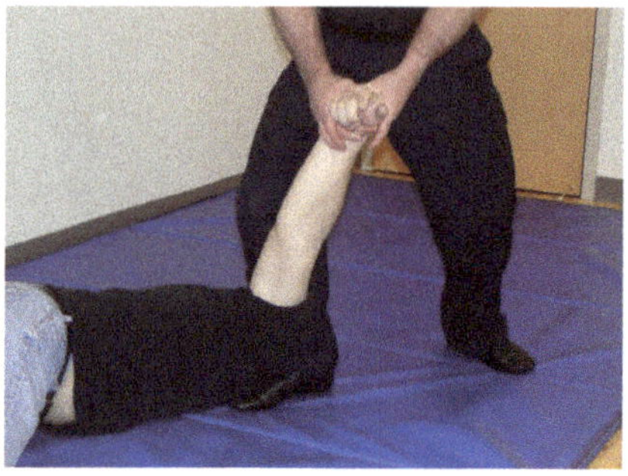

48K

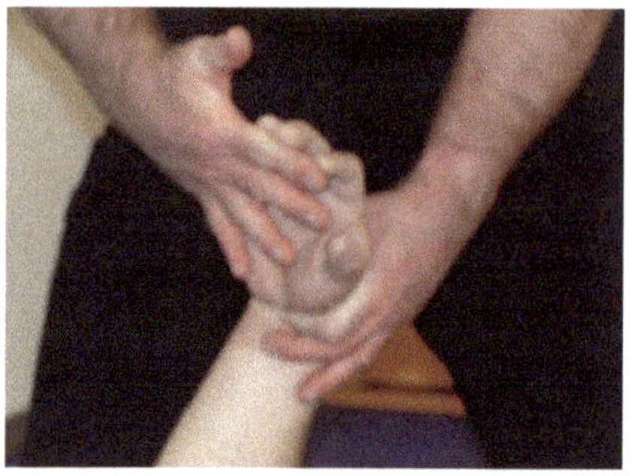

49K

Figure 47K. This is the evaluation position; looking up with good posture, slowing your breathing, which slows your heart and brings you back into focus, keeping you away from tunnel vision.

Figure 48K. From the "lockout position", you need to make sure your left grip is secure and the suspect's arm is locked out. Your right hand loosens at this time preparing to let go and open the suspect's hand.

Figure 49K. When removing your right hand from the suspect's wrist, place it palm to palm with the suspect's hand pulling it back opening it up.

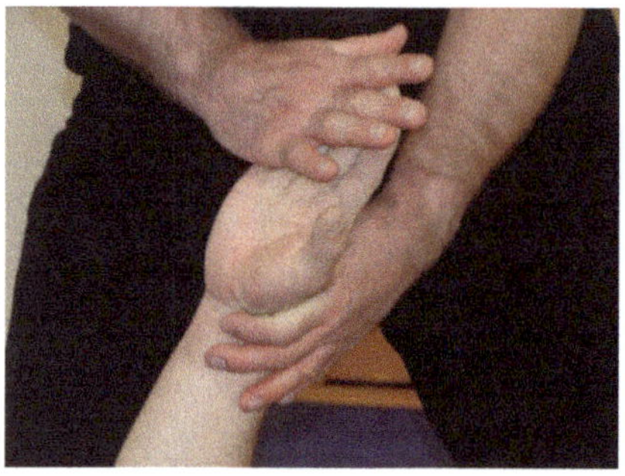

50K

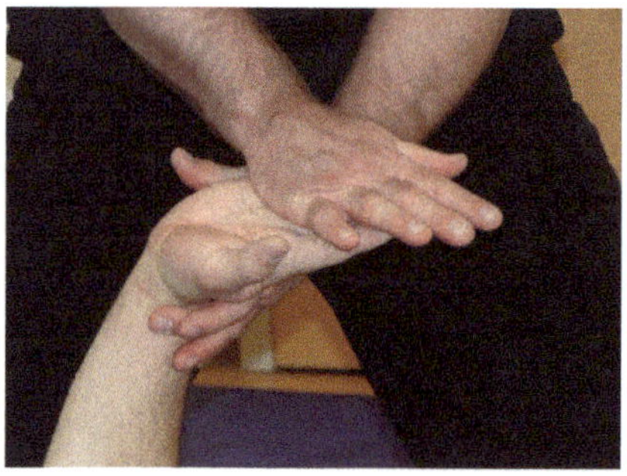

51K

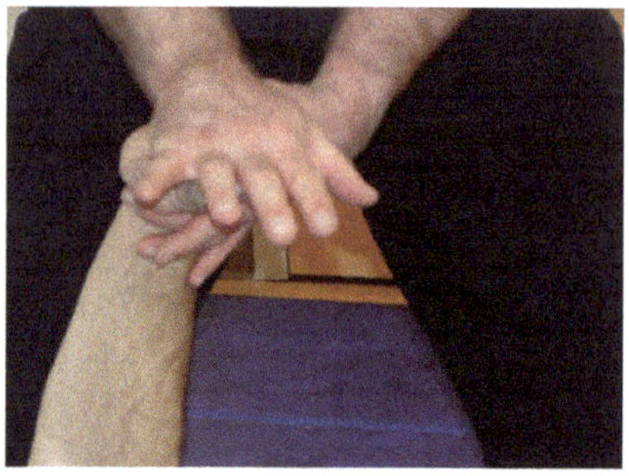

52K

Figure 50K, 51k, and 52K. Pull the suspect's hand back and keep the pressure on the palm side of the fingers and as you rotate his hand back to the left side. Turn the fingers and wrist around so the fingers point toward his feet. Your left grip is still at his wrist. Notice that as the suspect's hand turns over, the grip on

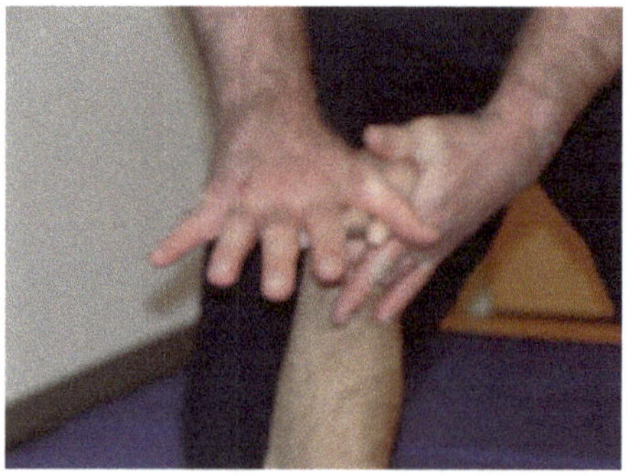

53K

Figures 53K and 54K. Press the suspect's fingers back with your palm to keep the hand open. The grip of the left hand changes from around the wrist to placing the thumb on the palm keeping the wrist back and flat.

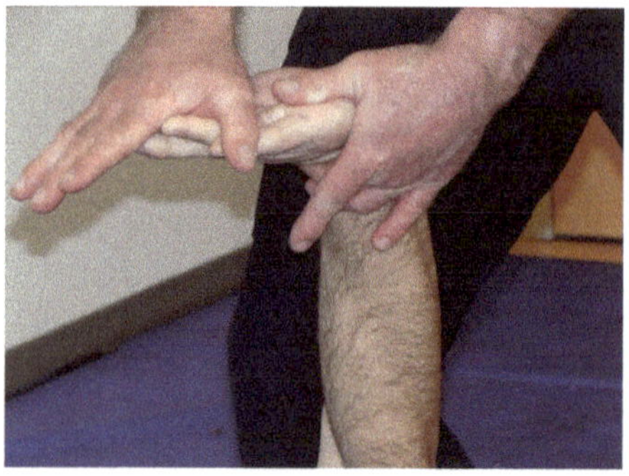

54K

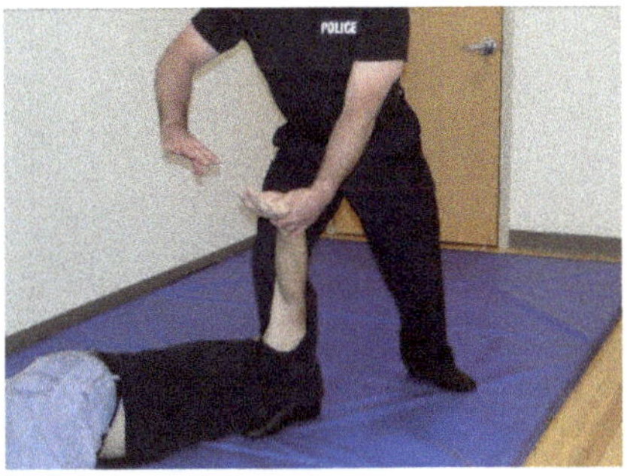

55K

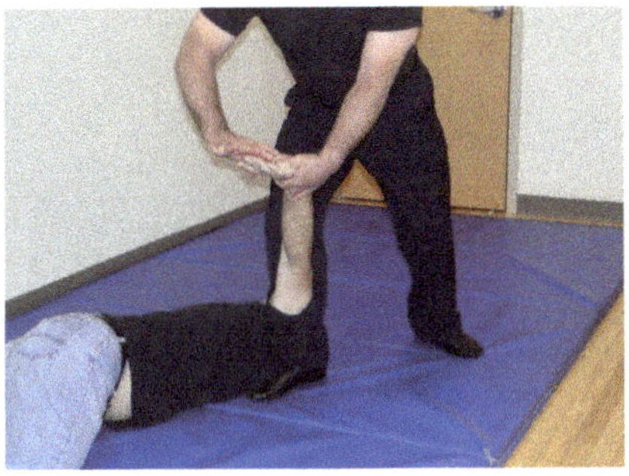

56K

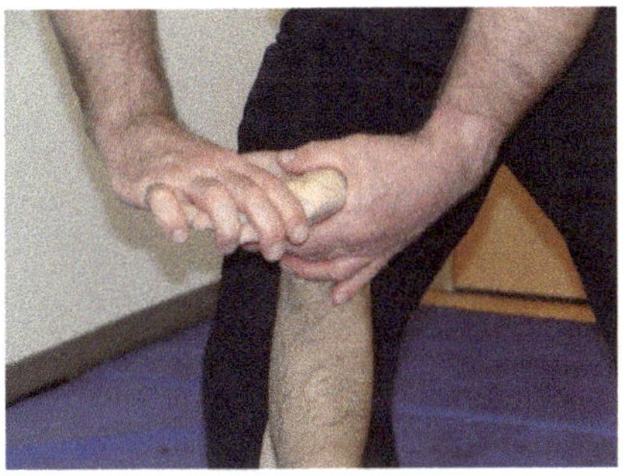

57K

Figure 55K. Reposition your right hand and take it away from the suspect's hand, and turn it in. Reach in to grab the suspect's hand as if to grip the hand in a handshake.

Figure 56K. Reach in with your right hand in the handshaking grip position, but in a deep grip on the suspect's hand so the web between the thumb and the index finger pushes tightly against the suspect's hand.

Figure 57K. The grip should also keep the suspect's hand bent back and your fingers should wrap around the fingers of the suspect's hand.

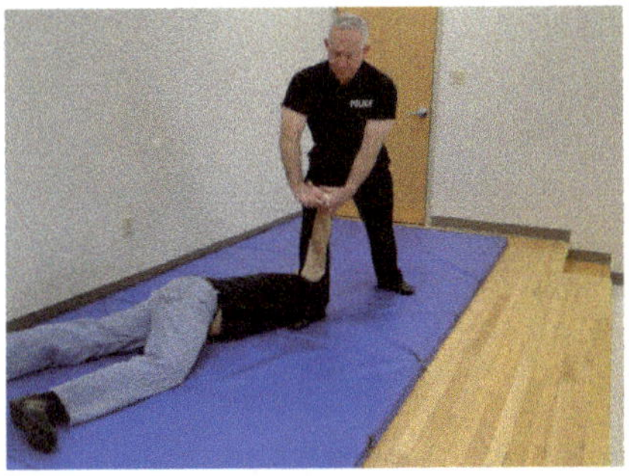

58K

59K

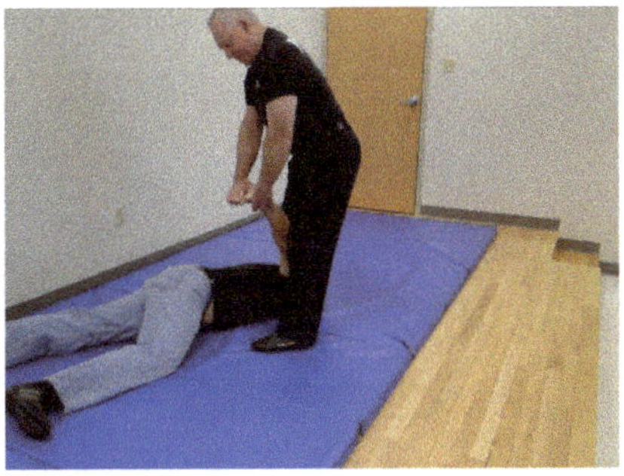

60k

Figure 58K. Once you have your grip, you are ready to take the suspect's arm to the suspect's back.

Figure 59K. As you start the takedown of the suspect's arm, your left hand still has support at the suspect's wrist. You start the movement with the twisting of the suspect's hand to the right as you keep the hand flat. The left leg is back and as the twisting of the suspect's hand starts, there is only one step from the back position to the suspect's waist. But to show you the movement of the suspect's arm, the step will be taken in several stop motion pictures.

Figure 60K. The suspect's arm comes down to the suspect's back as the hand and arm are turned back to the right, across his back. As your foot comes from the back position around to the waist, the suspect's arm comes down a little at a time.

NOTE: When in practice with a partner, this is the time to slow down and be cautious about your movements. DO NOT do this part of the movement fast in practice; be careful of your partner's joints!

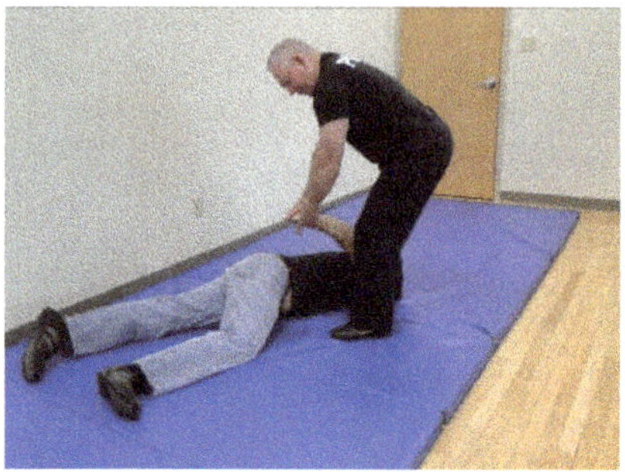

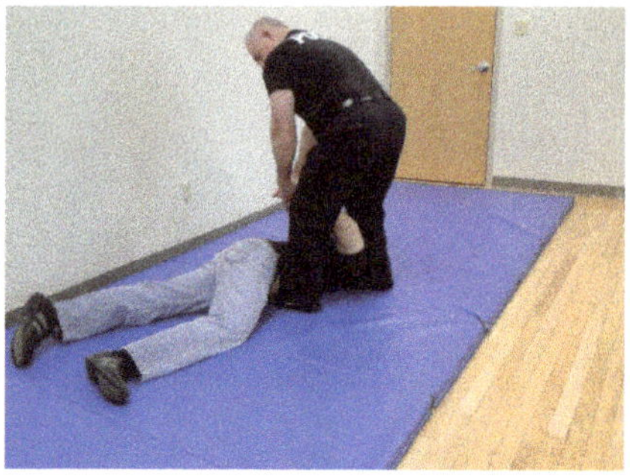

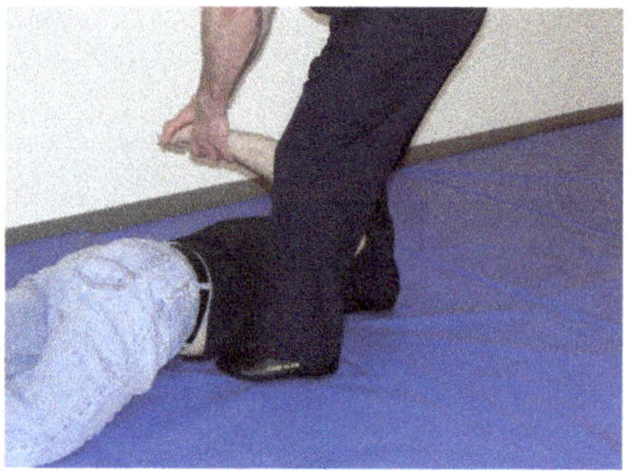

61K 62K 63K

Figure 61K. The closer you foot comes to the waist position of the suspect, his arm will be coming closer to his back making you bend over as it comes down.

Figures 62K and 63K. The single step from behind you reaches the suspect's waist. Remember that this is a single step. When your foot arrives at his waist, it is pressed in by his stomach. Now your leg is in position and is now at the bottom of his elbow. One hand is still in the handshake position, and the other is supporting the back of his wrist. When the arm comes down to the suspect's back his wrist will straighten out to lay flat on his back.

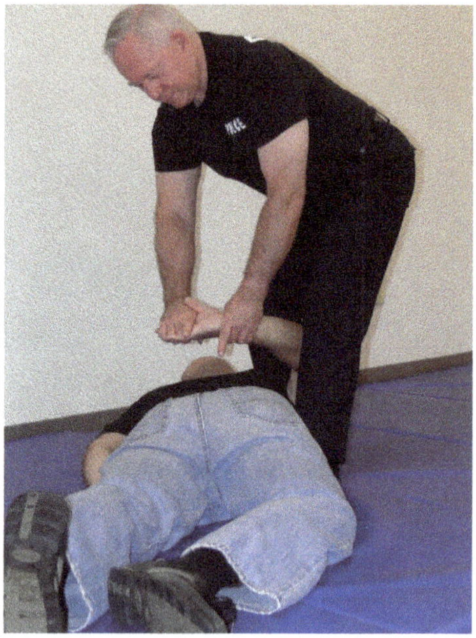

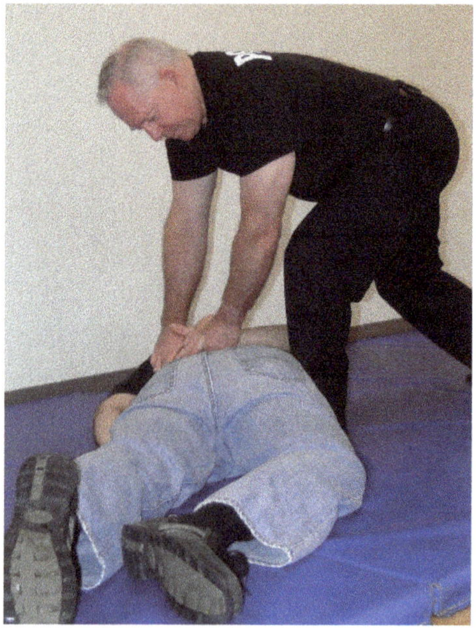

64K 65K

Figure 64K. Here is another view once you have made the step to the suspect's waist. Again notice that your left leg is in a position to the bottom of the suspect's elbow, and the suspect's hand and wrist are flat.

Figure 65K. When the suspect's arm comes in contact with his back, first place pressure on the hand and wrist to secure them from moving before they are secured by locking down.

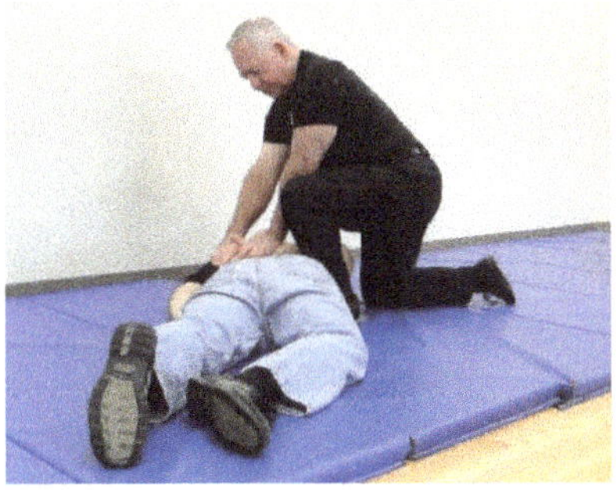

66K

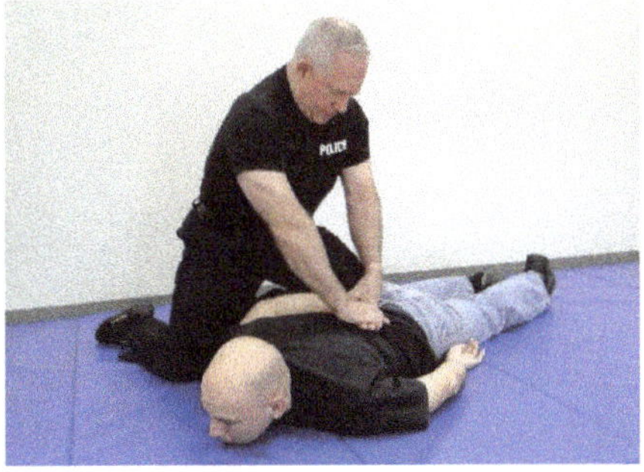

67K

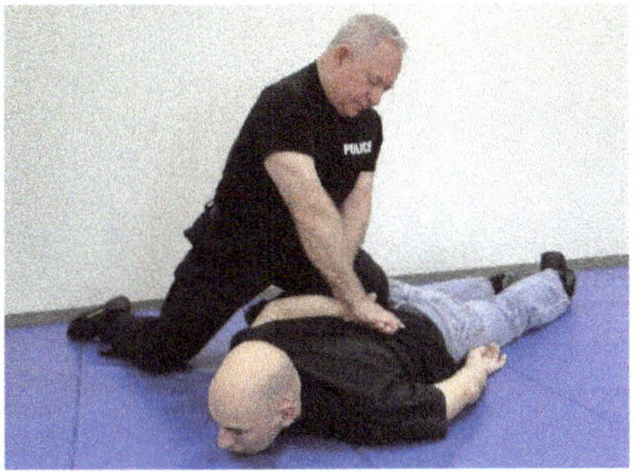

68K

Figure 66K. The pressure continues on the hands and wrist as you kneel down next to the suspect. Your left foot stays in place at the suspect's waist, and the right knee goes slightly back.

Figure 67k and 68K. Now that you are next to the suspect, push your knee forward across the small of the back. The knee will secure the arm from being pushed down. While your knee is being pushed across the suspect's lower back, you are leaning forward and your right leg is extended behind you.

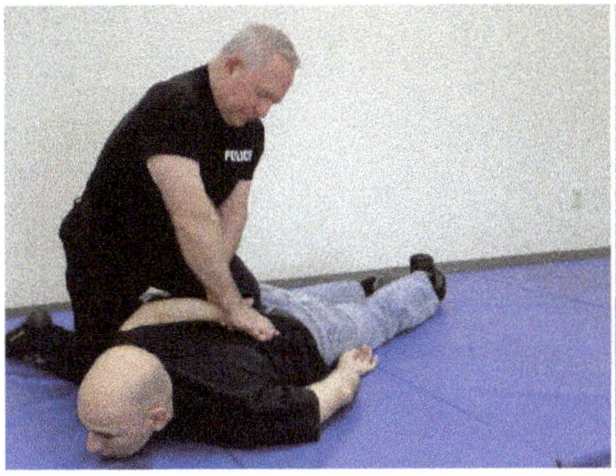

69K

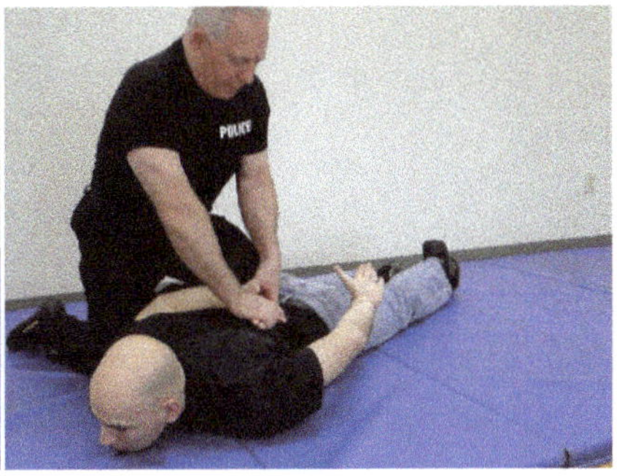

70K

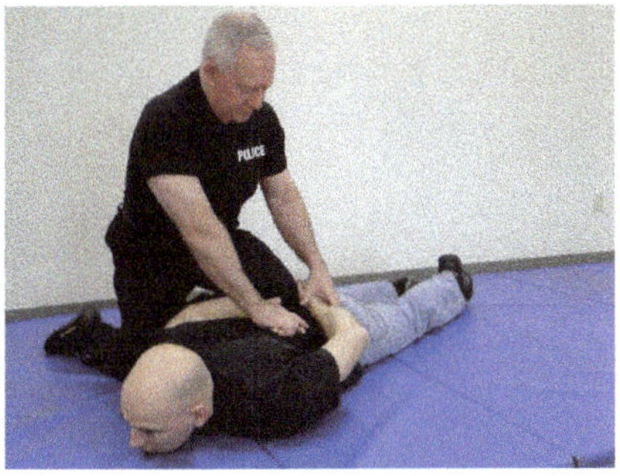

71K

Figure 69K. When the left knee is secure, now bring the right knee forward behind the suspect's elbow. The right knee will serve two purposes. First when the right knee is brought forward, it will make contact with the suspect's left elbow and push his arm across his back giving you the extra distance you will need for his wrist to be handcuffed. This is beneficial when you have a suspect that is broad across the shoulders or very obese. The second purpose is that your knee will now lock his arm from being pulled out to the side.

Figure 70K and 71k. While keeping the suspect's hand and wrist straight and flat, now give the command for him to give you his other hand. If by chance he is not cooperating, a small amount of pressure turning his hand sideways toward his head will allow you to place him under a great amount of pain, which will make him a willing and more cooperating subject. Even if the suspect happens to be laying on the other arm at this point, he will find a way to get his arm around to his back for you to handcuff. When the hand is brought back, you will be able to let go with your left hand to secure it. ***DO NOT REACH FOR THE HAND.***

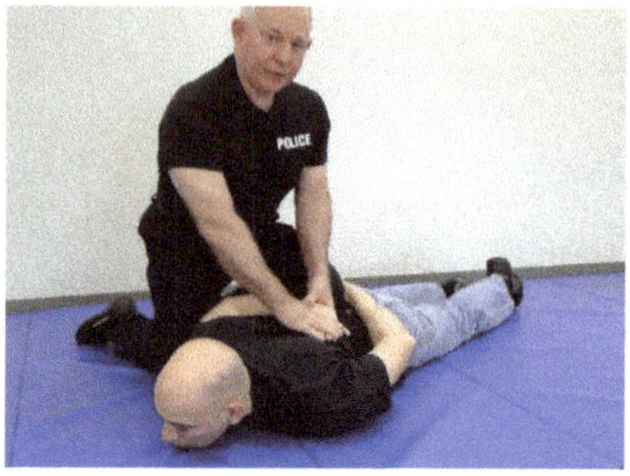
72k

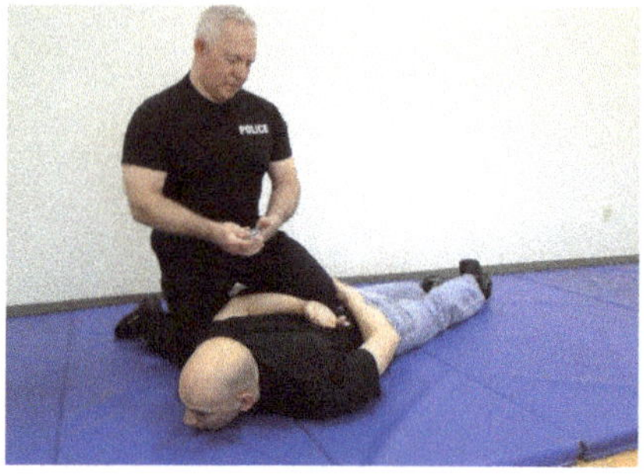
73k

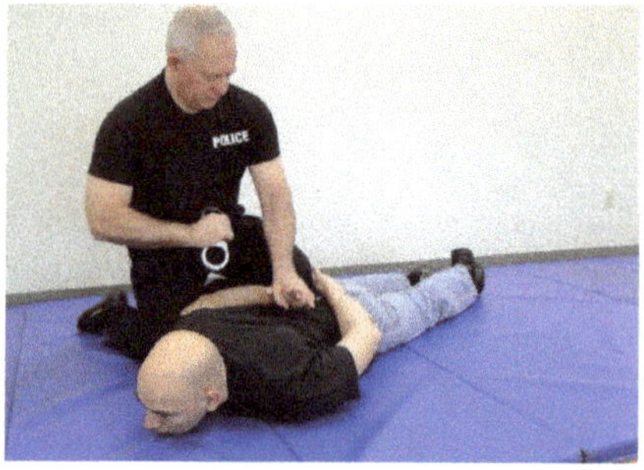
74k

Figure 72K. When the suspect's arm is locked from bring pushed down and being pulled back, you have plenty of time to handcuff.

Figure 73K. Not only do you have time, the suspect will not be able to get away from this position, and you will have both hands to get your cuffs.

Figure 74K. Now, you are ready to handcuff your suspect. Grip your handcuffs in the center so the opening to the cuffs are away from your hand and grip the suspect's hand.

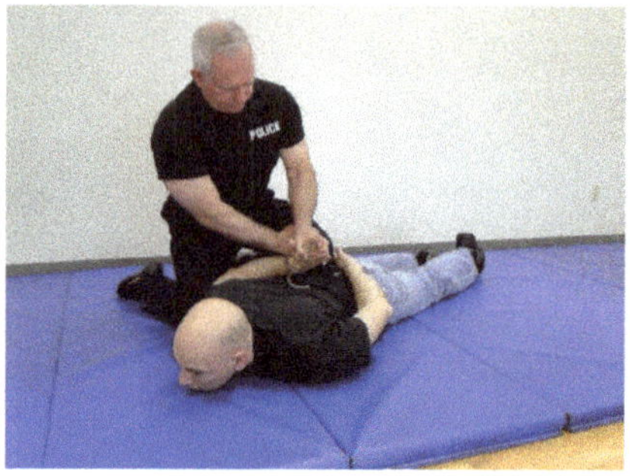
75K

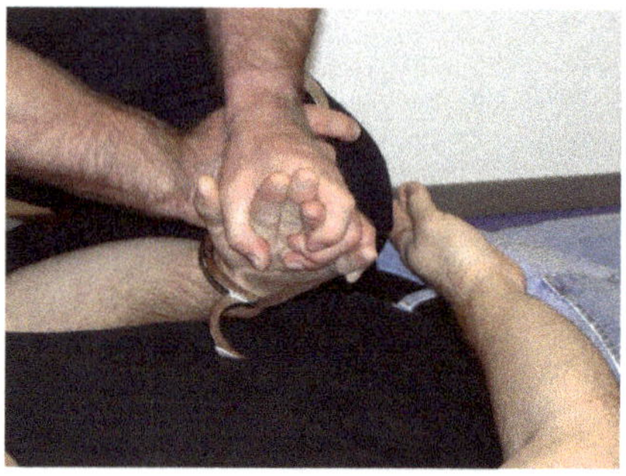
76K

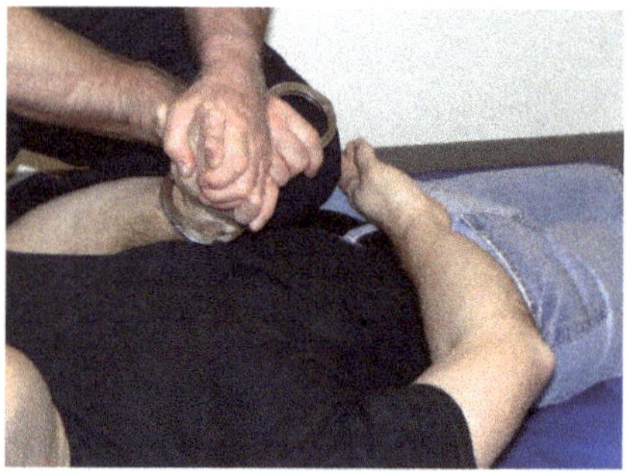
77K

Figure 75K. Grasping the suspect's hand with your left hand, lift it off the suspect's back to allow you room for the cuff to go around the wrist without snagging on his clothing. Continue the same knee locks on the suspect's arm while handcuffing.

Figure 76K. Lift the suspect's hand with your left hand in a "palm to palm" grip. Lift high enough so that when you press the handcuffs to the suspect's wrist, the cuff will open and spin around freely without hooking on his clothing. The cuff is held so that the cuffs are vertical and the bottom of the cuff is the first cuff placed on the suspect's wrist.

Figure 77K. Shows when the cuff comes in contact with the suspect's wrist, and the wrist is lifted high enough, and taking into consideration that your cuffs are lubricated occasionally, and are in good working order. The cuff will spin around smoothly and lock. Make sure the cuff is tight enough around the suspect's wrist so he is not able to slip his hand out of the cuff before you let go with your left hand.

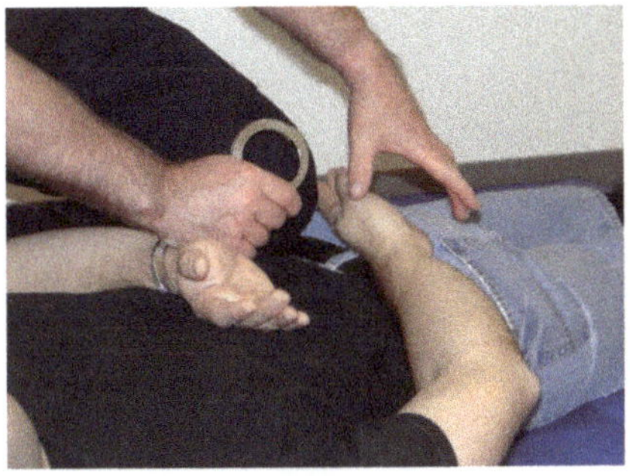

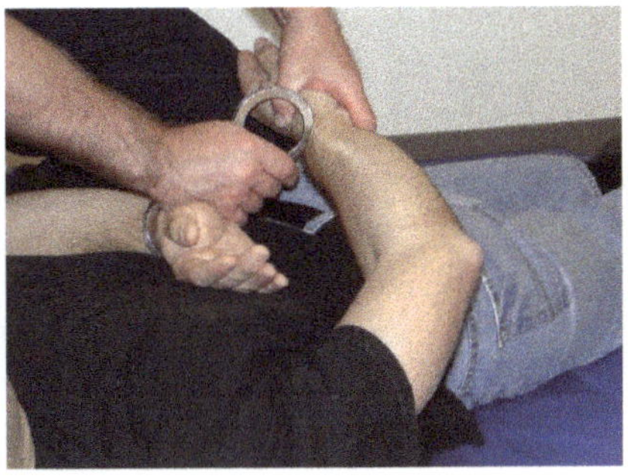

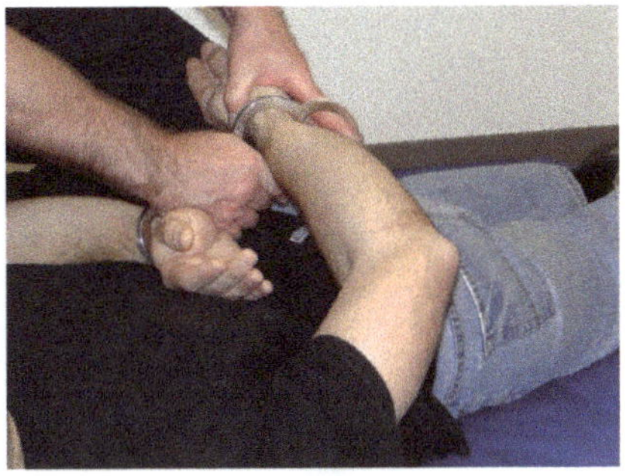

78K 79K 80K

Figure 78K. When you release your left hand grip on the suspect's hand to grasp the left wrist of the suspect, continue to have a good grip on the center of your cuffs.

Figure 79K. Grab just above the wrist on the base of the suspect's hand to allow you plenty of space for the next cuff. Bring the suspect's arm to the cuff. Press the suspect's wrist against the cuff, and at the same time, push your right hand forward to give a fast spin to the handcuff to the locking position around the wrist.

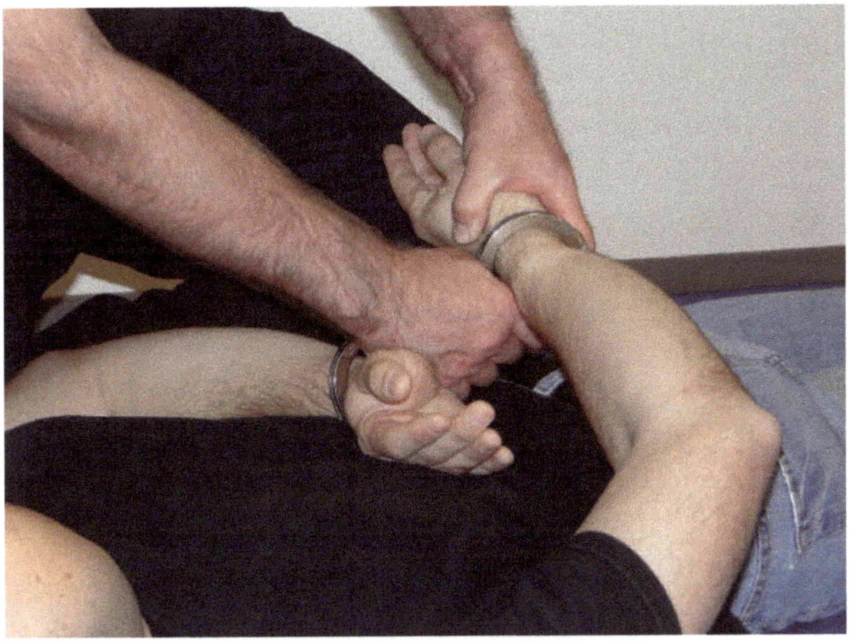

81K

Figure 81K. This shows a close up look at the grip on the suspect's hand. When the second half of the cuff is pressed on, your left hand grasps the heel of the hand with your fingers. and the thumb squeezes the suspect's thumb forward into his palm. This grip will not allow his to grab onto you at the last second.

NOTE: There are many companies that make handcuffs, some better that others. When choosing a pair of cuffs, think about control of the cuff and whether it is loose in your hand and flops around and turns. These are some things you may think about on your next purchase. The cuffs used in these pictures are a "hinge style" cuff.

HITCHHIKER I

Cross-Wrist Grab Left Hand

1L

2L

Figure 1L. The suspect reaches out and does a cross-wrist grab with his left hand onto your left wrist.

Figure 2L. Use a fast response to reach out to cover the suspect's hand with your right hand.

3L

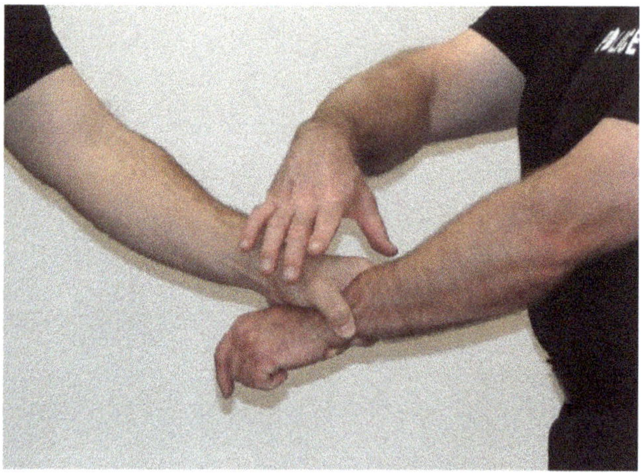

4L

Figures 3L and 4L. The placement of your hand on the back of the suspect's hand is specific. Your grip needs to be in the correct position on the back of his hand. In the hitchhiker technique, your hand reaches over the top of his hand with your fingers extended, the hand open, and the palm down. With the practice of a partner, your grab will become instinctive and to the point that you will not have to look. You will be able to know what technique to use as soon as your hand touches the hand of the suspect.

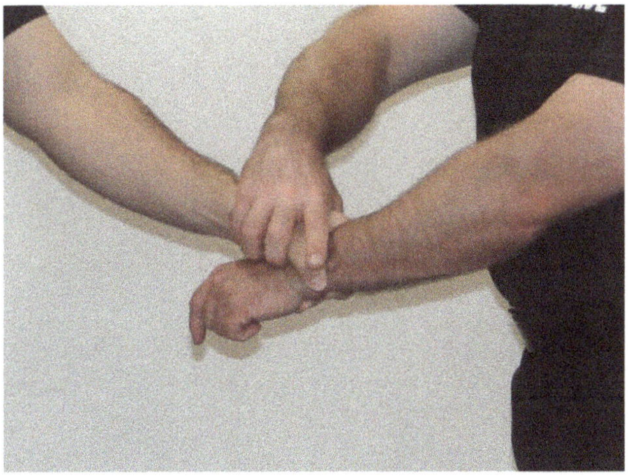

5L

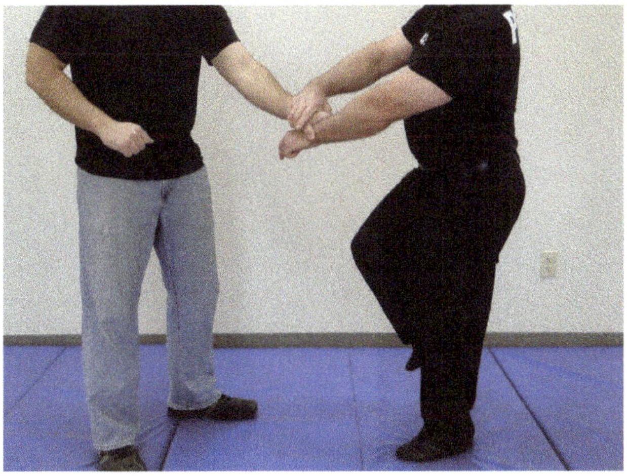

6L

Figure 5L. With your right hand used as the cover hand, it should cover the back of the suspect's hand. Your hand grips the suspect's hand and fingers by first gripping the meaty portion of his thumb. Your thumb is placed on the back of his hand between the knuckles of the middle finger and his ring finger just below the base of the knuckles.

Figure 6L. When your cover hand is secure so his hand will not be pulled away, the distract will start by using your right foot.

7L

8L

Figures 7L and 8L. The right foot is used for a quick snap kick to the suspect's shin. Remember that the distract does not have to be painful. The contact of the foot striking his shin will give you the time you need to start your hitchhiker technique. Like we had mentioned before, timing is the important thing at this point. When your foot makes contact with the suspect, you have to be ready to pull his hand away from your wrist.

9L

10L

Figure 9L. After the "quick snap" for your distract with your right foot, it is brought back as fast as it was struck. You need to bring the foot back to establish your balance as your technique starts in motion.

Figure 10L. By the time your foot is back on the ground, you should have the suspect's hand away from your wrist; pulling your left arm away at the same time your are pulling his hand off.

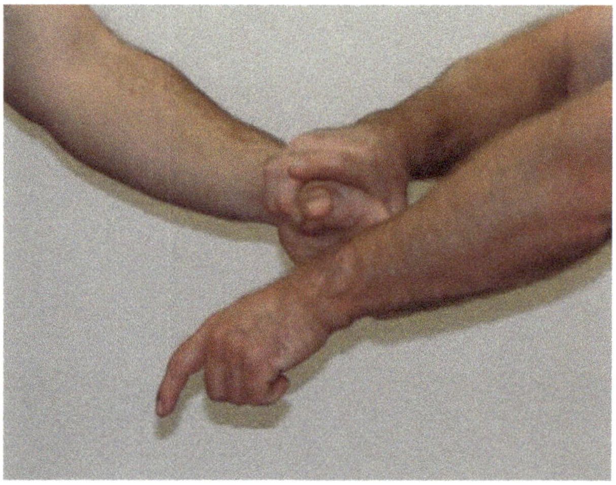

11L

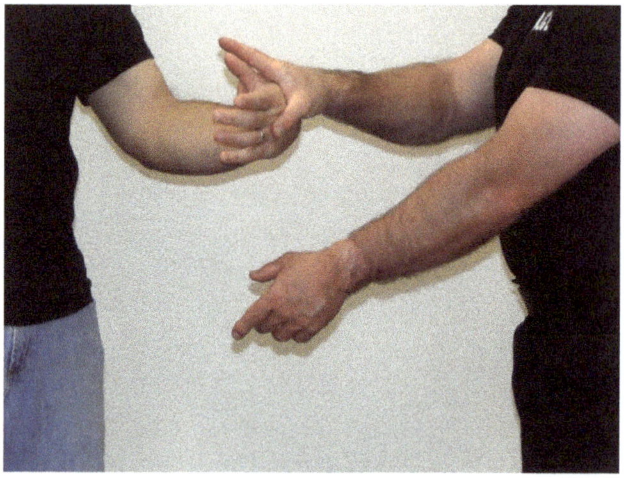

12L

Figure 11L. This is a closer look at the point that the hand is being pulled away. Notice that your hand is not pulled back toward your body, but twists toward the thumb side of the suspect's grip and away from this hand.

Figure 12L. Your left arm is pulled far enough away so there is no chance of the suspect to grab your wrist again. Your right hand has locked the suspect's hand back and twisting his fingers upward toward the second locking position. The tension is kept on the suspect's wrist as you keep his hand in motion.

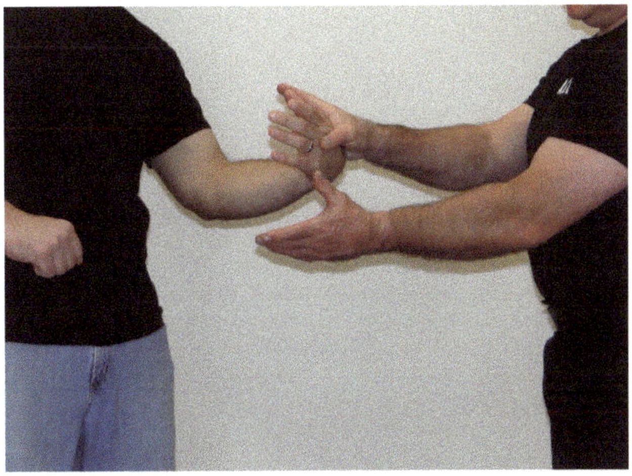

13L

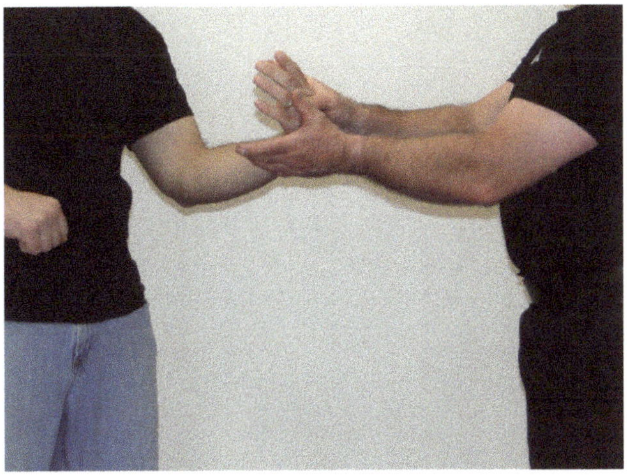

14L

Figure 13L and 14L. While you are locking the suspect's wrist back toward him, you should bring your left hand back in play to give power and support to your grip and to assist in the locking of the suspect's wrist.

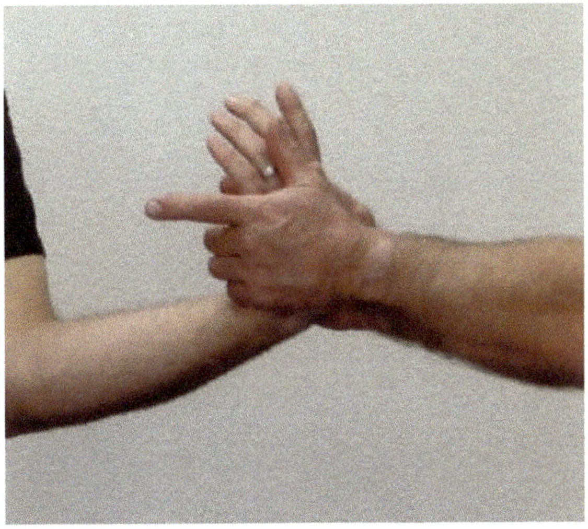

15L

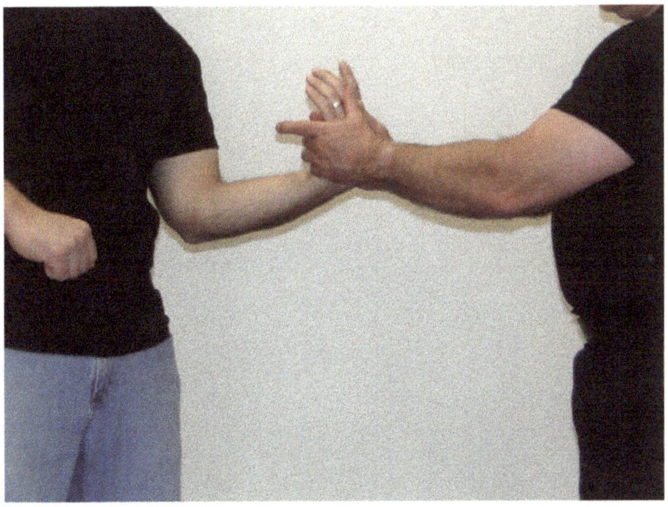

16L

Figure 15L. The close up shows the left hand meeting the suspect's hand in support of your right hand. The hand is placed on the back of the suspect's hand, and the fingers are grabbing the heel of the hand. Your thumb is on the back of his hand about in the center. Both of your hands are pushing his hand back, locking the wrist as it is being turned back to the left side.

Figure 16L. Your left hand catches up as soon as you can with your right hand in support of the "locking and turning" of the suspect's hand. The left hand grips on the side of the suspect's hand as soon as it makes contact. The left hand assists in locking the wrist back by using a forward twisting motion, by pulling back with your little finger side of your hand and pushing forward with the thumb.

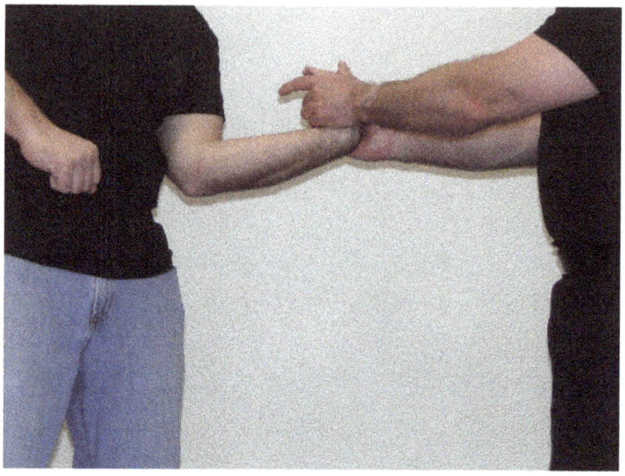

17L 18L

Figure 17L and 18L. When the left hand is brought in to assist your right hand, the technique continues placing pressure on the suspect's wrist turning it back to his left side. The suspect's elbow will start turning inward toward the suspect's body.

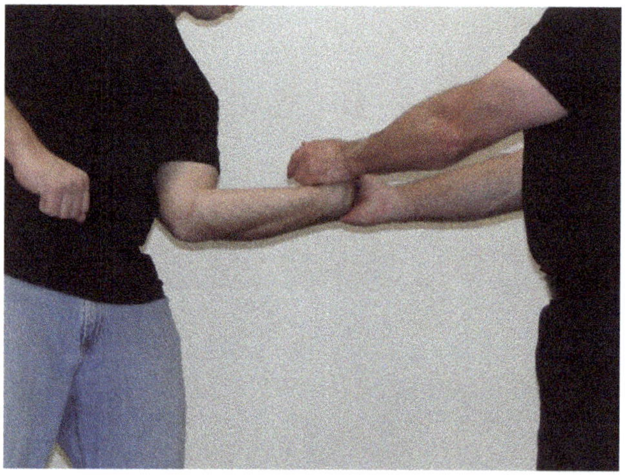

19L 20L

Figure 19L and 20L. When the pressure continues on the suspect's wrist, you will see that the elbow turns in almost to the midline of his body. His shoulder will drop down on the left side, and he will bend at the waist. He will shift his weight over his left hip which will lock out the hip, and he will no longer be able to step in any direction with his left foot. His left knee will start to bend as the pressure continues on his left wrist. At this point, the suspect's balance is broken. The pressure that is placed on the suspect's wrist is not just straight across from side to the side, but in a semi-circular motion. When his balance is broken, the suspect's hand is pulled back toward your center.

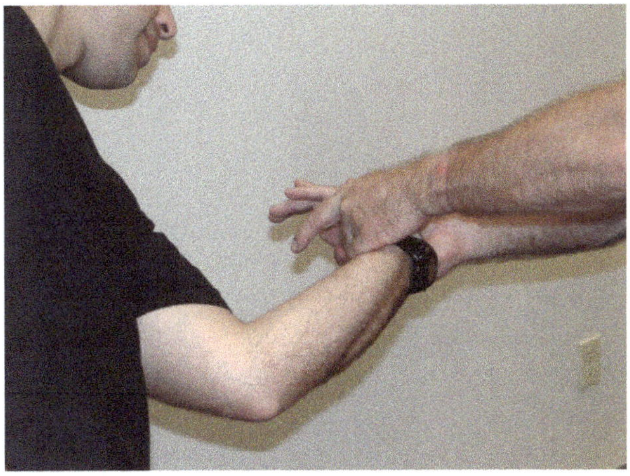

21L

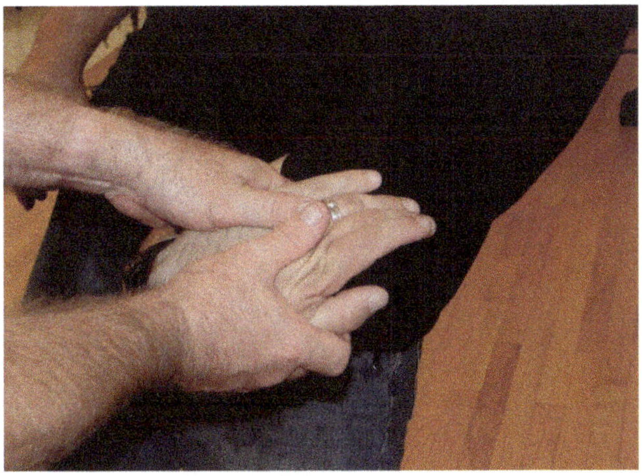

22L

Figures 21L and 22L. These figures show from both sides, the hand positioning of locking the suspect's wrist back and to the side, as it breaks down his posture and balance. Both your right and left hands are putting pressure on the wrist while it is being taken to his left side. The grip with your fingers is on his palm, and the thumbs are placed on the back center of his hand at the first knuckle.

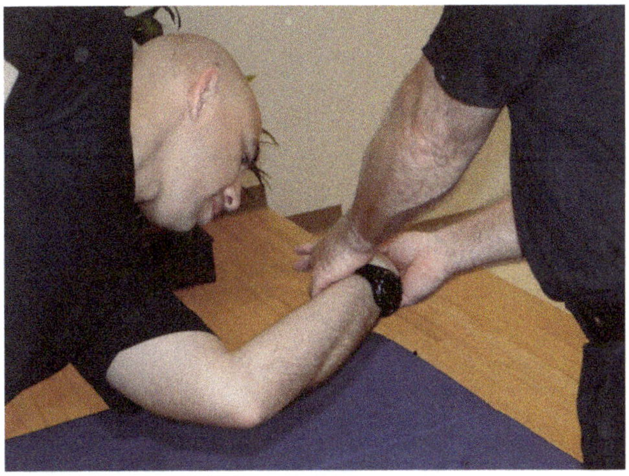

23L

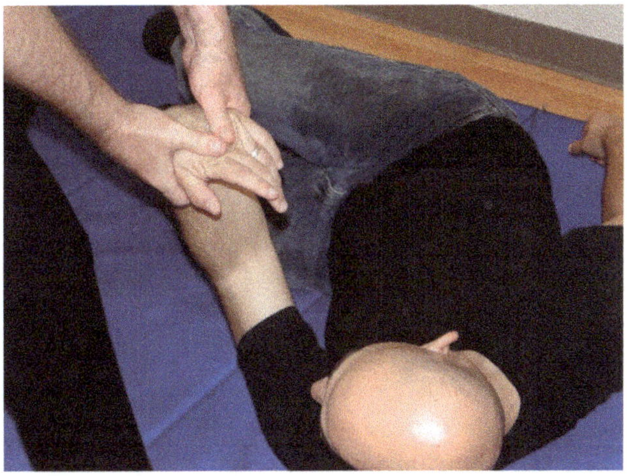

24L

Figure 23L. The balance has been broken to the left side at about waist high, the attacker's shoulder will lead as he falls toward the ground.

Figure 24L. As the suspect falls toward the ground, you control his fall to allow you to place his body in the correct position. You keep tension on the wrist and pull his hand back to your center. By bringing your hands back to your center, this will cause his left shoulder to come forward which will prevent him from falling directly onto the shoulder. As his shoulder now moves forward, it will keep his torso in the air a little longer, giving his left hip enough time to touch the ground first. With Hitchiker I, this will allow his body weight to settle into the ground.

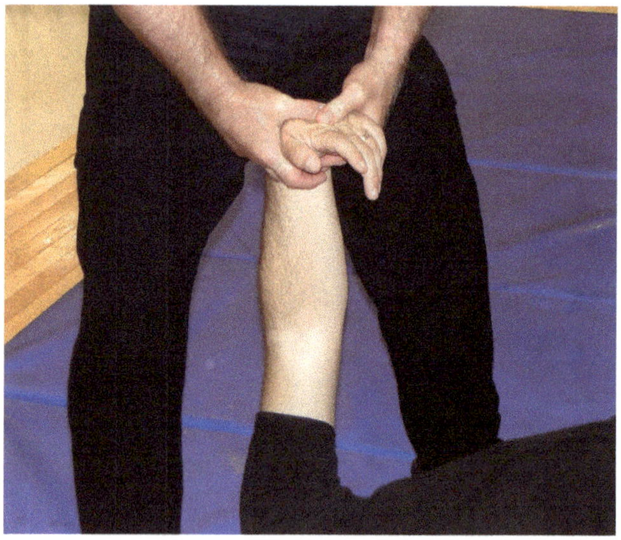

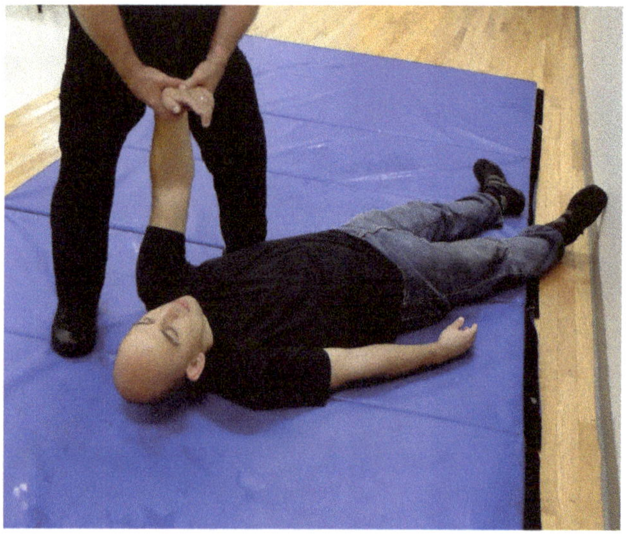

25L 26L

Figures 25L and 26L. When his body weight settles onto the ground, widen your stance to develop a good base. Pull the suspect's hand up to your center, while still keeping his wrist locked down. The object of pulling his arm up is to straighten your back and to prevent him from trying to pull you forward down on top of him. Keeping his arm in a straight position, presents a problem for him, which will not allow him to use stronger muscles in his arm and chest to attain leverage and strength.

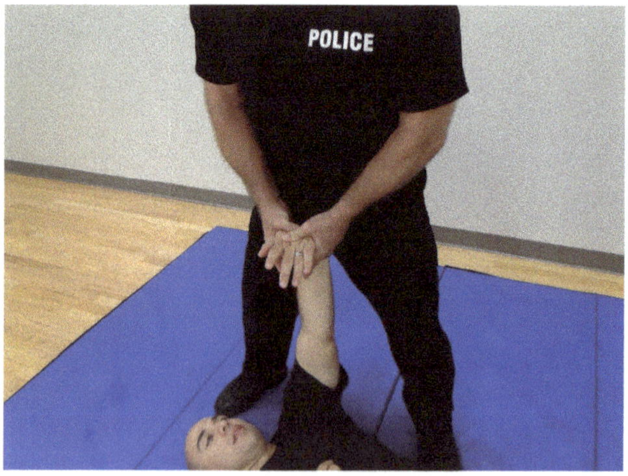

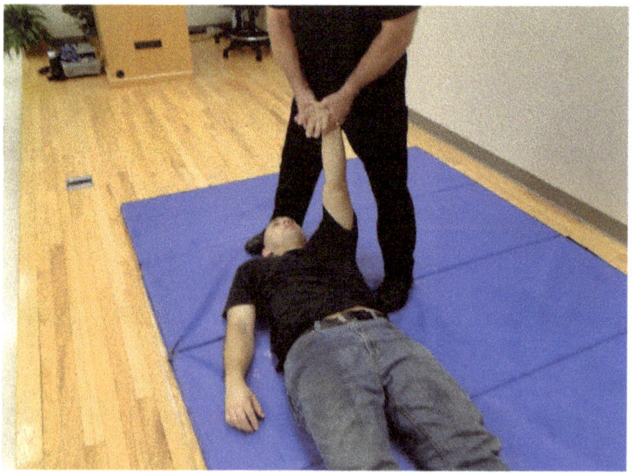

27L 28L

Figure 27L. With your wide stance and the suspect's arm pulled tight, the tension still is on his wrist; his fingers are pointed directly in front of you at a ninety degree angle.

Figure 28l. The first step in the "follow foot" is taken to your right, close to the suspect, about six inches to the top of the suspect's head.

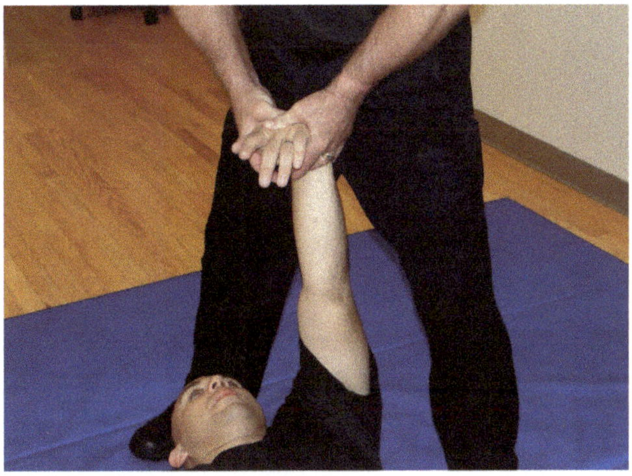

29L

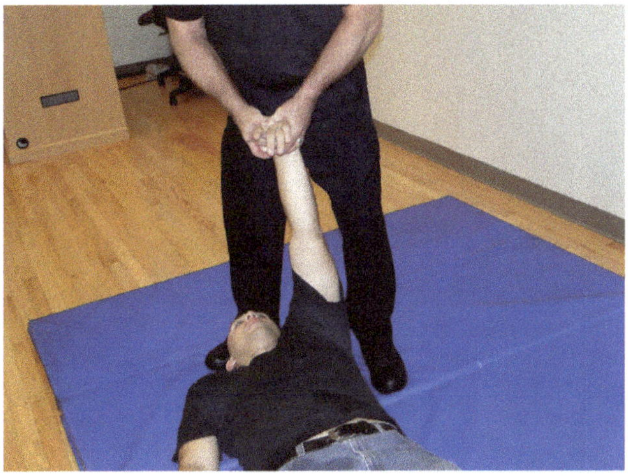

30L

Figures 29L and 30L. When doing the "follow foot", the suspect's hand remains in front of your center as you move around the head of the suspect, stepping six inches now with your left foot.

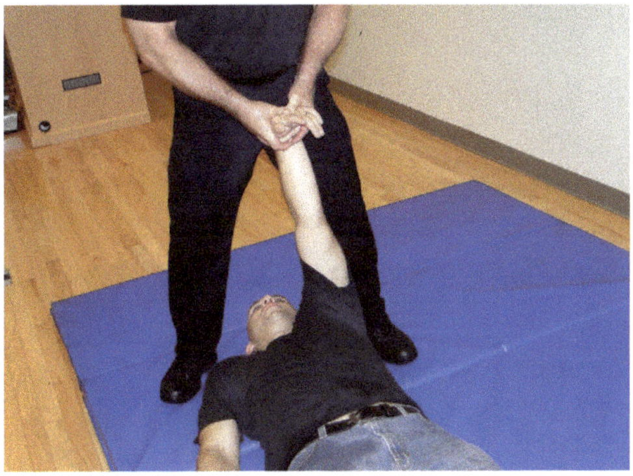

31L

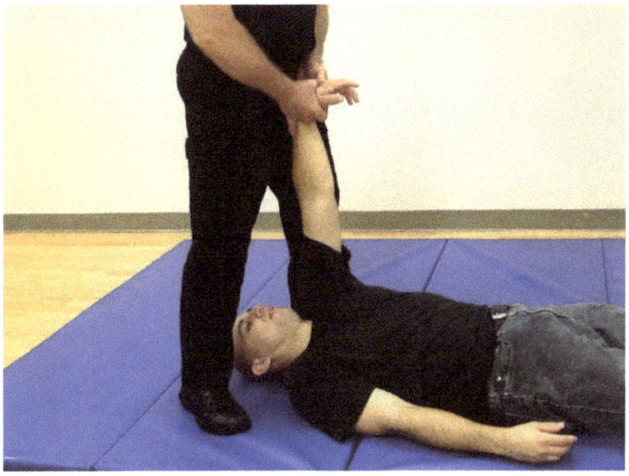

32L

Figures 31L and 32L. Take another six inch step with your right foot around the top of the suspect's head, keeping it close to his right shoulder. The suspect's arm should remain straight as you move around him. Keep his wrist locked down and straight in front of you. As you follow foot around the top of his head, your body will keep turning toward the suspect, as you get to his right side. Once you have reached over the top of his head, you will see that his left shoulder will start coming off the floor. This is a natural progression in turning the suspect over onto his stomach. You may notice that my grip on his wrist shows my little finger split around to the back of his wrist. This is a personal preference. I place my little finger around to allow me to get a tighter and stronger grip, allowing me to have even more control on the bend in the suspect's wrist.

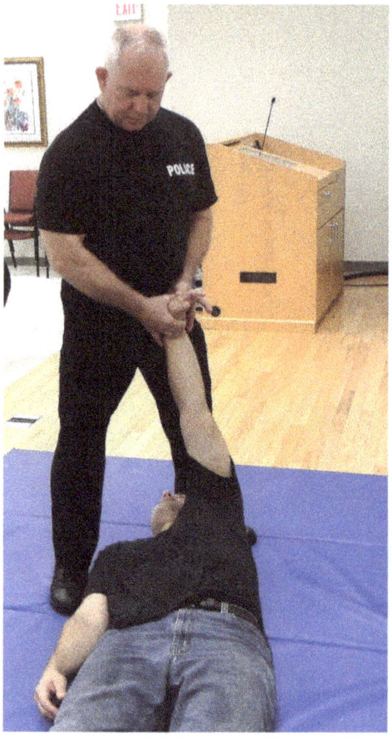

33L

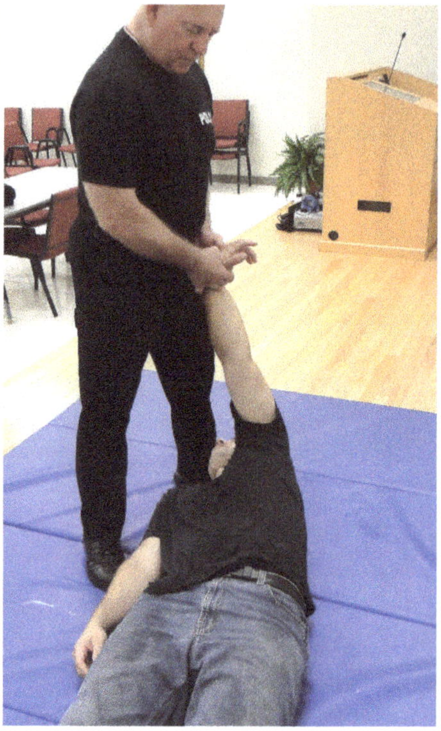

34L

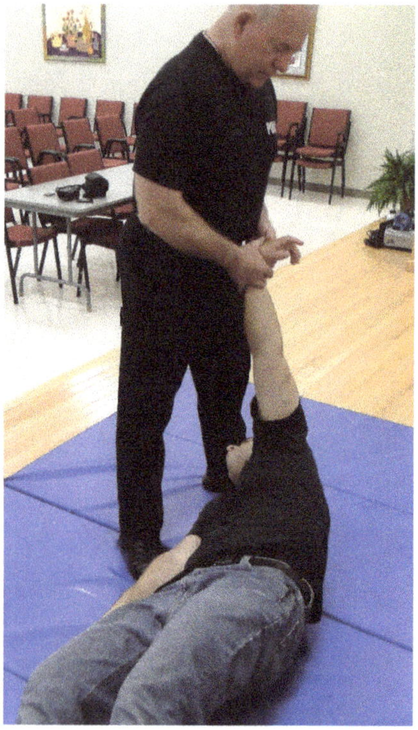

35L

Figures 33L, 34L, and 35L. Notice when “follow footing” around the suspects’s head. His wrist is kept at your center. The actor’s left arm will raise as he turns over onto his right shoulder, but make sure that it remains straight as you move

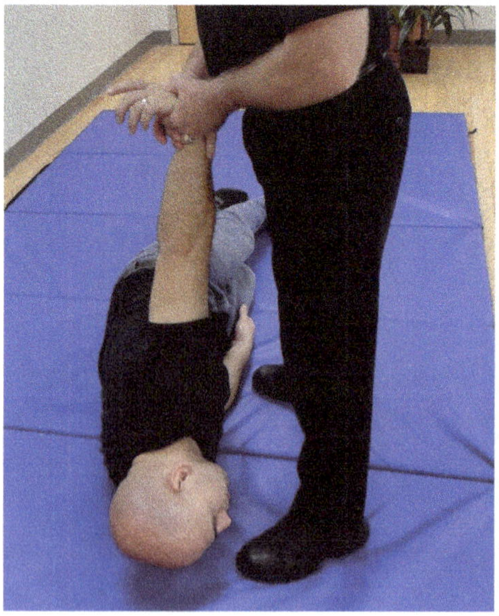

36L

Figure 36L. When the actor has hit the high point in being turned over, take up the slack by pulling higher.

Figure 37L. The actor’s shoulder needs to go all the way to the ground before going to the next step. If it he keeps his shoulder up, just rotate his wrist toward his head and apply a small amount of pressure downward. He will comply.

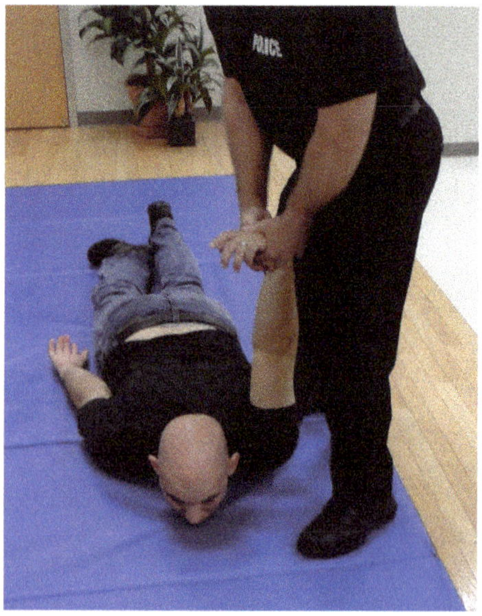

37L

38L

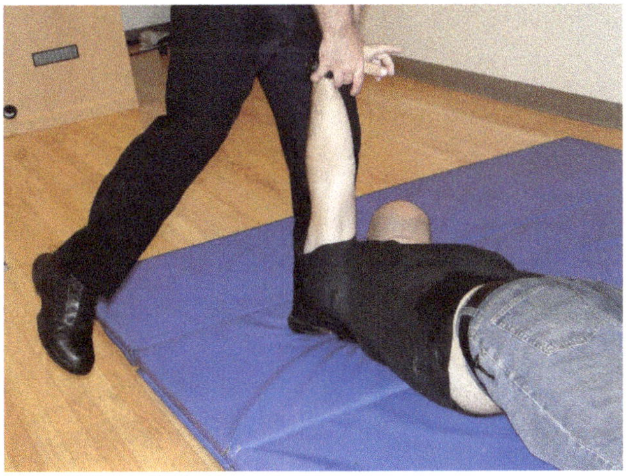

39L

Figure 38L. When the actor's shoulder has been placed flush against the ground, step around to the top of his shoulder with one step using your left foot. Place the toe of your boot or shoe next to the actor's neck under the shoulder; still maintaining control with both hands on his arm.

Figure 39L. Shift your weight to your left foot, and step back with your right foot in a swinging motion.

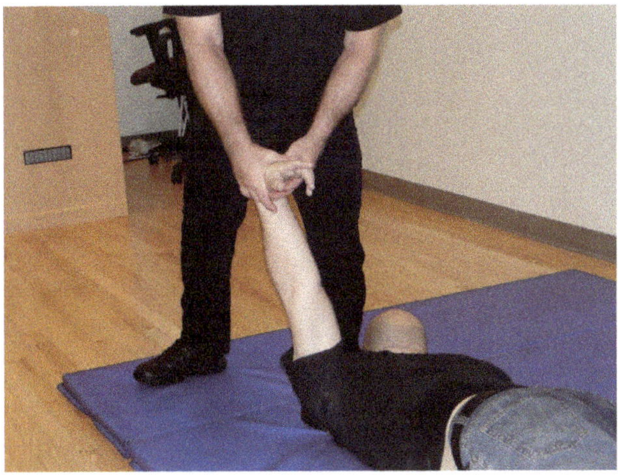

40L

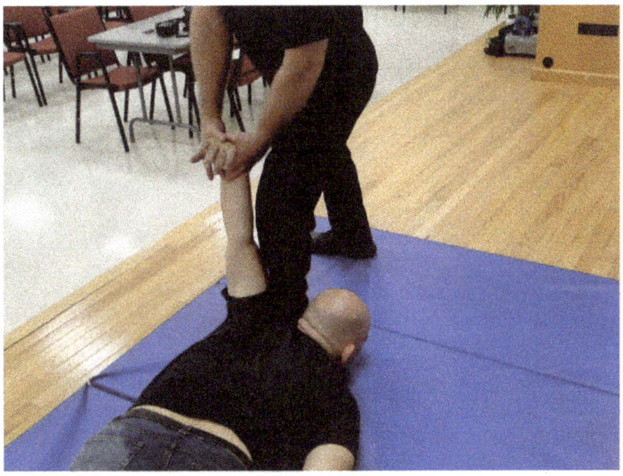

41L

Figures 40L and 41L. In the one step back with your right foot, place it behind you at least a shoulder widths distance. Your left knee will be inside the actor's left elbow. Allow your left knee to bend forward and pull back on the actor's arm until it is tight. This "pulling back" motion will lockout the arm putting pressure on the shoulder and elbow. When applying this in a real life situation, this is the point that you should slow down and evaluate the situation. Take a few deep breaths to bring your heart rate down and prevent you from having tunnel vision on the suspect. You have your suspect secure at this time, so look up and make sure there are no other persons that may cause a threat to you.

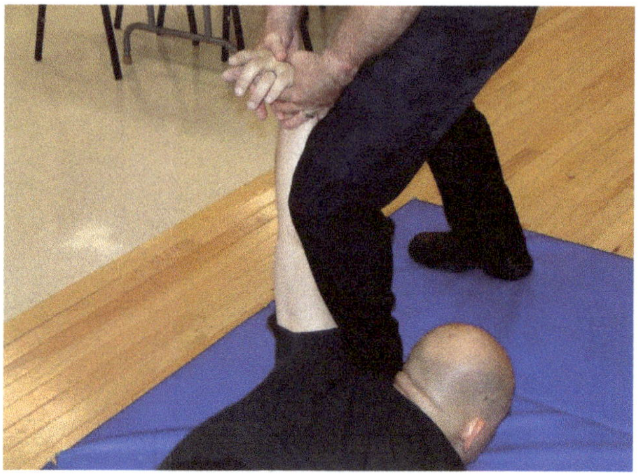

42L

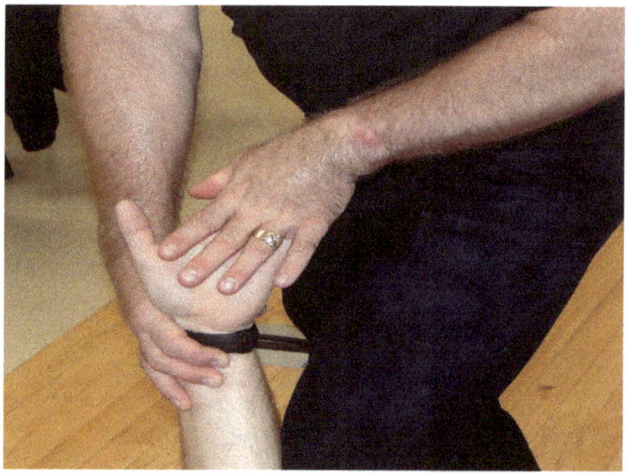

43L

Figure 42L. Tension on the actor's arm is important when evaluating; making sure that the suspect knows that you are in control. Don't become laxed. You are slowing down to evaluate and bring yourself down from the excitement.

Figure 43L. Making sure you have a good grip with your right hand on the suspect's wrist, release your left hand to pull the suspect's hand back and open. Keeping pressure on the fingers of the suspect for control.

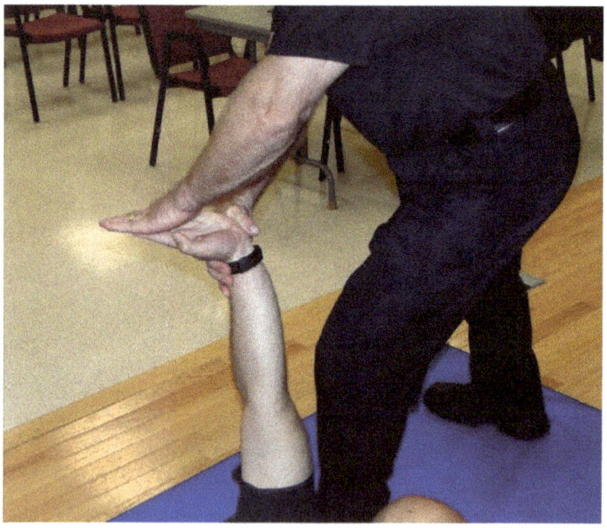

44L

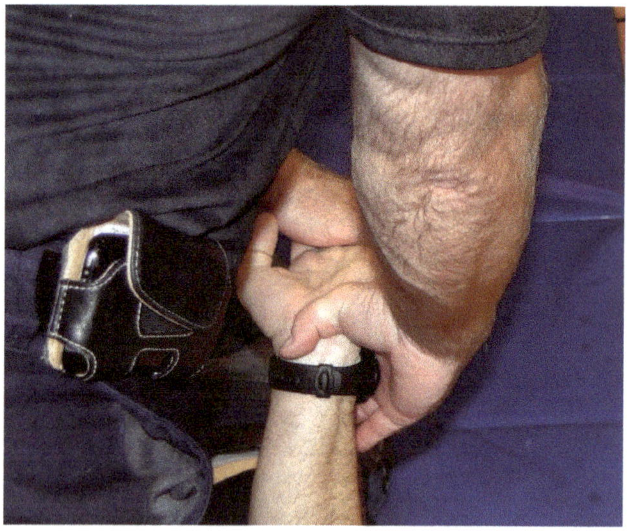

45L

Figures 44L and 45L. Controlling the wrist with your right hand, rotate the suspect's hand back to your right, still in the open position. Allow his wrist to turn in your right hand as it rotates. Maintain pressure on the fingers so he will not be able to clench his fist . When his fingers are pointing toward his feet, no more rotation is required of his hand. Keeping your hand open as you turn the actor's hand will help in keeping his hand open. When his fingers are pointed in the correct direction, your palm should be across the suspect's fingers.

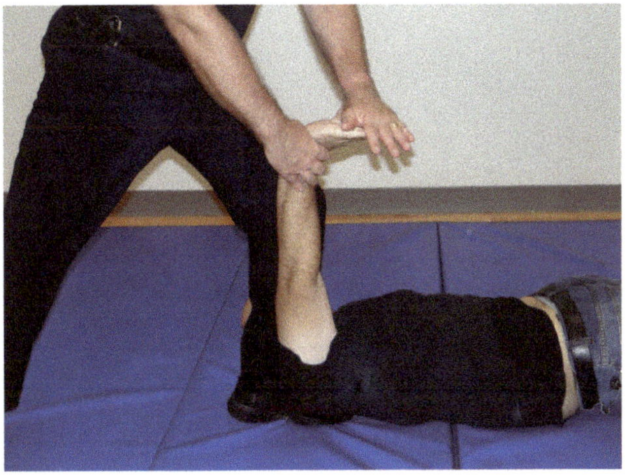

46L

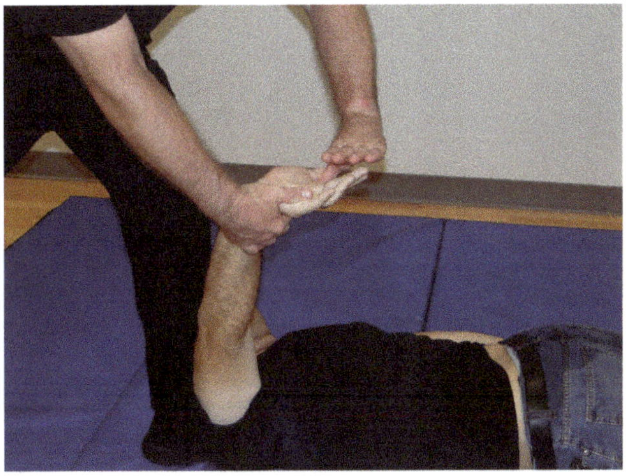

47L

Figure 46L. After the suspect's hand is pointed in the correct position toward his feet, apply pressure to the arm by leaning forward with your left knee and pulling back with your right hand until tight. This will allow you to release with the left hand.

Figure 47L. Release your left hand and open your hand so the palm is facing down. Your fingers are together and the thumb is away from your hand. Reach into the suspect's hand as if you were going to shake his hand.

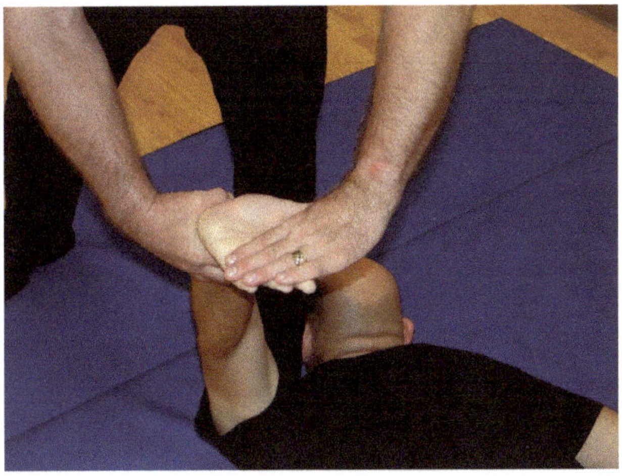

48L

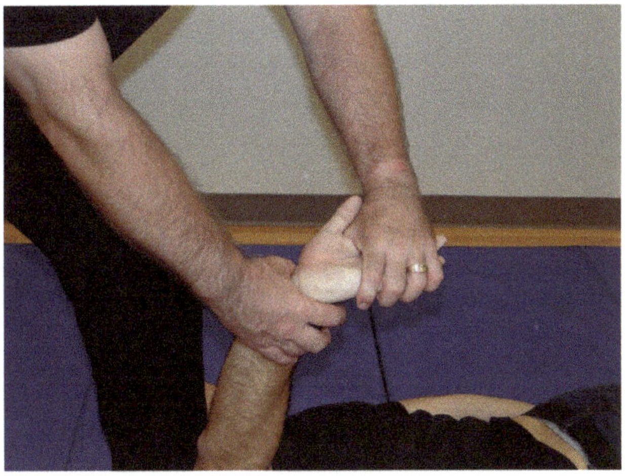

49L

Figure 48L. Reach in with your left hand in the handshaking position pressing the web portion of your hand tight against his. Your right hand index finger is right at the bend of his wrist as it is kept bent back.

Figure 49L. The grip on the suspect's hand is tightened, and his wrist is kept back. Turn your left hand back to the left, keeping his hand flat. In practice, do this slow so you do not injure your partner's wrist or elbow. The amount of pressure on the wrist and arm will cause the actor's arm to bend back across his back, so allow it to move.

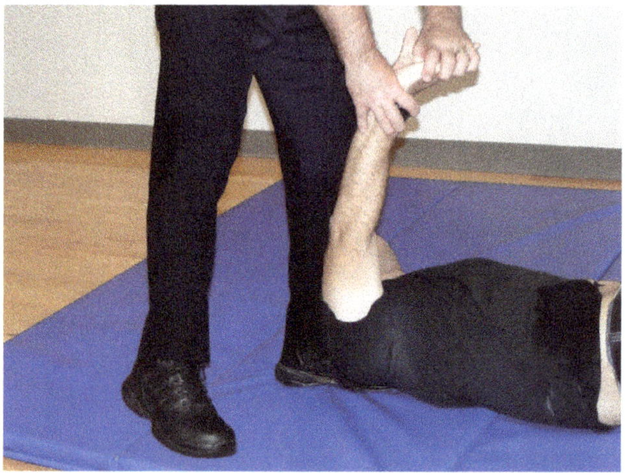

50L

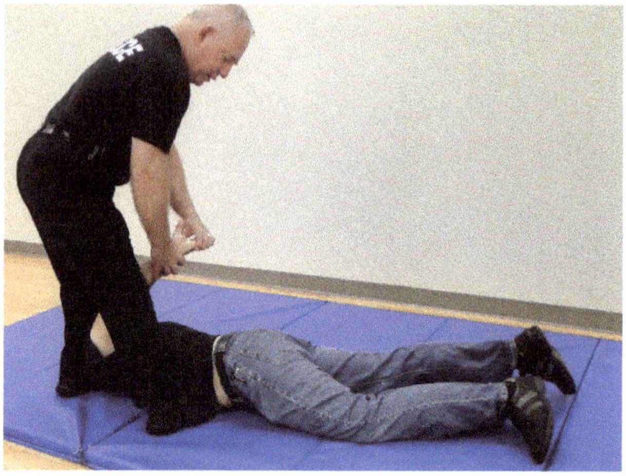

51L

Figure 50L. As the pressure is being applied from the turning of the suspect's hand, bring the left foot from the back position around in one step.

Figure 51L. Your left foot is brought around in one continuous motion to the waist of the suspect, as you allow his arm to bend down across his back.

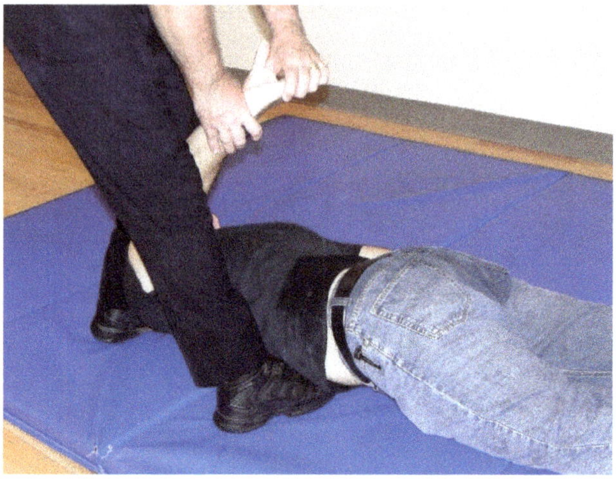

52L

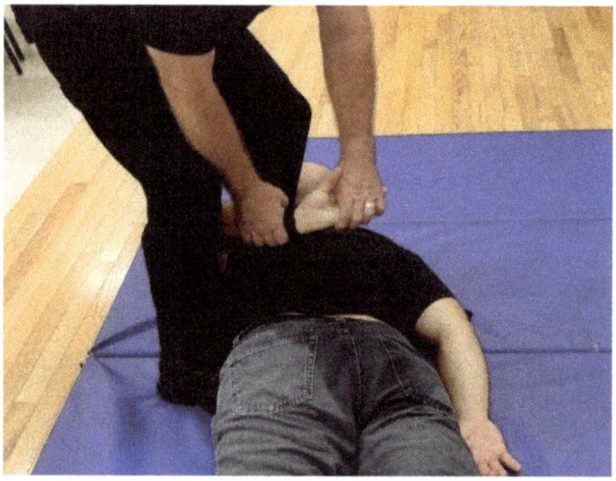

53L

Figure 52L. When in practice with a partner, take the actor down to his back easy and slow so as not to cause injury to his elbow or shoulder. Allow his arm to come back and down toward his feet to release the pressure on the shoulder then allow it to bend at the elbow. Give the hand and wrist support using your right hand on his wrist and the left with the grip on his hand.

Figure 53L. Bend down when placing his hand across his back, preparing to move the left foot back. The right foot remains at his waistline under his stomach area. In real life action with a suspect, you could place the arm across the back and allow pressure to be applied on top of his arm with your bodyweight to secure it in place as you prepare to move your left foot back. But, remember to keep the suspect's wrist and hand flat when placed on his back, so allow it to move.

54L

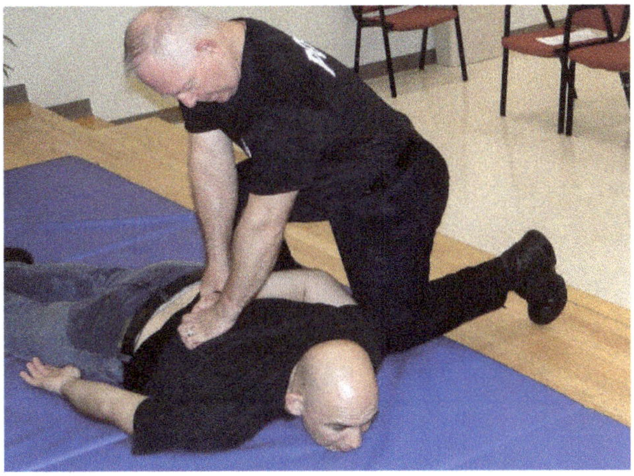

55L

Figure 54L. The step you have taken with your right foot to the waist will be behind the arm across his back. This prevents him from pushing his arm down. Step back from the neck area with your left foot placing pressure on the arm of the suspect.

Figure 55L. Bring your left knee forward striking the elbow on the suspect. This will push his arm further across his back and tighter to his side. This will allow his arm to be closer to the other side which will give you plenty of room when the other hand is brought up to be handcuffed.

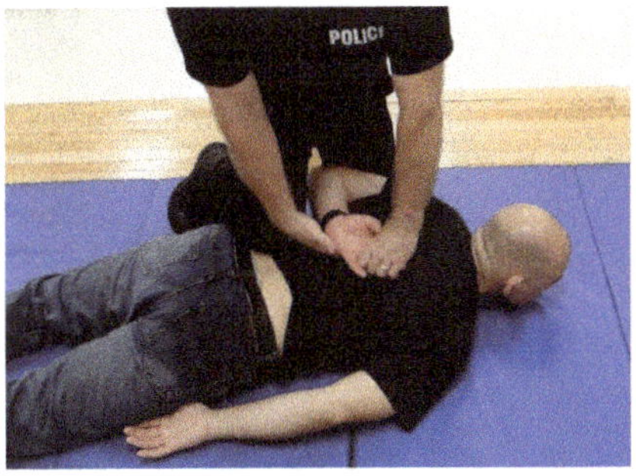

56L

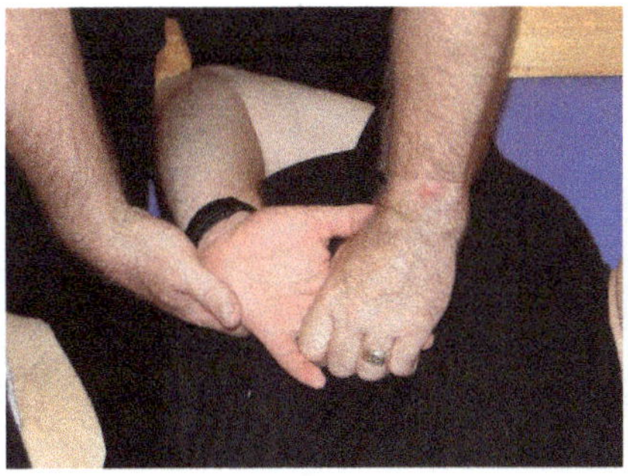

57L

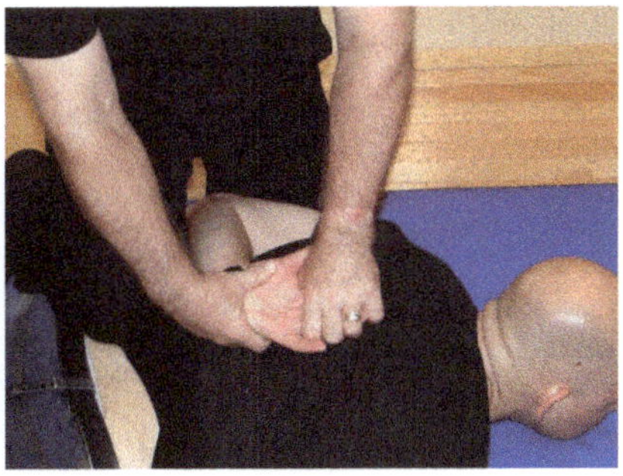

58L

Figure 56L. Still applying pressure down onto the suspect's hand, bring your right knee down on the suspect's lower back just below his arm. This will secure the arm from being pushed downward, and the left knee is behind his elbow which will prevent the arm from being pulled out to the side.

Figure 57L. Keeping the suspect's wrist flat while it is on his back is important when pressure is needed to be applied to the fingers. The pressure is applied by turning your hand counterclockwise. This will place the pressure on the joints of his fingers where they are not made to bend.

Figure 58L. ***DO NOT*** allow the wrist to just bend back. When you attempt to apply pressure, the fingers are just bent where they are much more flexible.

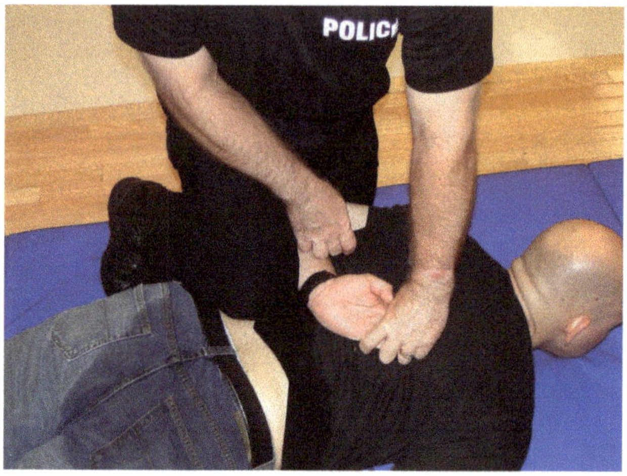

59L

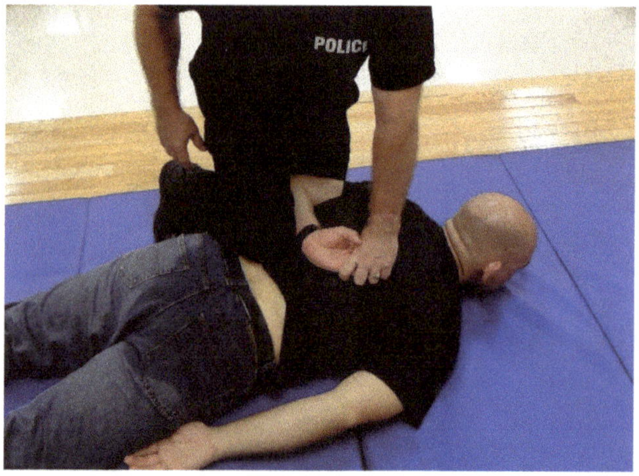

60L

Figures 59L and 60L. Applying the pressure to the fingers counterclockwise with the wrist flat will allow you to release your hand support from under the suspect's wrist. This will give you the freedom you need to reach back behind you for your handcuffs and still maintain control over the suspect.

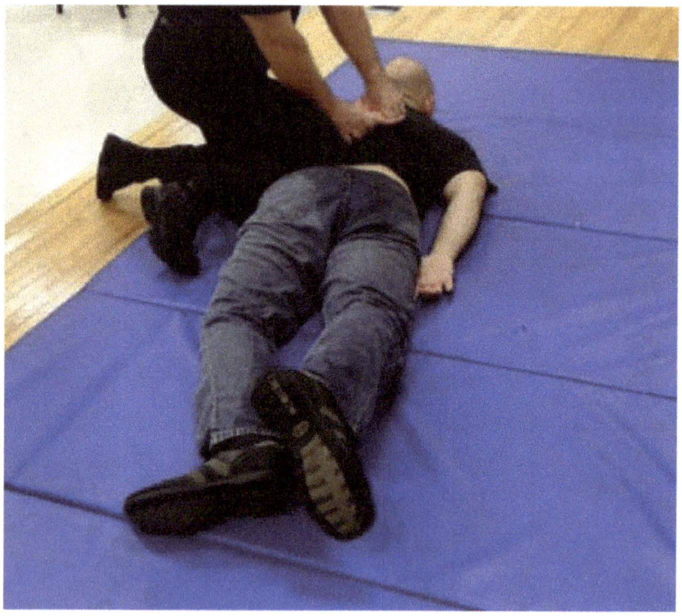

61L

Figure 61L. ***REMEMBER THE TEST*** !!! Apply pressure to the fingers to get cooperation due to him being unruly, not listening to your commands, or just plain stubborn. As you apply pressure to his fingers, watch his feet for a reaction. If you are doing it correctly, his feet will react in a "tell tale" way. Either one foot or both feet will twist or raise when the pressure is applied, and may be accompanied by a yell or groan. The torque of the fingers to the side is painful, and you will get a reaction.

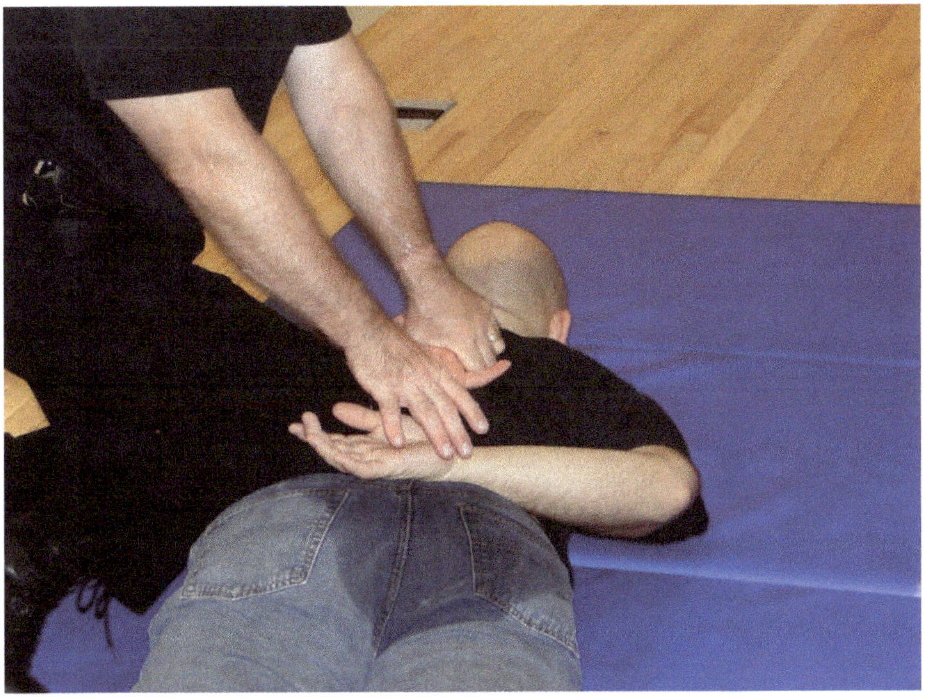

62L

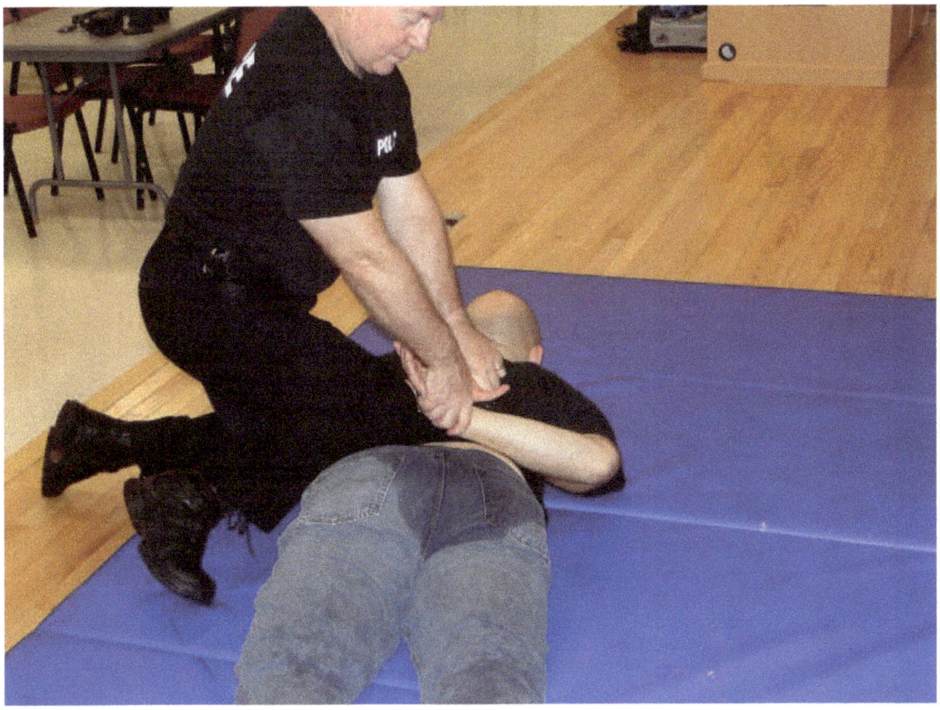

63L

Figures 62L and 63L. After the compliance is met, the order is given for the unsecured hand to be brought up to his back. Even if the actor may have been laying on his arm, he <u>will</u> find a way to get his hand to his back for you to take control and handcuff his hands.

HITCHHIKER I

Uniform Grab

1M

2M

Figure 1M. When a suspect grabs your uniform to pull you or intimidate you, the use of the hitchhiker is a great defense. In this case, the suspect is grabbing with his left hand.

Figure 2M. The response to the suspect's grab in this case is a right hand cover. The right hand is brought up reaching over the top of the suspect's hand.

3M

4M

Figure 3M. Your response should be quick to cover the suspect's hand. Reach over the top of his hand with your fingers extended and your thumb open.

Figure 4M. Grip the meaty portion of the thumb area of the suspect's hand with your fingers, placing your thumb on the back of his hand between the middle finger and the ring finger. Make sure that your grip on his hand is secure right away, so if he should try to pull his hand away, you will be able to start your technique.

5M 6M

Figures 5M and 6M. After the cover hand has been properly placed, your weight is shifted to the left leg for the distract using a front snap kick with the right leg in this case. Remember that when using a front snap kick that the foot used in the kick comes directly from the floor to the kick. The knee is not brought up first which may telegraph your kick.

7M 8M

Figure 7M. After the distract of the front snap kick, the foot is withdrawn as fast as possible. This will place both feet on the ground for a better balance allowing you to start your technique.

Figure 8M. The right hand peels the suspect's hand from your uniform by gripping with your fingers and pushing with your thumb. The turning of the suspect's hand will be to the inside toward his thumb. This should clear his grip on your uniform and open up his hand.

9M

10M

Figure 9M. When the suspect's hand has cleared your uniform, the left hand is brought up to assist in the grip and the locking of the suspect's wrist.

Figure 10M. The left hand grips the little finger side of the suspect's hand with the fingers placed on the inside of his palm and the thumb on the back of his hand. Both hands should be pressing his wrist back toward him locking him in that position as you continue turning it back to your right.

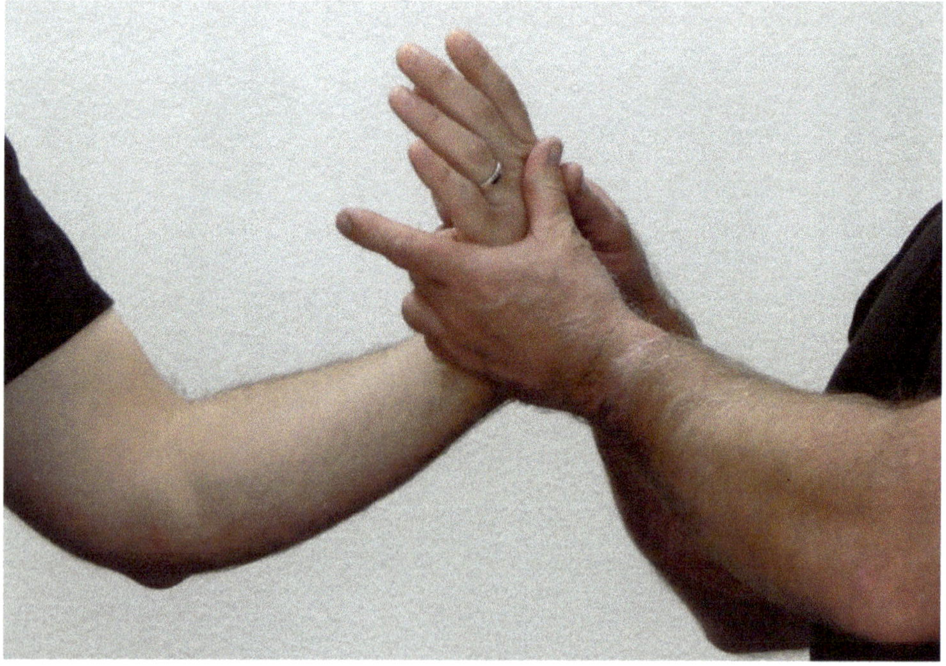

11M

Figure 11M. This is a close up of how the left hand assists the grip of the suspect's hand. The suspect's hand is being turned to the right and at the same time, being pushed forward locking it down.

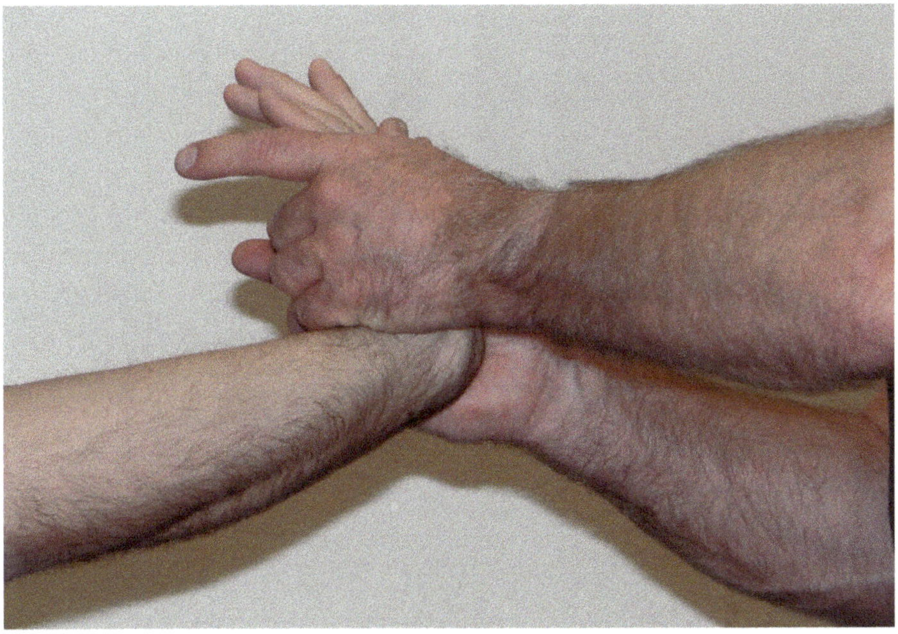

12M

Figure 12M. This close up shows the locking out of the suspect's wrist both forward and to the side. This is where the wrist is stopped in both the back and the side positions. Remember that flexibility will vary from person to person. You will be able to tell when the wrist locks by the feel when you are placing the wrist in this position. At this point, the body's posture will start breaking down.

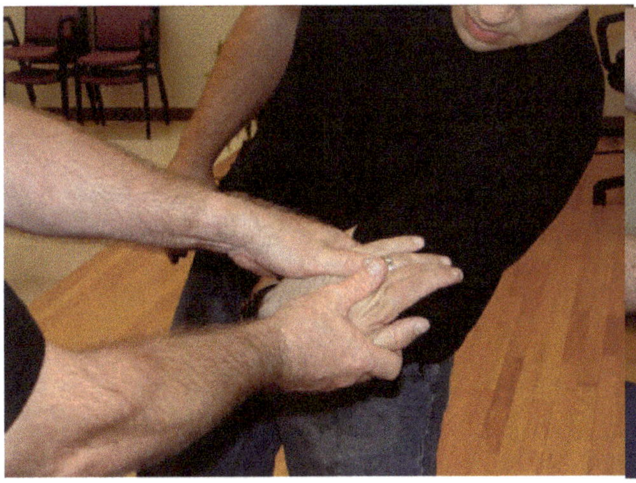

13M

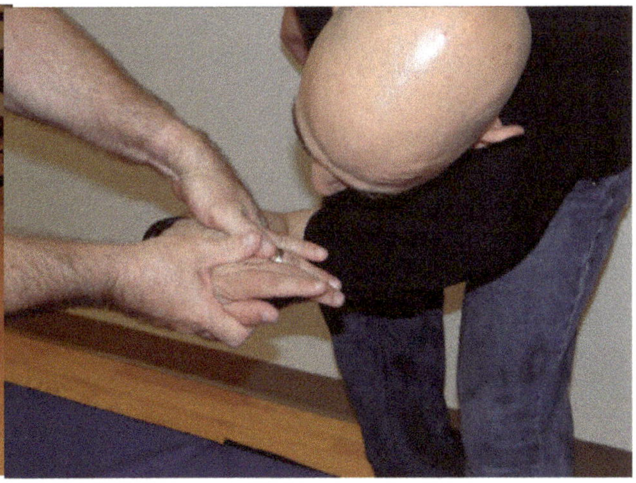

14M

Figures 13M and 14M. The posture breaks down when the wrist locks out to his left side. First, the suspect's elbow will turn in, and the shoulder will drop to the left side as the body weight will shift over the hip. With the body weight shifts, all of his weight will be on the left hip. He will not be able to take a step or move the left foot to regain his balance.

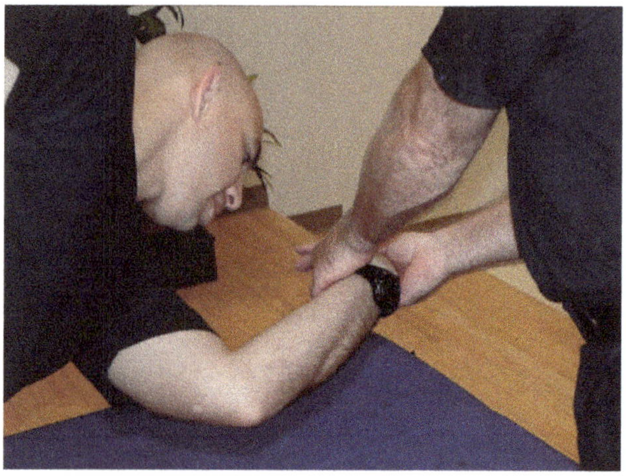

15m

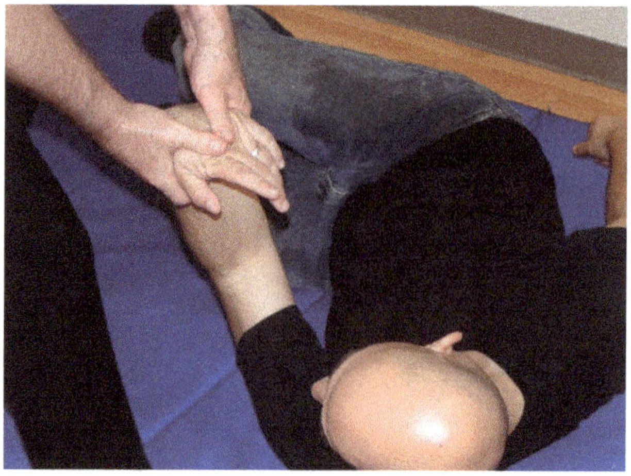

16M

Figure 15M. After the shift of the weight to his left hip, he has no choice, as you continue the pressure to his wrist, but to fall to his left side.

Figure 16M. When he falls to his left side, you assist the way he falls. Continue to keep your grip on the actor's hand and pull back to your center with his hand. This will eliminate the problem of the suspect falling directly onto his shoulder without the support of his hand. The fall then will be directed onto his left hip where you want him at this time.

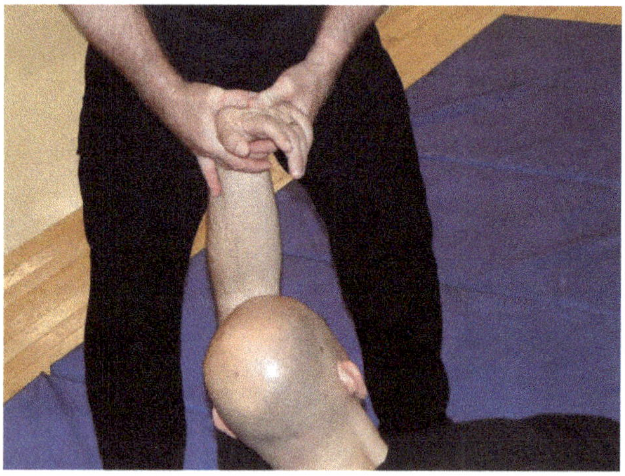

17M

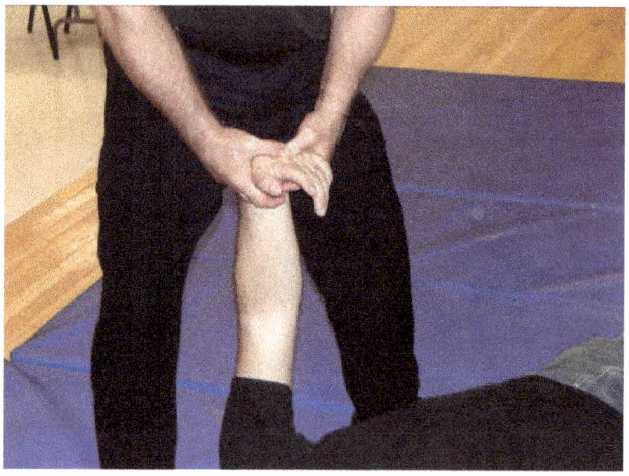

18M

Figures 17m and 18m. The pulling of the suspect's hand back to your center, allows the his weight to settle onto his back. The pulling of his hand back to your center also keeps his arm straight as his total weight settles on the ground. Keeping the arm straight is important so he does not have a chance to bend his arm and pull you forward. As soon as you pull his hand to your center, your knees should be partially bent and your back should be straight with no bend at your waist. This position will give you balance so that he will not be able to pull through.

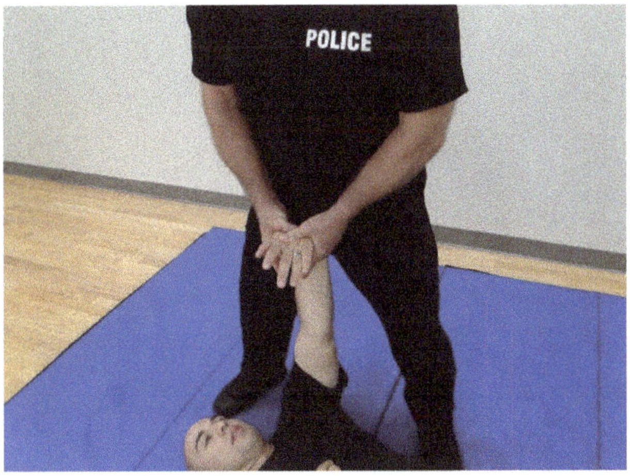

19M

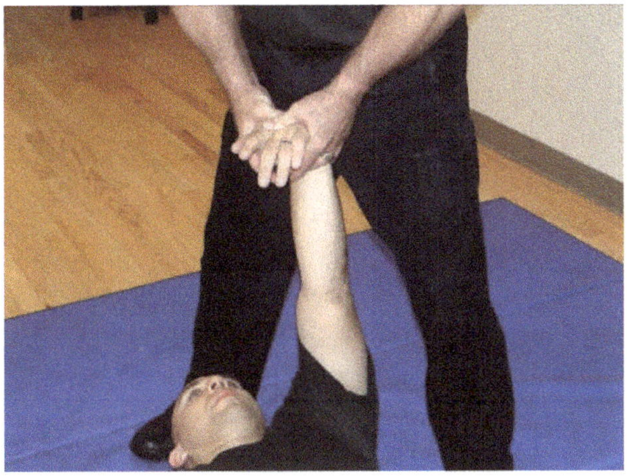

20M

Figure 19M. Centered in this position, the actor's wrist is locked forward, and his arm is straight up.

Figure 20M. Take your first step of the "Follow Foot" technique with your right foot. This step should be only 6" to 8" and kept close to the suspect as you start the move around the head of the suspect.

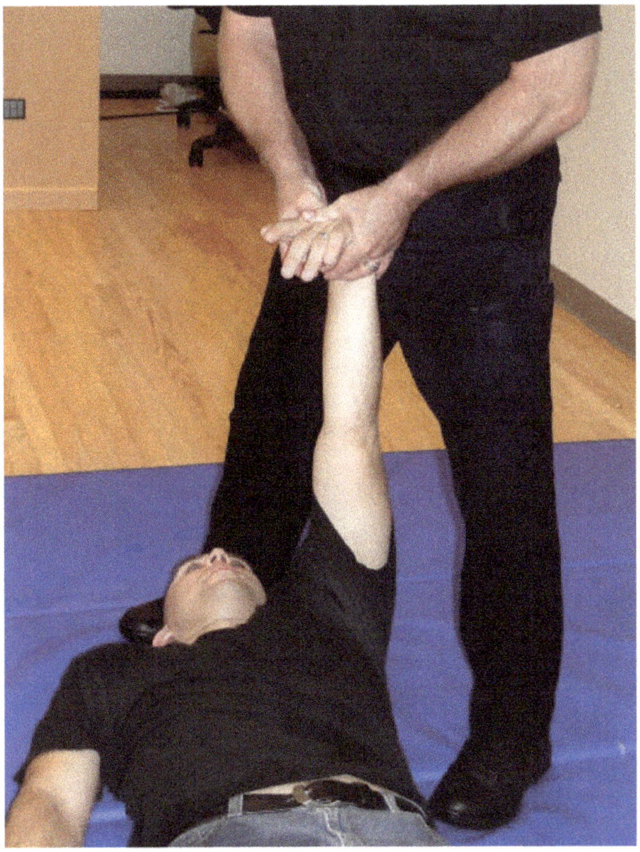

21M

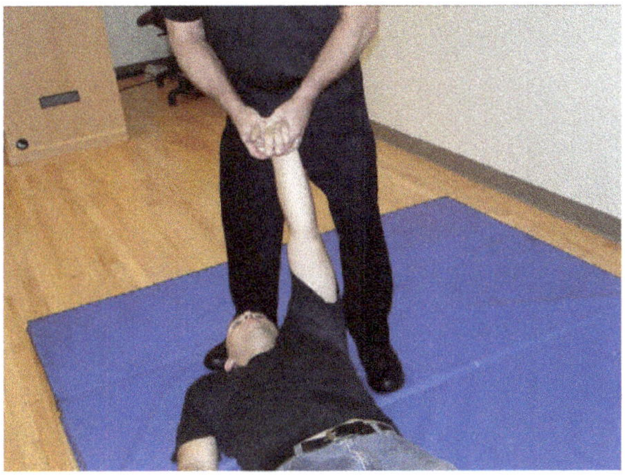

22M

Figures 21M and 22M. When taking your first step with your right foot, there should be only a small shift of weight when stepping. The shift in weight is brought back right away as you pull the same distance of 6" or 8" with the left foot. Keep the suspect's hand at your center and at a 90 degree position from your body.

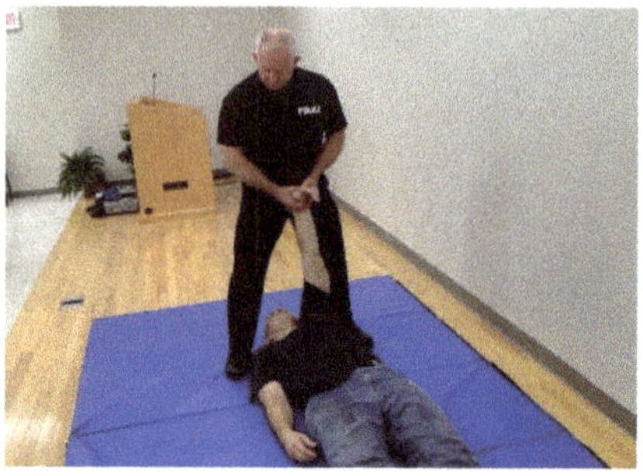
23M

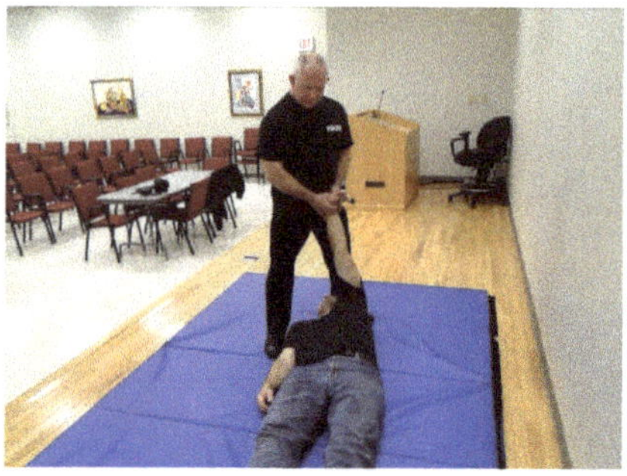
24M

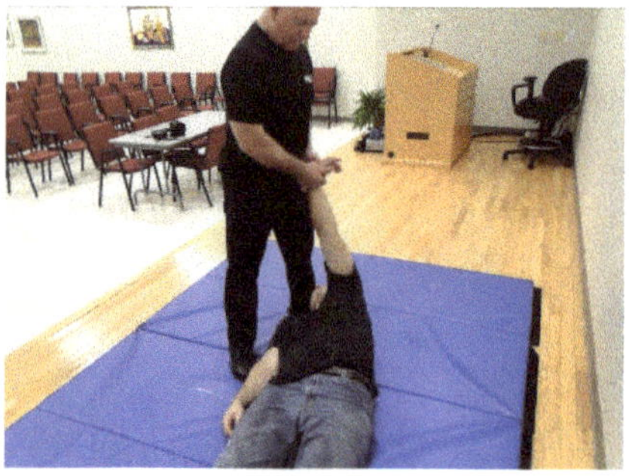
25M

Figures 23m, 24M, and 25M. Continue the "Follow Foot" around the head of the suspect, stepping 6" or 8" and pulling at the same time. Keep close to the actor. Keep his arm straight and his hand at your center and straight out at a 90 degree angle.

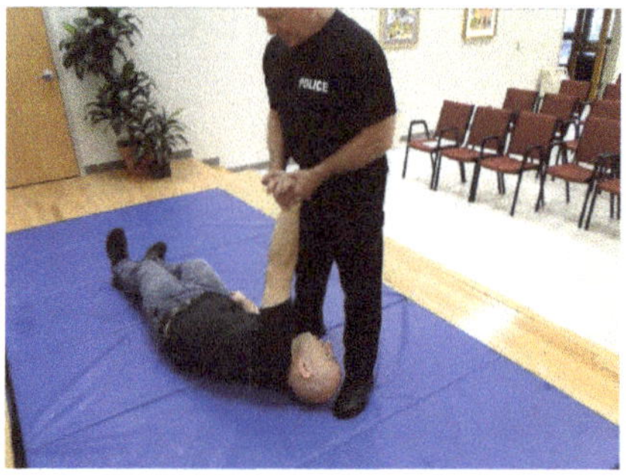
26M

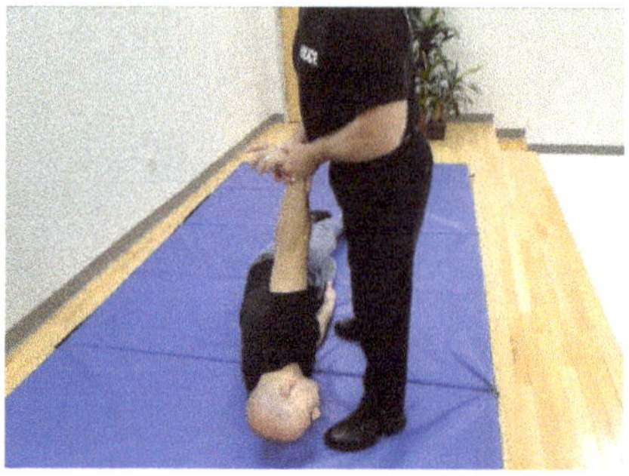
27M

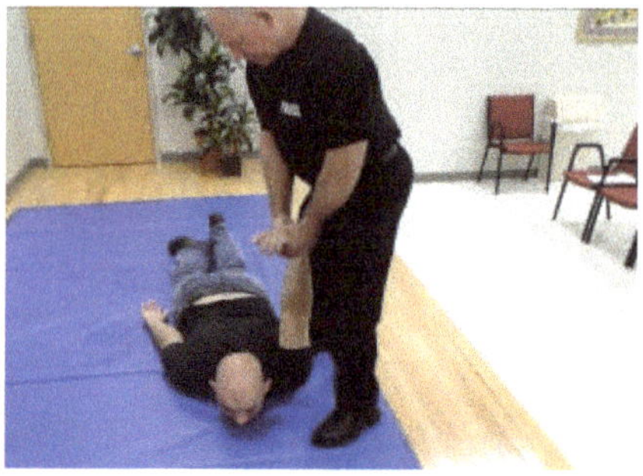
28M

Figures 26M and 27M. When you reach the left side of the actor, his arm will extend up several inches due to the actor rolling over his shoulder. You will need to take up the slack by continuing to pull upward and maintain a wide stance to maximize you base and balance.

Figure 28M. Most of the time, the actor will roll over onto his stomach with no problem while you do the Follow Foot. Of course, there is that 1 or 2 percent that will attempt to give you a problem. This will not be a problem for you.

NOTE: If by chance the suspect stops just prior to going flat onto stomach or attempts to grab your foot with the other hand and you have done everything right and are in the correct position, "the remedy" is simple. Standing along side of the suspect, rotate the his hand slowly toward his head. This will rotate his arm putting a great deal of stress on his shoulder. The actor will cooperate and have no other choice but to push his shoulder into the floor where you want it.

The next step of course is the "stepping over" the shoulder and locking the arm, in preparation for taking the hand down to the handcuffing position across his back. This step should be familiar to you and will be not shown again to prevent the repetion.

HITCHHIKER I

Front Choke

I had mentioned previously in this book with words of wisdom saying "Attack the attacker and not the hold." This is a small counter diction to the rule for the reason that the hand has to be grabbed in the demonstration of the hitch-hiker I. BUT, please understand that you are not really attacking the hold. You are just placing your hand in position in preparation for this technique. When an assailant attacks you in a choke attack, your response has to be as quick as possible to prevent you from losing consciousness.

1N

2N

Figure 1N. When anattacker seizes you around the neck, your response has to be as fast as you can respond.

Figure 2N. Respond by bringing yourright hand up in an open position over the top of the attacker's grip.

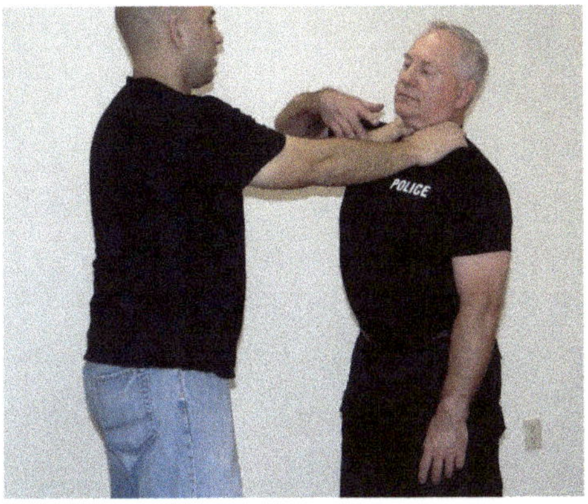

3N

Figures 3N and 4N. Your right hand comes over the top left of his hand. Your fingers grip around the meaty portion of his thumb, and your thumb is placed on the back of his hand between middle finger and the ring finger.

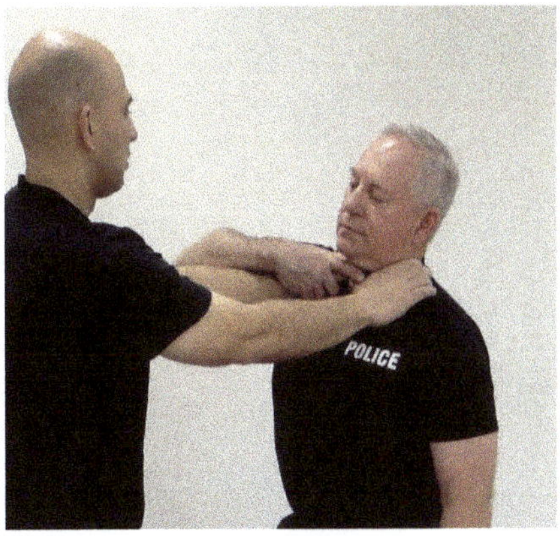

4N

5N

6N

Figures 5N and 6N. When your grip is secure on the attacker's left hand, use your right foot for the distract to strike the attacker's shin area.

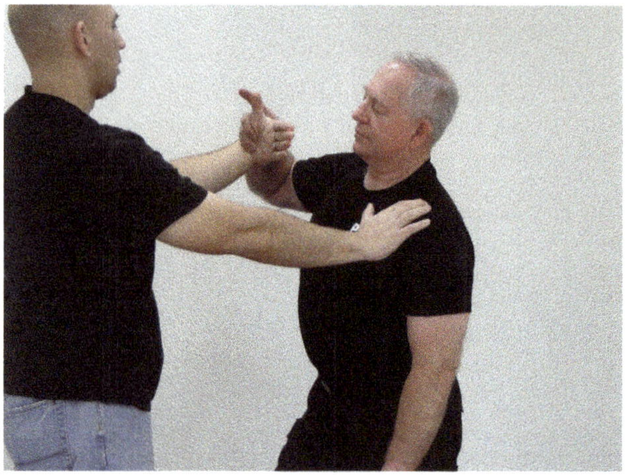

7N

8N

9N

Figures 7n, 8N and 9N. The right hand removes the attacker's hand from your neck as soon as the distract is accomplished, and the right foot is brought back to the floor for stability. The attacker's hand is pushed back to the locking position as it is being turned back to your right side. At the same time, your left hand is being brought up between the attacker's arms to assist your right hand in locking the attacker's hand.

10N

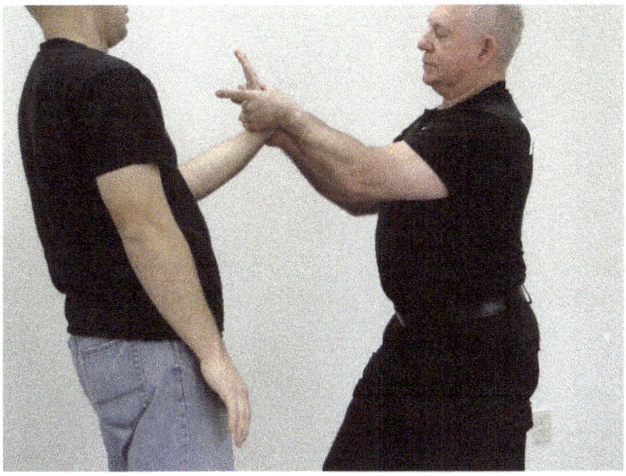
11N

Figures 10N and 11N. When your left hand catches up with your right hand, it is placed on the back of the attacker's hand and gets the grip on the little finger side of the his hand. It reinforces your power in locking the attacker's hand back. The attacker will not be able to continue to hold on around your neck when his balance is broken.

Applying the Hitchhiker technique in this manner is not fighting the hold as I have mentioned before not to do. "**Fighting the hold**" would be trying to remove the strangle hold the attacker is putting on you by trying to pull his hands away from your neck. In this case, this is preparing for the start of the technique.

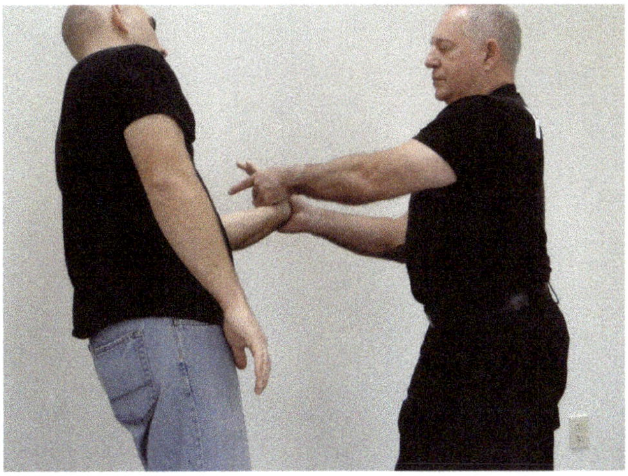
12N

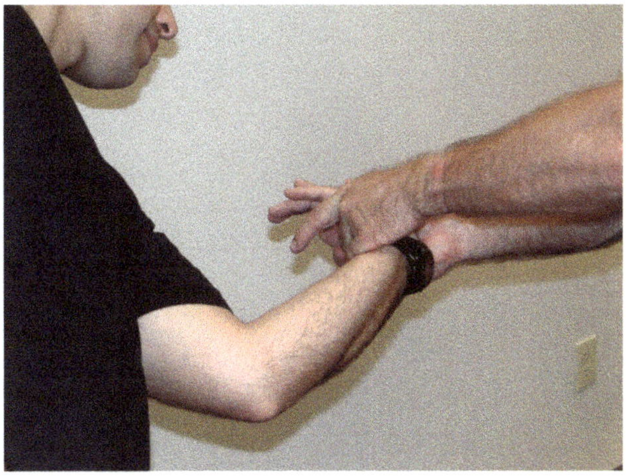
13N

Figure 12N. When the attacker's hand is taken to your right side, and his hand reaches a point that it can go no further the breakdown of his balance will start. The left elbow will turn in toward his waist, and the shoulder will drop to the left side. When the shoulder drops, it will cause his weight to shift to the left side putting the weight over the left hip.

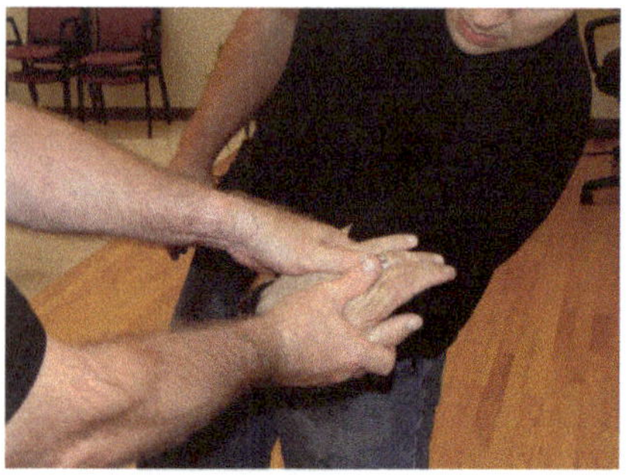

14N

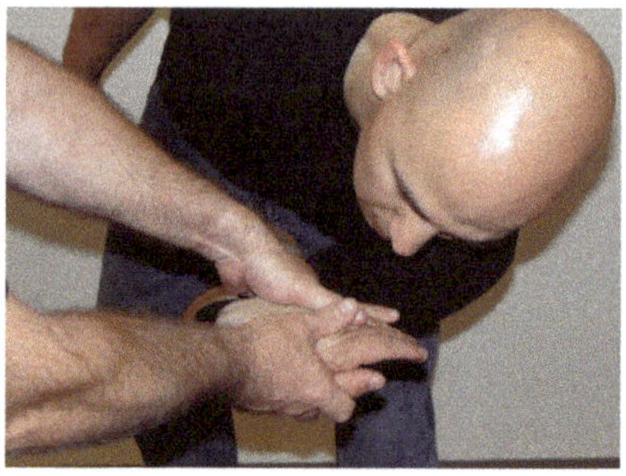

15N

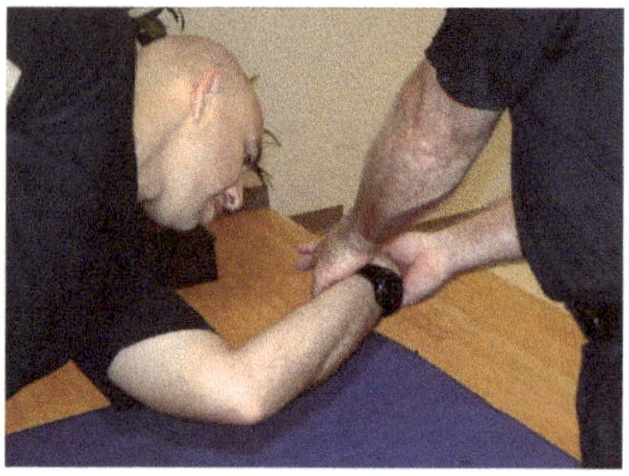

16N

Figures 14N,15N, and 16N. Once the weight has shifted over the left hip, he will not be able to step in any direction with his left foot to catch his balance. Continue pushing the attacker's locked wrist to your right side which will continue the breaking down of his balance. The elbow will continue to turn inside, and the shoulder will continue to drop to the side, until there is no other option but to fall to the ground to his left side. Notice that the elbow in figure 16N comes forward away from his body just before he falls to the ground.

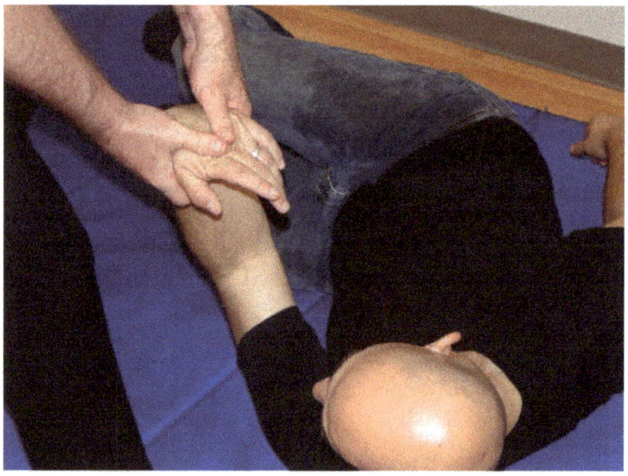

17N

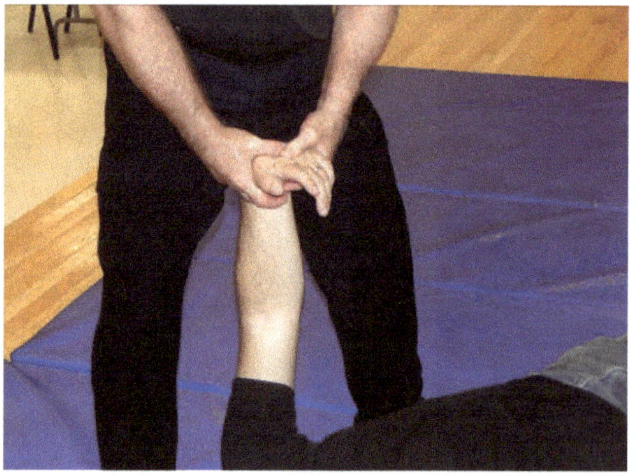

18N

Figure 17N. When he falls to the ground, his hip will be the first part of his body to touch. Keeping pressure on the wrist and pulling back so he doesn't pull you down with him, will keep his arm in front of him. By keeping his arm in front of him, prevents him from falling directly onto the shoulder, shortening the time he spends on his hip.

Figure 18N. As soon as he lays on the ground, you should pull back to your center. Again, keeping your back straight and using a wide stance for a good base. Your grip on his wrist is the same. The pressure is pushing his wrist forward with your thumbs and the pulling back pressure is at the bend of his wrist using your fingers. The pressure does increase on his wrist when it comes back to your center. Keep the attacker's arm straight and perpendicular to the ground.

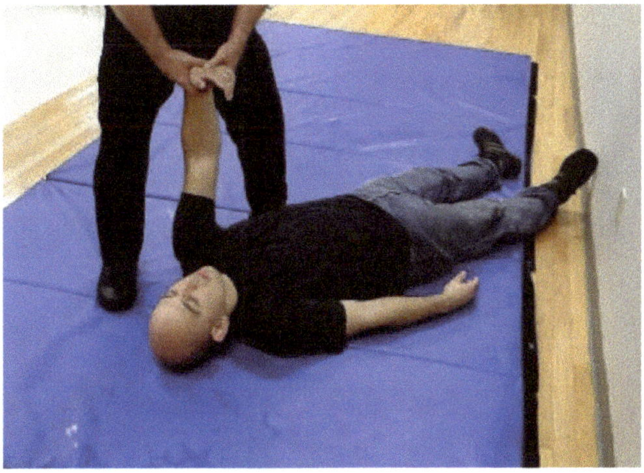

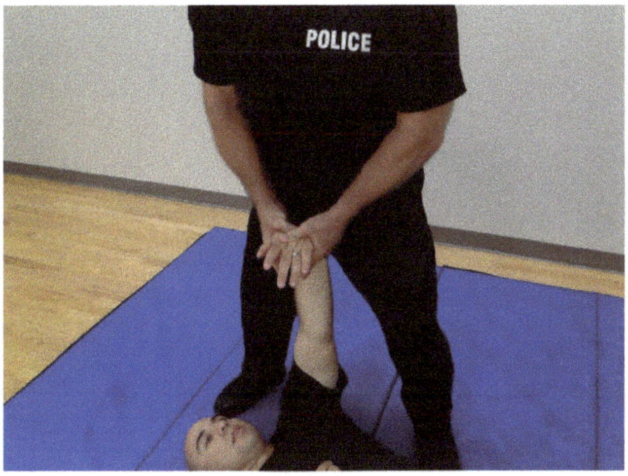

19N 20N

Figures 19N and 20N. These figures show the wide stance alongside of the attacker and that his arm is pulled up so that it is straight. The wrist of the attacker is pulled up close to your center and bent forward so the fingers are away from you at a 90 degree angle.

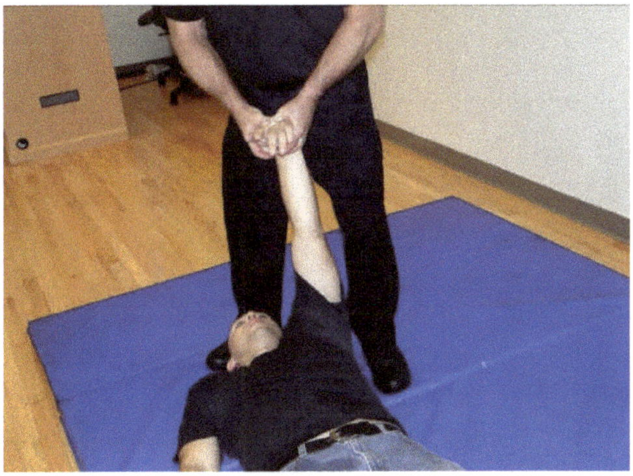

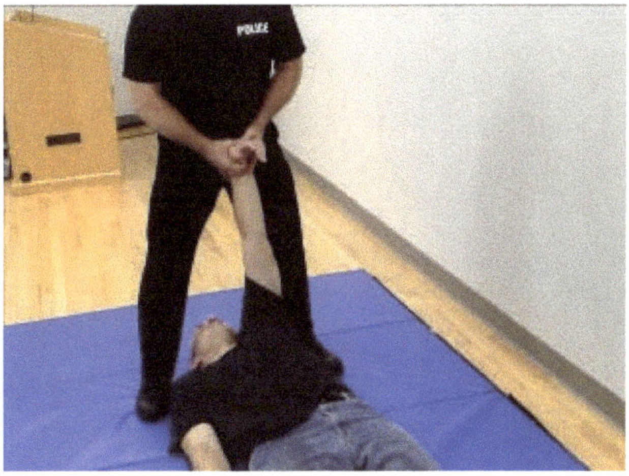

21N 22N

Figures 21N and 22N. The "Follow Foot" technique starts with your right foot when on the attacker's left side. Step 6 inches with your right foot then pull 6 inches with your left. The step is low, just slightly above the ground so little change when shifting your weight is needed. When pulling the second foot, it drags on the ground even lower, requiring even less shift of weight. As you move around the top of the actor's head, you need to keep as close as possible to the actor's body. While moving, it is important to keep the actor's hand straight in front of you and remain pulled up to your center. Notice that as you are going around the top of the attacker's head, once you get midway, his shoulder will start to extend up as he starts to roll over his other shoulder. Just take up the extra length by pulling up.

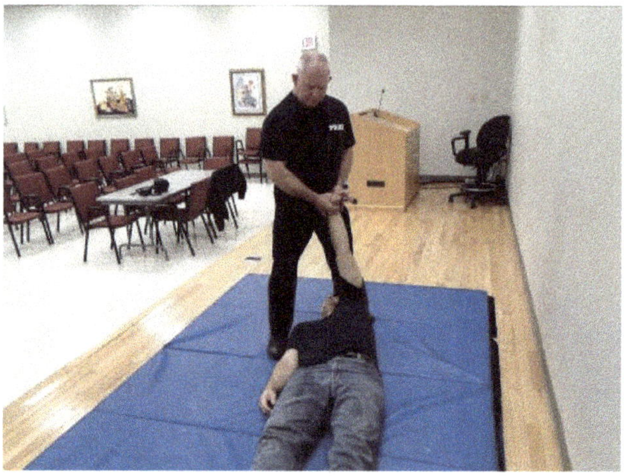

23N

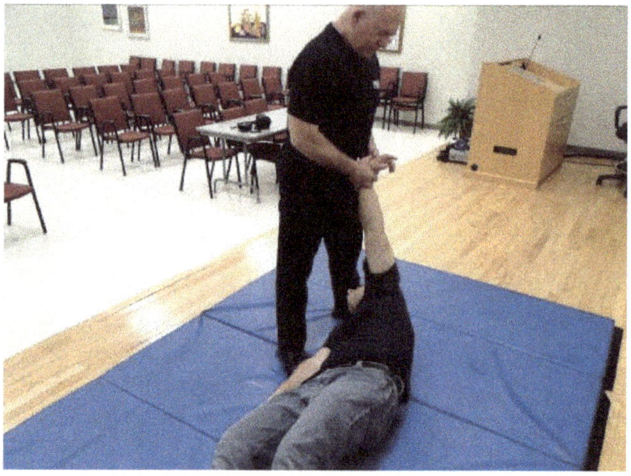

24N

Figures 23N and 24N. Continue the "Follow Foot" Technique around to the other side of the actor, stepping 6 inches and pulling 6 inches, all the way around always keeping your feet apart for balance. Keep your back straight as well as the attacker's arm while he is rolling over his other shoulder.

25N

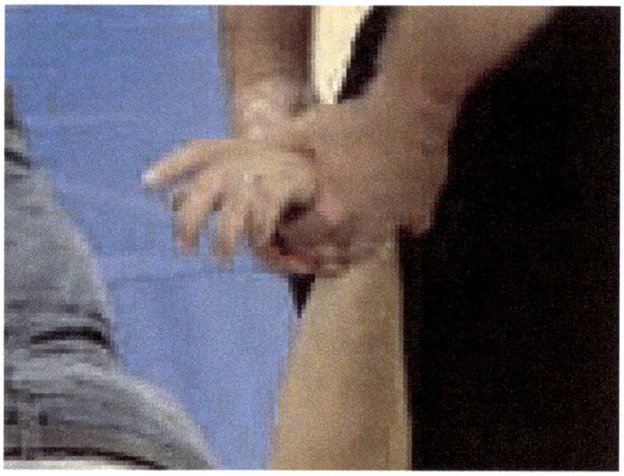

26N

Figure 25N. When the attacker is on his side directly over his other shoulder, this will be the highest point that you need to continue to maintain the upward pull.

Figure 26N. After he has reached his peak in height, he will turn onto his stomach. This is a critical part of the movement. Most of the time the actor will roll flat onto his stomach with his shoulders down on the ground, <u>***but***</u> *THERE ARE-THE FEW THAT WANT TO MAKE IT DIFFICULT; TRYING TO KEEP THEIR SHOULDER UP OFF THE GROUND.* The difficult part will be on them not you. There is an easy remedy for this problem. When his shoulder does not touch the ground, rotate his hand and fingers toward his head and apply pressure down. This movement rotates the shoulder forward and directly onto the ground.

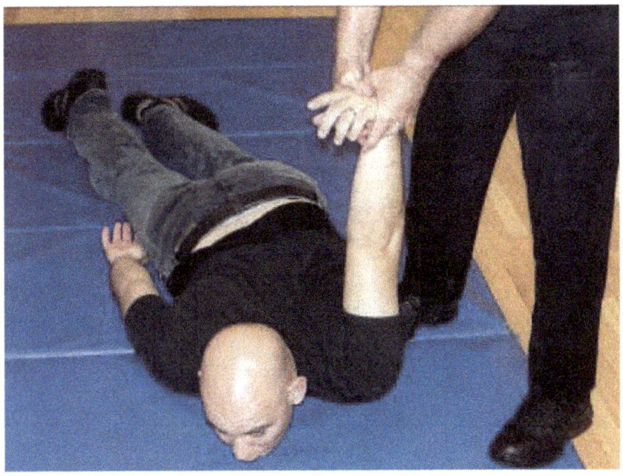

27N

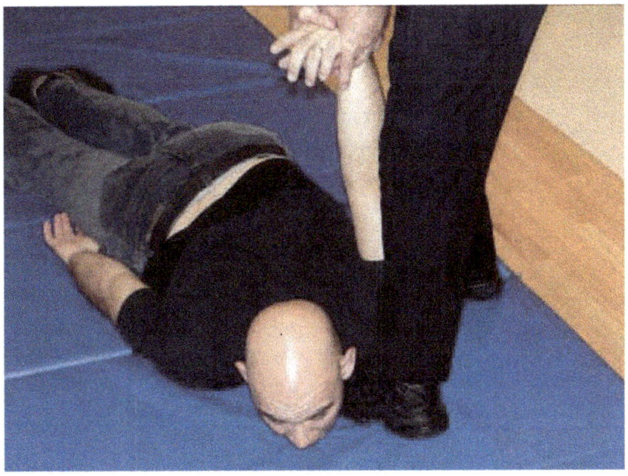

28N

Figure 27N. When the shoulder of the actor is pressed into the ground, he will be in a stable position that will keep him flat on the ground and makes him ready to lockout the arm.

Figure 28N. Step around and over the top of his left shoulder with your left foot. Place the toe of your left foot under the attacker's left shoulder next to his head and neck. Still keeping the attacker's arm straight up and pressure down on his bent wrist.

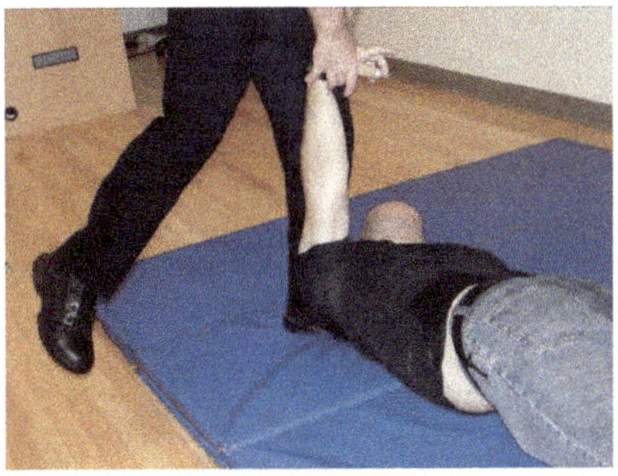

29N

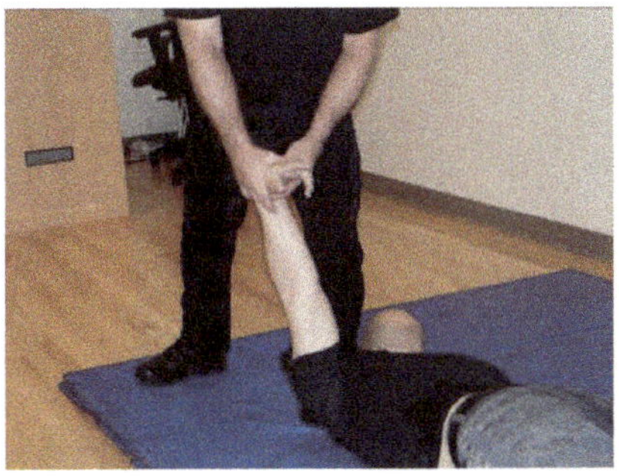

30N

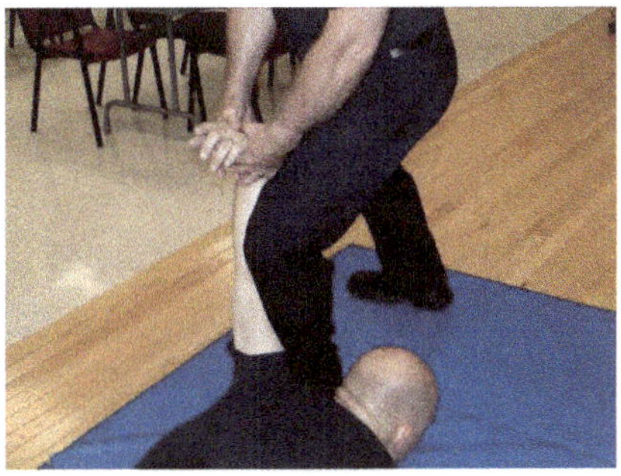

31N

Figures 29N, 30N, and 31N. After your left foot is in place, your right foot is brought around behind you while maintaining minimal pressure on the attacker's wrist. As you step around behind yourself, your body will turn back toward the attacker. The attacker's wrist will turn back so his fingers point toward his feet. The twisting of the attacker's wrist makes it almost impossible for him to bend his elbow. Your left knee is placed inside his elbow, where you pull back on his arm to put a hyperextension on his elbow as well as an increase of forward rotation of the attacker's shoulder. This is the point he is locked out. You need to **STOP**!!! **Evaluate the situation**. You need to take your direct focus off the attacker and look up. Look to see if there is anyone else involved. *Does he have a friend out there?* Also, this is the time to bring yourself down. Take at least three deep breaths. Remember the "Ten Cycle Method of Control?" Use it. This will lower your heart rate and help you regain your awareness.

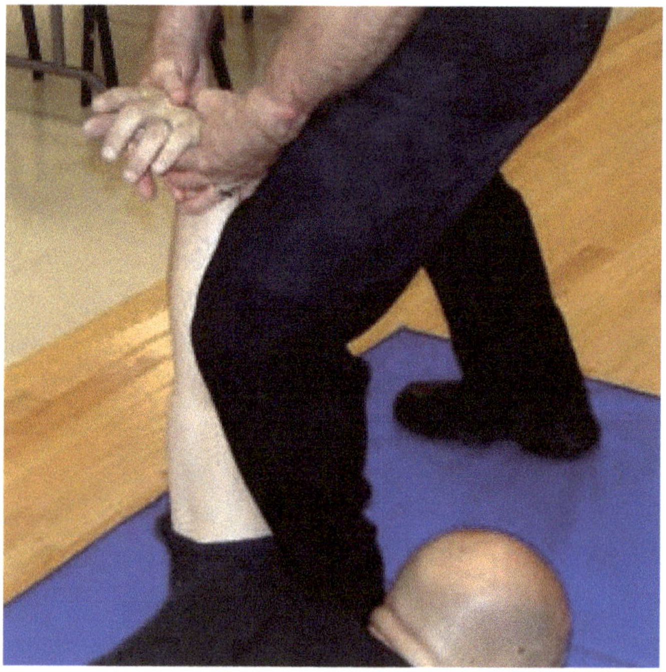

32N

Figure 32N. Notice where the knee is placed. It is not on the elbow itself but to the inside. The pressure on the arm is applied by pressing your knee forward on the inside of the elbow and pulling the actor's arm back to your center. The pressure is on the elbow and the shoulder of the attacker. ***CAUTION:*** **The pressure should be applied slowly. If applied fast, this will cause damage to his elbow**

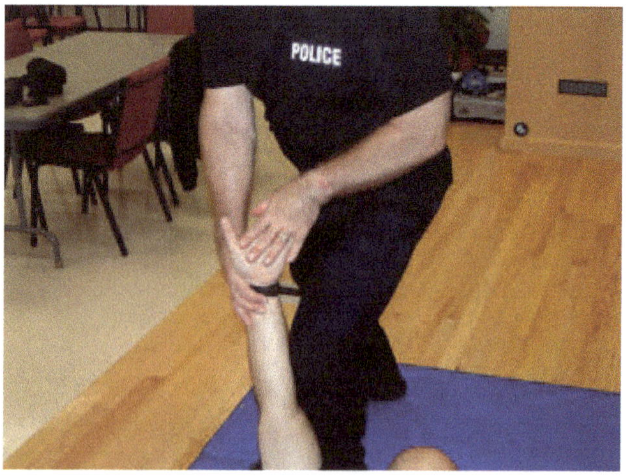

33N

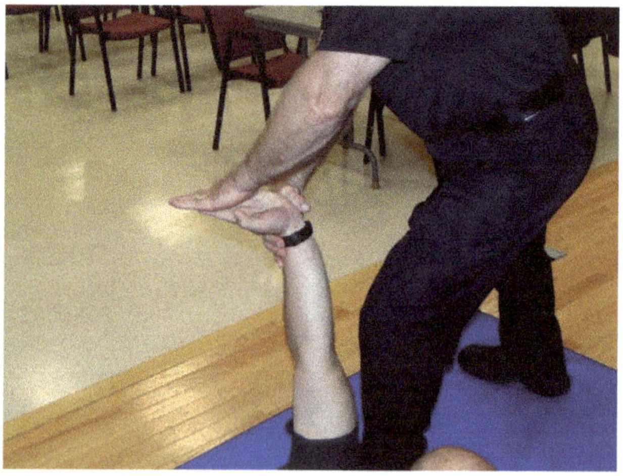

34N

Figure 33N. Change the grip of both hands. Your right hand is lowered to the attacker's wrist with the fingers forward, allowing his hand to be opened back by using the palm of your left hand. Stroke the palm of your left hand back across his palm opening, extending his fingers back.

Figure 34N. Rotate his flattened hand palm up around to the outside, keeping your palm down on his fingers.

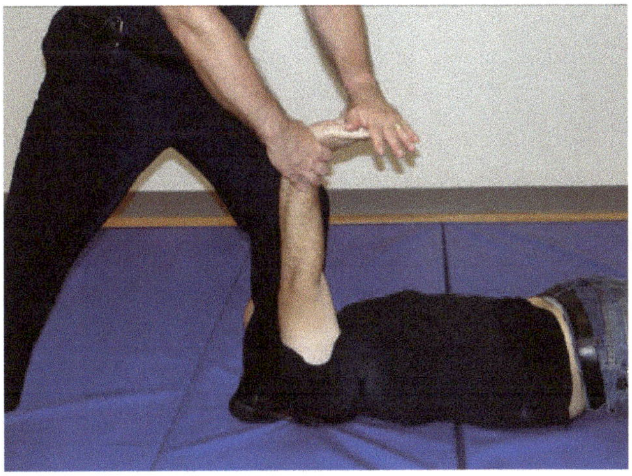
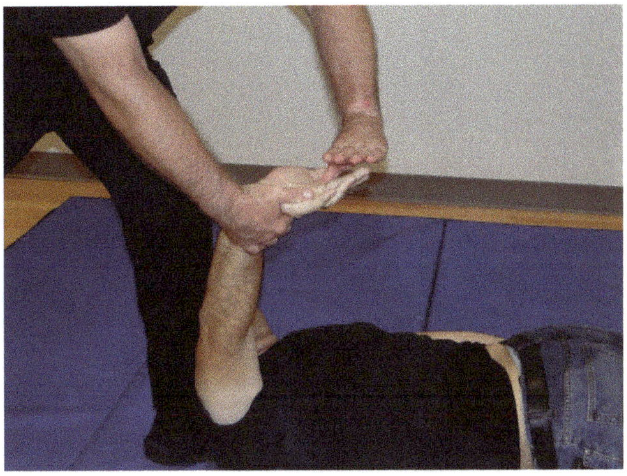

35N 36N

Figure 35N. Finish the rotation of the attacker's hand so that the fingers of the attacker are pointed back toward his feet. Your palm remains on top of his fingers keeping them extended.

Figure 36N. Slide the thumb of your right hand from his wrist up across the palm side and grip the heel of his hand. This will keep his hand open as you remove the left hand for just enough time to lower your thumb to reach across his hand to take a handshake type grip.

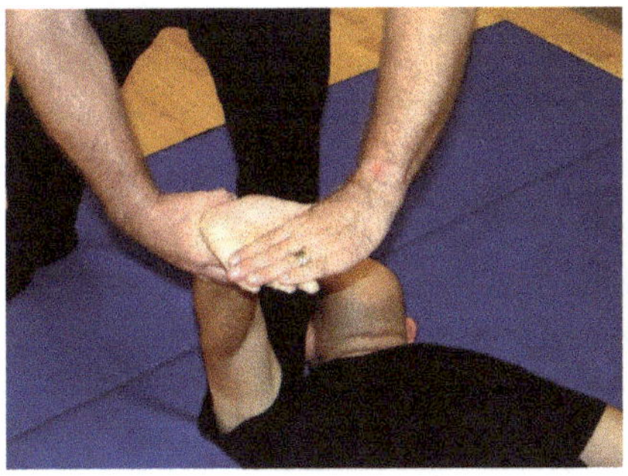
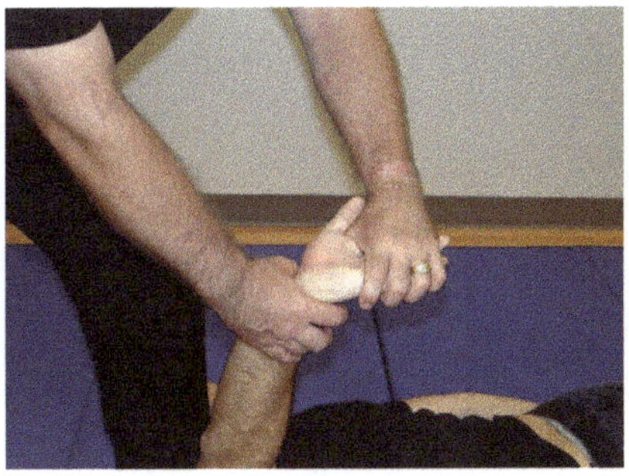
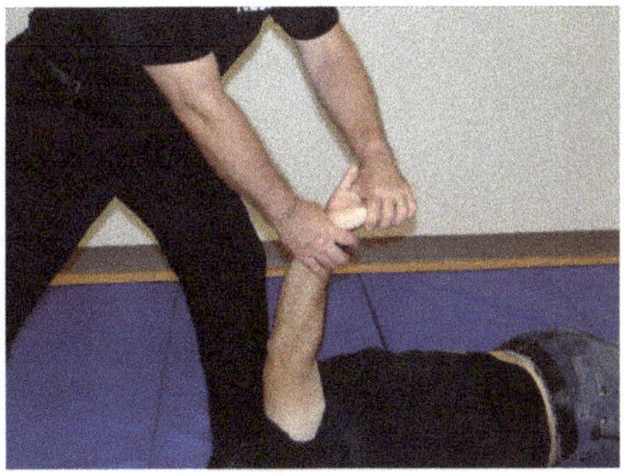

37N 38N 39N

Figure 37N. Reach across the palm of the attacker with your palm down. The thumb of your right hand is moved to the inside of his wrist, and the hand is kept pushed back over your index finger.

Figure 38N. The web portion between your thumb and index finger is pushed deep against the web portion of the attacker's hand as you grab the fingers. The attackers hand should remain pushed back and flat.

Figure 39N. Start turning your left hand back counterclockwise, keeping a tight grip on the attacker's hand. Keep the right hand on his wrist to support his wrist in the correct position. **NOTE: When practicing on a partner, be careful so you don't cause any injuries.**

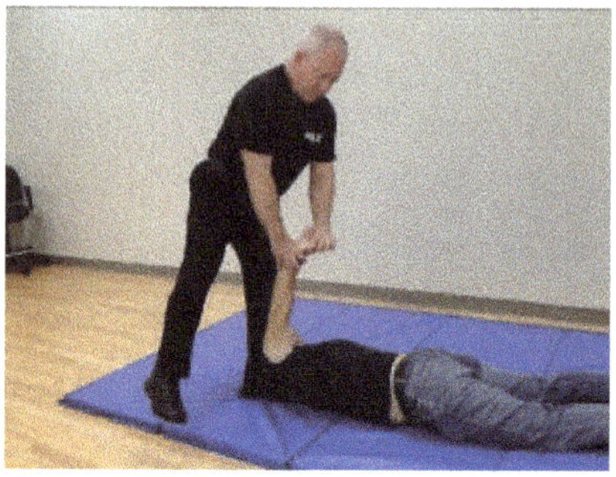

40N

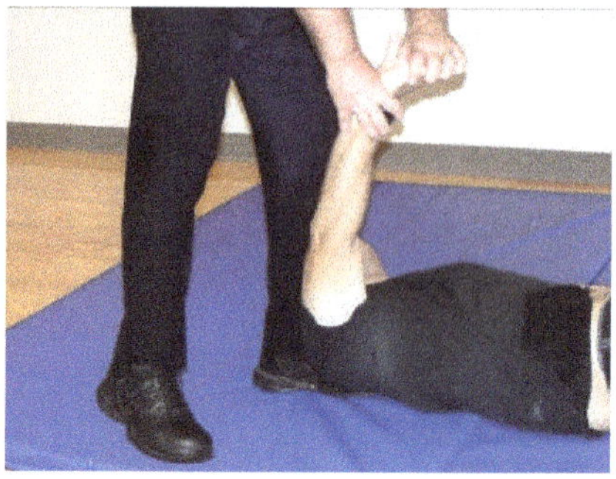

41N

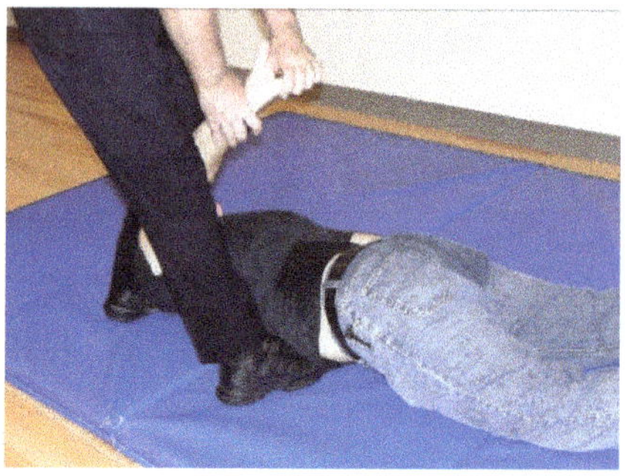

42N

Figures 40N, 41N, and 42N. When starting the counterclockwise turn with your left hand, your right foot takes **one** step from behind you around to your right. This step places the toes of your right foot under his waist. While the step is taking place, allow the attacker's elbow to bend by guiding it down as your body is twisting to your right side.

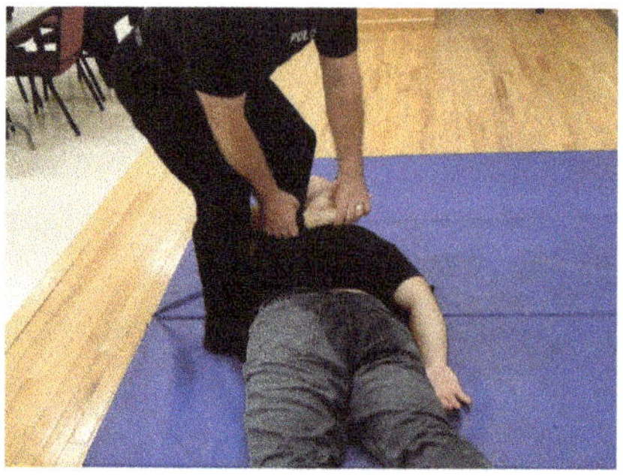

43N

44N

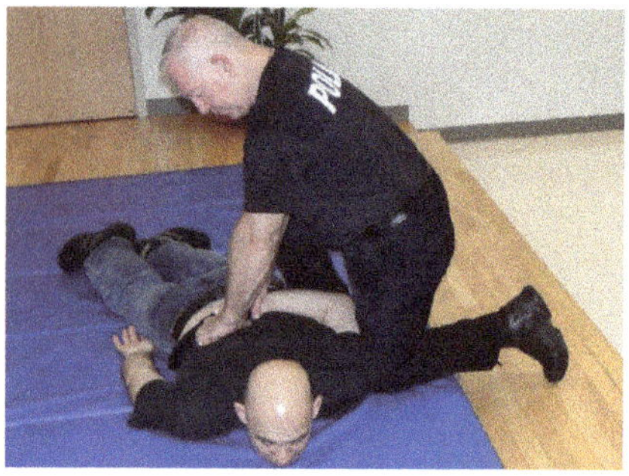

45N

Figure 43N. When your right foot is placed at the attacker's waist, you need to bend your knees to allow the his elbow to bend. **This is another point that needs some caution when practicing with a partner to prevent injury to his elbow.** The attacker's hand is placed as close as you can get it to the center of his back. Pressure is then placed down on his wrist and hand to secure it in place. The attacker's elbow will extend beyond his body a few inches, but your right ankle will be just below it to prevent the arm from pushing down.

Figure 44N. As you are applying pressure downward on his hand and wrist, your left leg is extended back behind you so you are repositioned directly beside him, and the pressure is balanced on his back.

Figure 45N. Pressure is lessened on the attacker's hands and wrist as your left knee is brought forward striking his elbow, which will push his arm further across his back. The arm is pushed across so that when it comes time to place him in handcuffs, his arm is over as far as possible to give you that extra room you may need when the right arm is brought up when you ask for it. If the actor's back is wide due to muscularity or obesity and the wrist is still not at mid back, it is usually a good indicator that two pairs of cuffs will be needed.

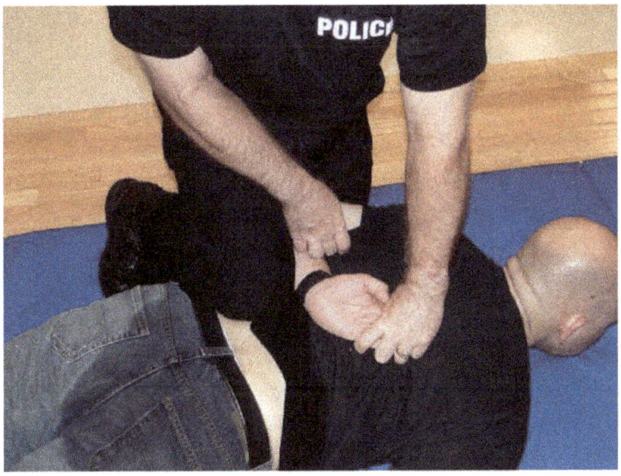

46N

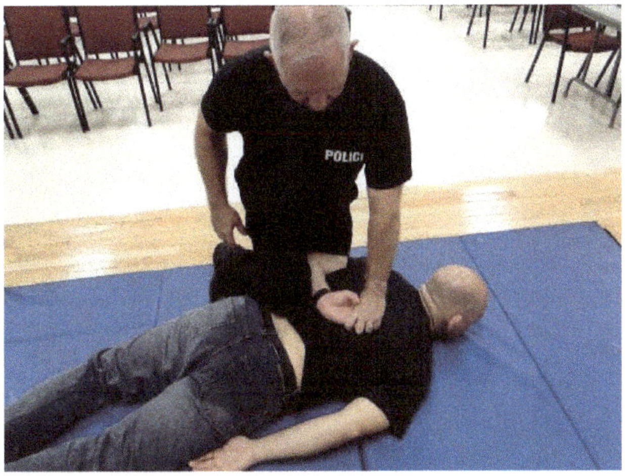

47N

Figures 46N and 47N. Lower the right knee onto the attacker's back, right behind his left forearm. This will lock it in position so his arm will not be able to be pulled out through the elbow area due to your left knee against his elbow, or down through the lower back area where you right knee is laying. This gives you plenty of opportunity to release your right hand and have complete control. Now you are ready to reach behind you for your handcuffs with your right hand.

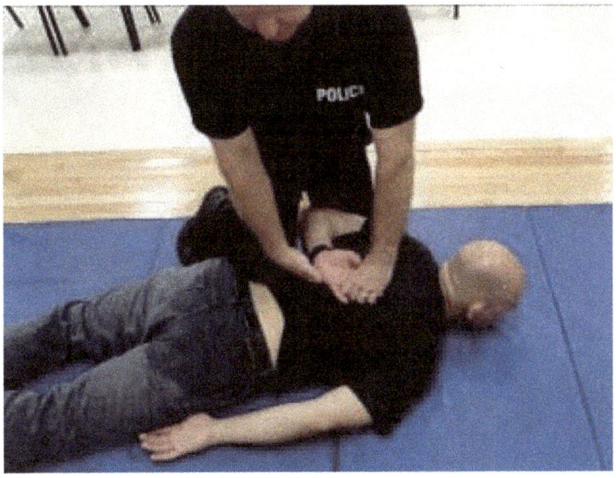

48N

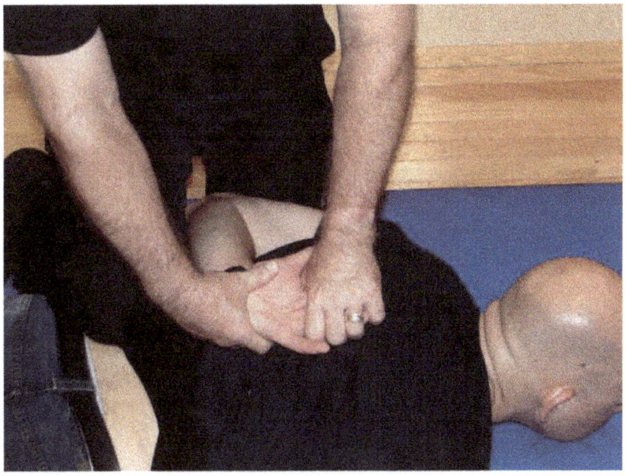

49N

Figures 48N and 49N. In preparation, inform the attacker that you want his other hand brought back to his back for handcuffing. Place your right hand under the attacker's wrist to lift up, keeping his wrist flat. With the left hand still gripping the fingers, torque should be applied sideways on the attacker's fingers with your left hand. This technique will get the attention and compliance of the attacker.

NOTE: *Finger flexibility varies from person to person when the fingers are pushed back.* ***BUT****, when the fingers have torque put on them sideways, it's a whole other story. There is very little flexibility if any when turned to the side and it is very painful. So Go Slow and Use Caution to Prevent Injury.*

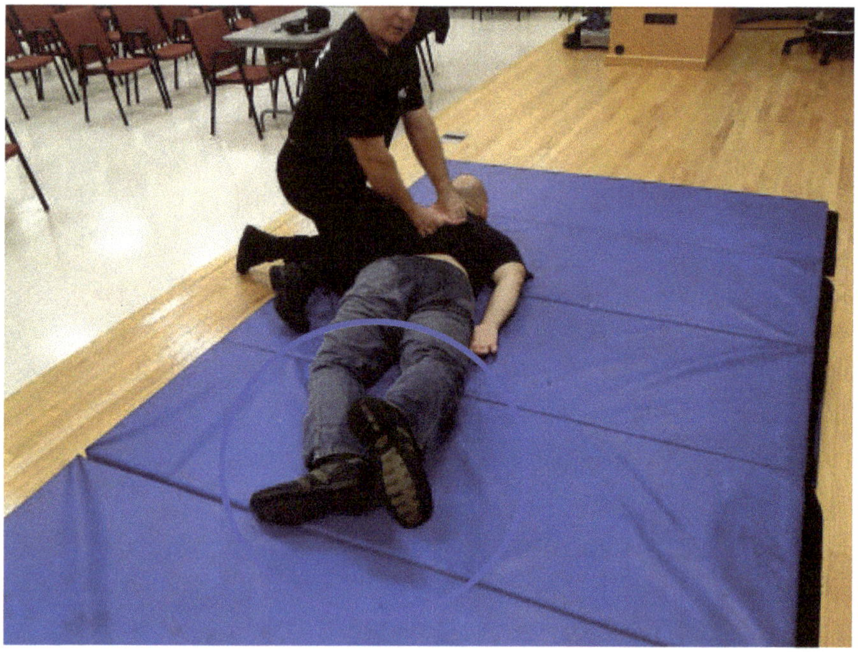

50N

Figure 50N. You will be able to tell if you have this technique correct by the "tell tale" sign that happens when applied. When the torque is put on his fingers sideways, his feet will lift or turn in as soon as the pain starts. Watch his feet to observe his response when you apply the side torque to his fingers. He will comply when you tell him you want his other hand, even if he is laying on it.

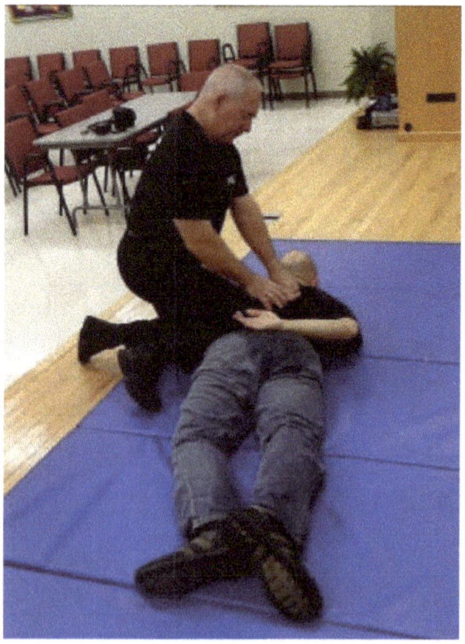

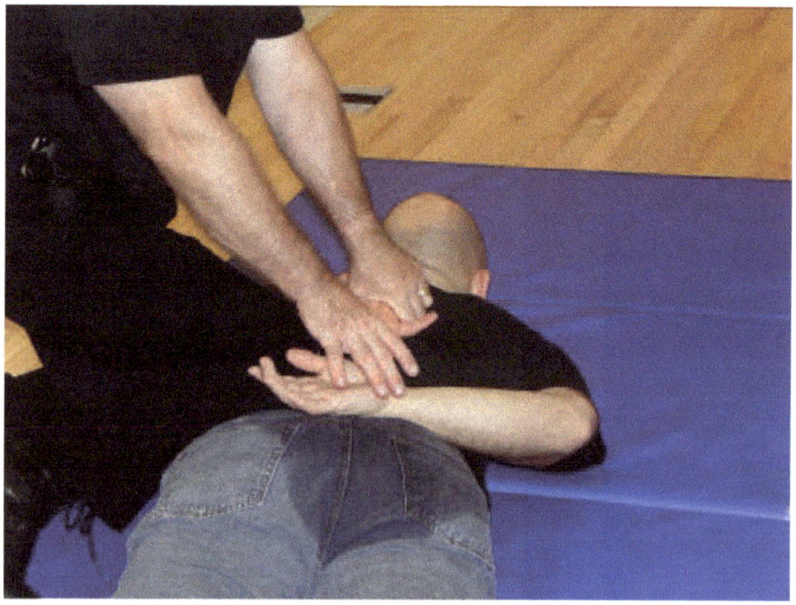

51N 52N

Figures 51N and 52N. After the attacker complies when you tell him you want his other hand to his back, keep control on his fingers and reach for his hand with your right hand to pull it close enough to be handcuffed.

CHAPTER 6

Moving Handcuffed Prisoner

STANDING A HANDCUFFED PRISONER

Multiple techniques have been used to move prisoners after being handcuffed. Some of which are a little unorthodox and may cause injury to the prisoner, as well as the officer. Keeping "your wits about you" and not losing your temper may be useful advice. But, we have been told this before. I know it happens that we get caught up in "the heat of the moment" and adrenaline is running through your body. But let's look at this sensibly and think of the damage this may do to you as an officer - injuries to various body parts, torn ligaments, muscles sprains - everything you could possibly imagine. Most of these problems are caused from officer's being in a hurry, or as I said before, getting caught up in "the heat of the moment".

Let's slow down for a minute and breath. Remember the "Ten Cycle Method of Breathing" from the front of this book and move your prisoner with control and intelligence. Now that your prisoner is handcuffed, in most cases, ***IT'S OVER.*** Let us say in a greater percentage of the time anyway. (Not that there aren't exceptions, because there are.) First, let's start by slowing ourselves down using the Ten Cycle Method, especially if you had to fight or chase a suspect. If the adrena-

STANDING A HANDCUFFED PRISONER TECHNIQUE 1

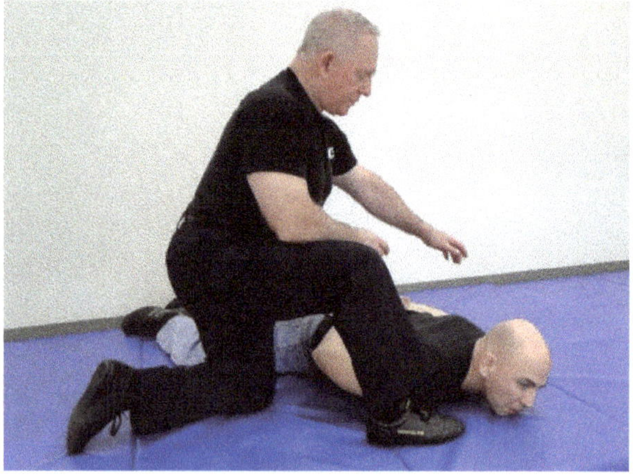

1L

Figure 1L. After your prisoner has been handcuffed, and you are ready to move him, there are two techniques that are very good to get him to his feet. This is technique 1. First, you need to be balanced and kneeling next to the prisoner. Then inform the prisoner what you are about to do. This will give him an idea of what is happening, and in most cases, the prisoner ends up assisting the movement which makes it much easier for you.

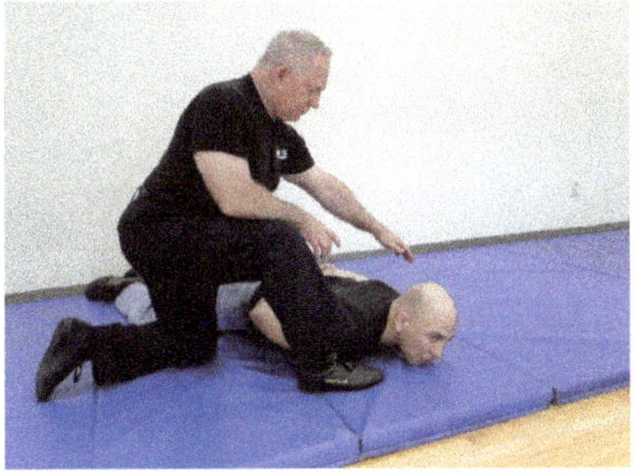

2L

3L

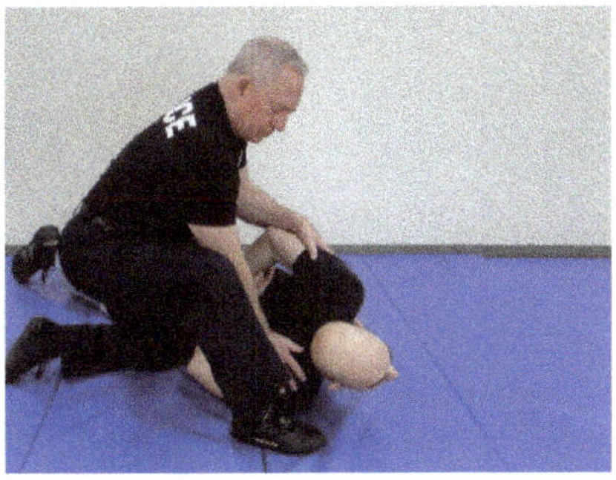

4L

Figure 2L. Spread your base out between your knee and your right foot, as you reach your prisoner's left shoulder.

Figure 3L. Grabbing his left shoulder with your left hand, and placing your right hand on the back of his right shoulder, **explain to him** that you are going to roll him back toward you as you sit him up.

Figure 4L. Pull back with your left hand, as you support your prisoner's right shoulder, so that it doesn't slide back with your right hand.

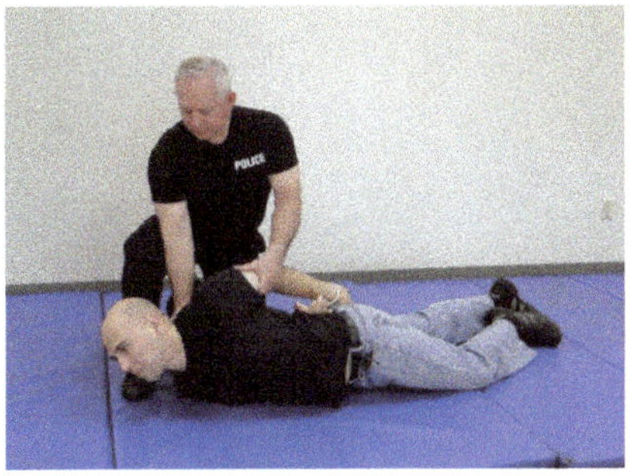

5L

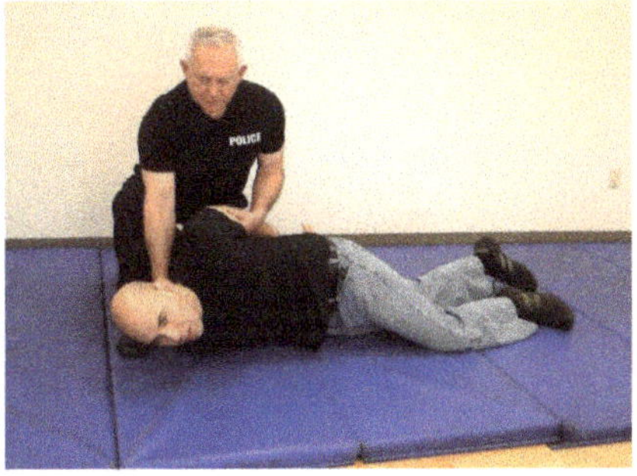

6L

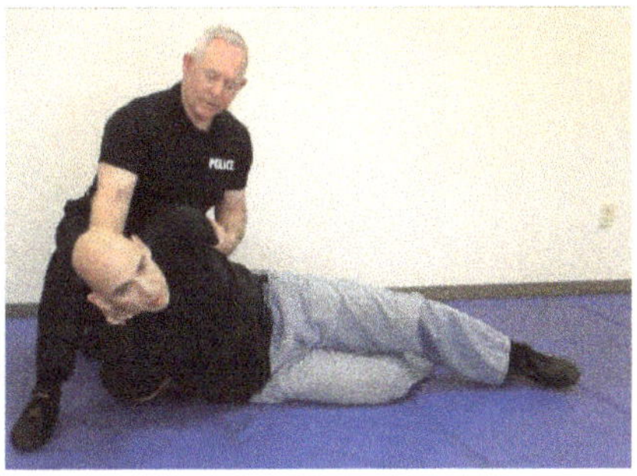

7L

Figure 5L. Pull back on the prisoner's left arm, assisting him in turning to his shoulder, and allowing his weight to roll back on his right hip.

Figure 6L. When the prisoner is on his right shoulder, move your right hand to the right side of his neck for support and control of his head. Your left hand is still on his left arm to prevent him from rolling forward onto his face.

Figure 7L. Lean back pushing with your right foot to prevent you from doing all the work with your arms and back. Pull the prisoner's left arm and support his neck. While you are pulling, **still explain what you are wanting your prisoner to do as you are doing it**. As you are pulling, he will be turning across the right hip, and his weight will be in his torso. Make sure that your base is wide, on your left knee, and the right foot is forward behind the head area. During the pull to get him up onto his right hip, most of the pull is done with your legs by shifting your weight back by pushing back with your right leg pulling his torso up off the ground with your arms.

8L

9L

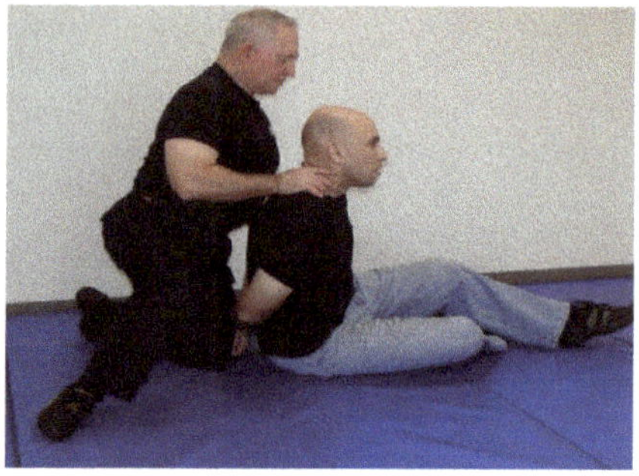

10L

Figures 8L and 9L. When the prisoner approaches the sitting position, continual support is given to his neck with your right hand until he is seated. You will be turning toward his back as he comes up.

Figure 10L. As your prisoner comes to rest on his behind, keep him leaning forward a little. Keep up over the top of him, keeping some weight on his back to allow your balance to have a forward posture. Your right leg will pivot and start to kneel on the ground.

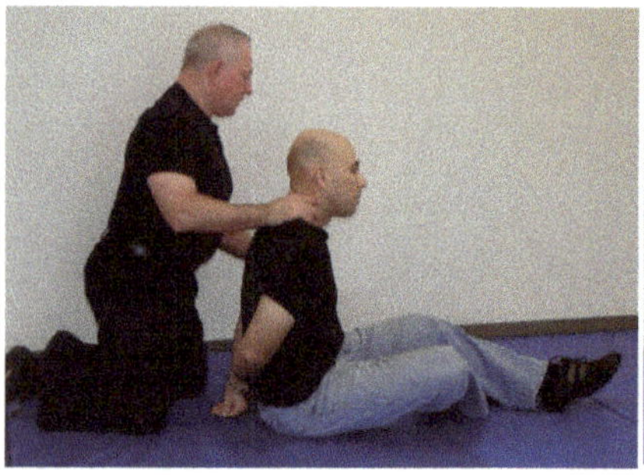

11L

12L

13L

Figures 11L and 12L. Once your prisoner is seated squarely on his behind, you should be in back of him, kneeling on both knees. Both your hands are still in place at his neck and arm to prevent him from pushing back at you.

Figure 13L. When you are ready, pick your prisoner up. You need to move your left leg forward, stepping alongside of his left hip with your foot. Your left hand now moves up to the shoulder area, and your right hand moves down toward his hands.

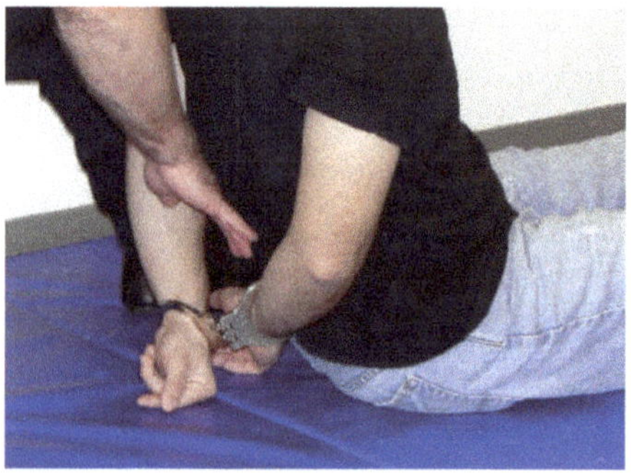

14L

Figure 14L. When reaching for the prisoner's handcuffed hands, open your right hand so the back of your hand will be against his back and your palm is facing you. Reach inside the cuffs, and the prisoner's hands so the back of the hand is actually touching the prisoner's lower back, and the inside of your hand will be able to grip his hand and ***NOT*** the center of the handcuffs.

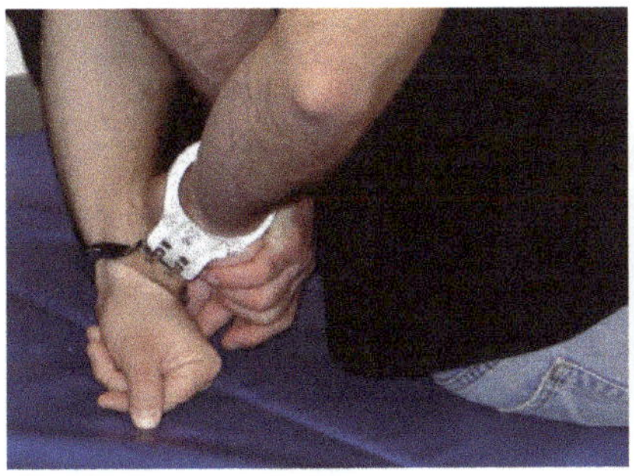

15L

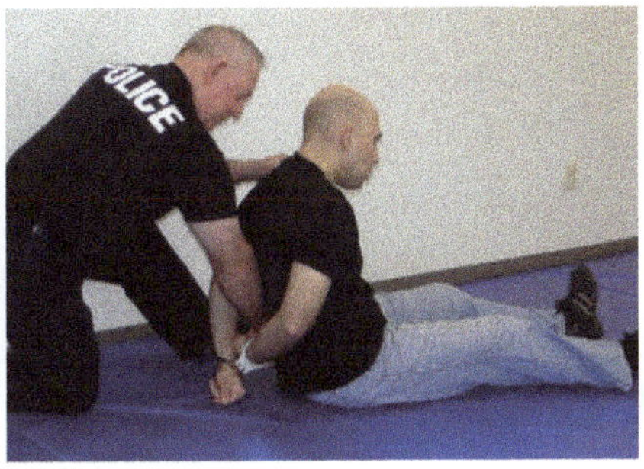

16L

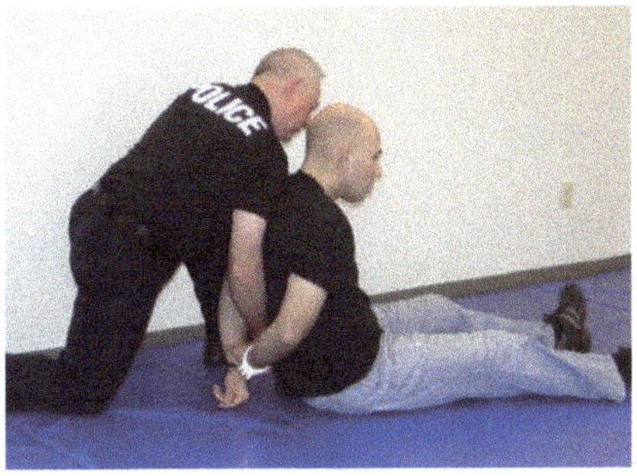

17L

Figure 15L. Look close at the grip as your hand reaches inside the cuffed hands. The grip is on the outside of the prisoner's hand, gripping the outer two or three fingers depending on the size of your hand. The thumb of your right hand will come between the fingers, making your grip tight around the fingers and not the hand.

Figure 16L. When your grip is tight, pull up enough to cause pressure on the wrist and fingers. This pressure is caused because when you start pulling up between the cuffs, his hand will turn back and lock his wrist against the cuff. If you should use hinge cuffs, you will find they lock out easier due to them not being able to swivel on the chain.

Figure 17L. Your grip is causing some discomfort to your prisoner, so don't pull too hard to avoid injury your prisoner. Lean forward, pushing you shoulder and arm against the prisoner's back and your head to the left side.

NOTE: DO NOT PLACE YOUR HEAD BEHIND YOUR PRISONERS HEAD IN CASE HE SHOULD THROW HIS HEAD BACK INTO YOUR FACE! THIS MAY CAUSE INJURY TO YOUR FACE.

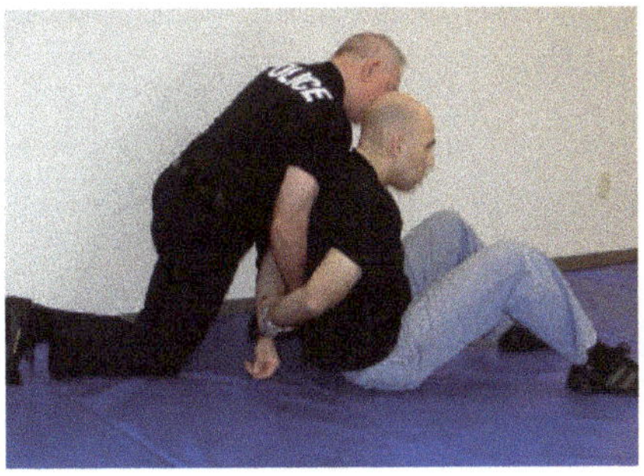

18L

19L

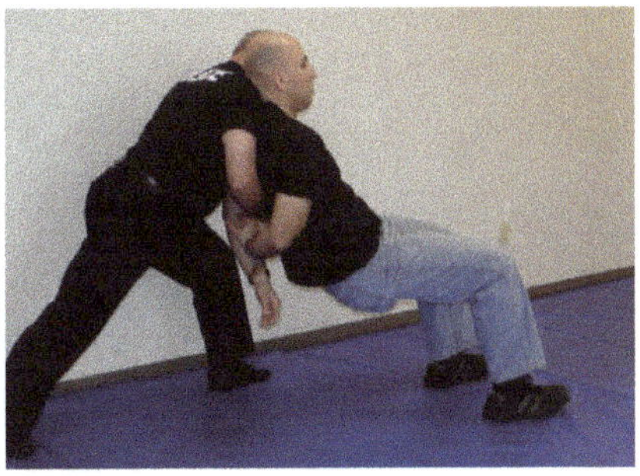

20L

Figure 18L. After leaning against your prisoner, advise him to bend his legs and to prepare to push back against you.

Figure 19L. Tell your prisoner to push back against you, as you push forward with your right shoulder against his back. If you push forward with the same amount of pressure as him, you will see that it will start lifting him up.

Figure 20L. Keeping an equal amount of pressure forward as he is pushing back, you can now just stand up as he helps raise himself.

21L

22L

Figure 21L and 22L. As your prisoner stands, less and less pressure is required to be applied. When he is standing, there is no pressure required. Using this lift is greatly beneficial to prevent officers from injuring their backs by lifting their prisoner by the arms.

STANDING A HANDCUFFED PRISONER TECHNIQUE 2

This technique is designed for prisoners that are very heavy, or overweight that do not have the flexibility of the average person. Standing your prisoner while handcuffed in Technique 1 required your prisoner to bend both legs and push back against you to stand. If you should come across a person that is very heavy, he may not be able to be in a sitting position and bend his legs at the same time. This would be a problem for you if you didn't have an alternate plan, well here it is, - ***Technique 2***.

The first part of this Technique 2 from moving the prisoner from the handcuffed position on their stomach to the seated position will be the same. The pictures will start in this section from the seated position of your prisoner, and the officer again leaning against the back of the prisoner. To refresh your memory on how to turn your prisoner over from the stomach position, look back a couple of pages to figures 1L through 13L. This will cover the turning of your prisoner. This technique works well for anyone that you may be trying to stand, not just overweight people.

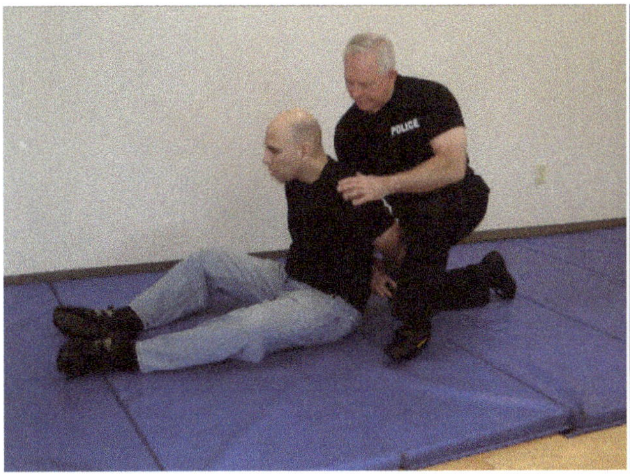

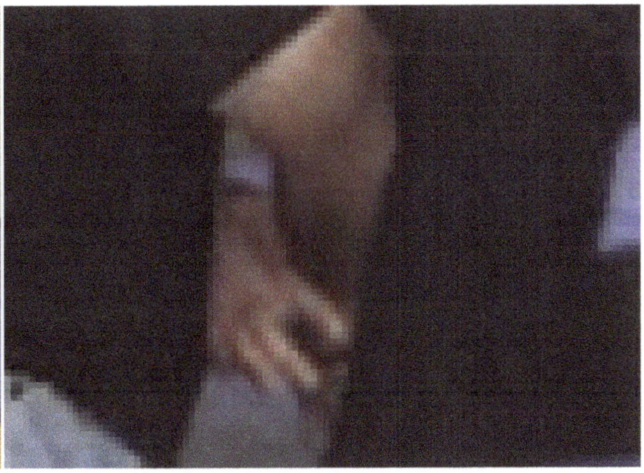

23L 24L

Figure 23L. This figure starts ***Technique 2,*** by reaching through the inside of the handcuffed hands, with the back of your hand against the prisoner's back. Grip the little finger side of the right hand with a deep tight grip.

Figure 24L. This is a close up of the grip, showing that your thumb separates his fingers as it pulls the hand of the prisoner up.

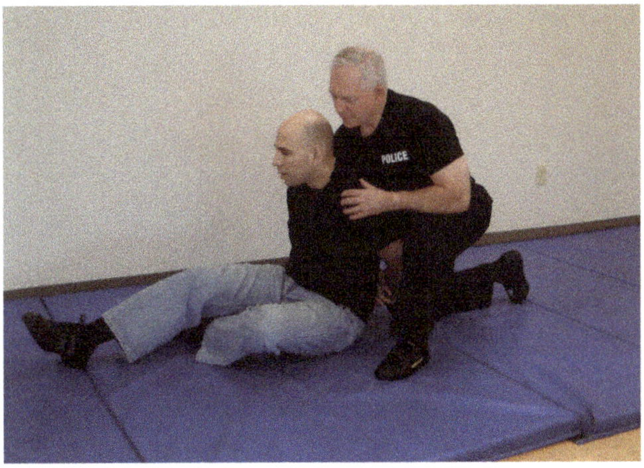

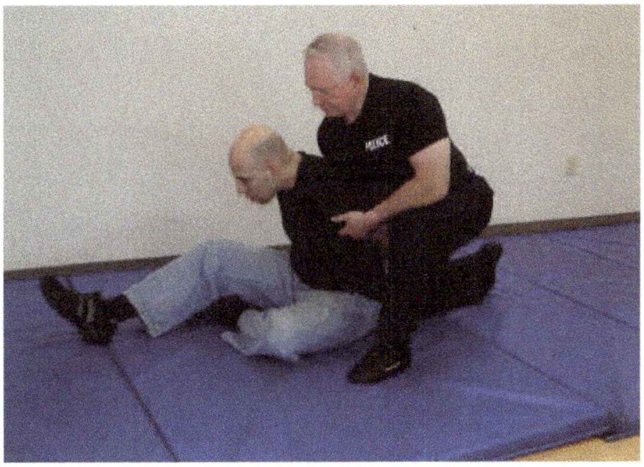

25L 26L

Figure 25L. Give the command for your prisoner to bend his left knee sideways; bending the leg under his right leg. When he is finished, explain that you are going to push him forward onto the bent knee, then ask him if he understands, so that he is not confused.

Figure 26L. Stay tight against the prisoner's back, keeping a wide base in your kneeling stance. Keep your head away from the back of the prisoner's head so you don't get hit in the face, if he should throw his head back. With a steady, firm push start him moving forward. He will be moving at an angle to his left side in order for him to kneel on the knee. Depending on his weight, he may only be able to lean; it is up to you to make sure that he gets onto the knee.

27L

28L

29L

Figure 27L. Place your shoulder against your prisoner's back, pushing forward to get him on his left knee.

Figure 28L. Prepare to push forward by coming off your knee to give you the best balance, and maximize you pushing power.

Figure 29L. Explain to your prisoner what you are doing, and what you need from him in order to be done. Tell him that when you push him up to his knee, that he should bring the other knee down so he is on both knees. This will alleviate any further pressure on you, and allow you to get onto your feet.

NOTE: Observe the grip of the left hand on the shoulder of the prisoner. You see that the hand is in front of the shoulder. This is a safety measure for your prisoner to prevent him from losing his balance and falling forward onto his

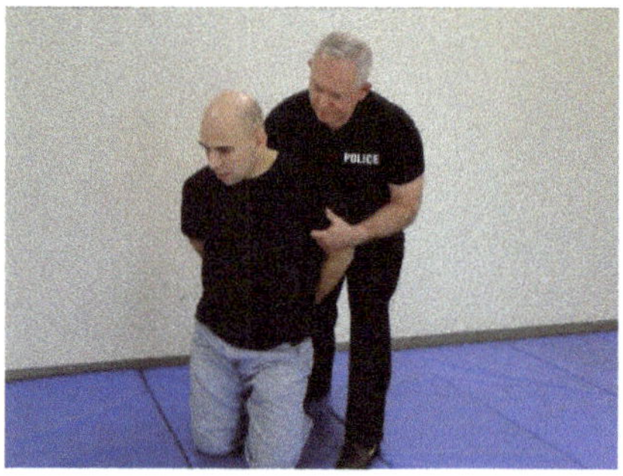

30L

31L

32L

Figure 30L. Prepare to give assistance in the standing of your prisoner and command him to stand up.

Figure 31L. Have him place one foot forward, as you assist in keeping his balance, **still being conscious that your head is not behind his**.

Figure 32L. Once he is steady with the one foot forward, tell him to stand up. This is where there may be a little bit of assistance to push him forward. Be prepared to move with him as he stands; keeping control of him with your left hand in front of his arm. Your hand will prevent him from losing his balance forward and falling, and once he is up to his feet, he may try to bolt forward trying to get away. As he stands up, you should move to his left side for better visibility forward and better control.

33L

34L

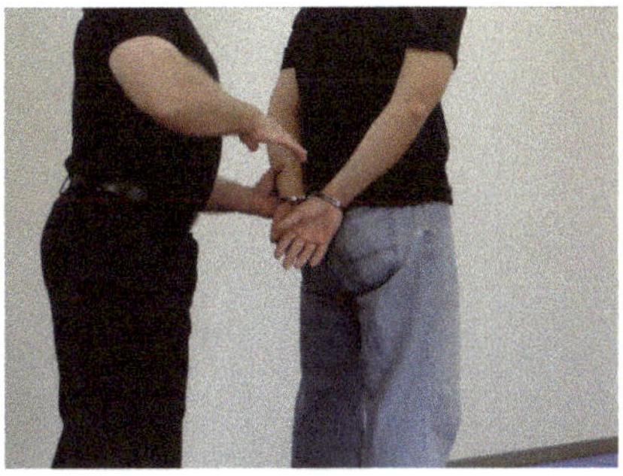
35L

Figure 33L. In the assistance of standing your prisoner, pull back with your left hand after he gets stood up, to bring his torso erect for balance and to prevent forward movement.

Figures 34L and 35L. Once he is stood up, you are ready to move him. There may be some time between standing your prisoner and walking him whereever you need him to go. Move your left hand to the outside of his left wrist, and prepare to grip his fingers.

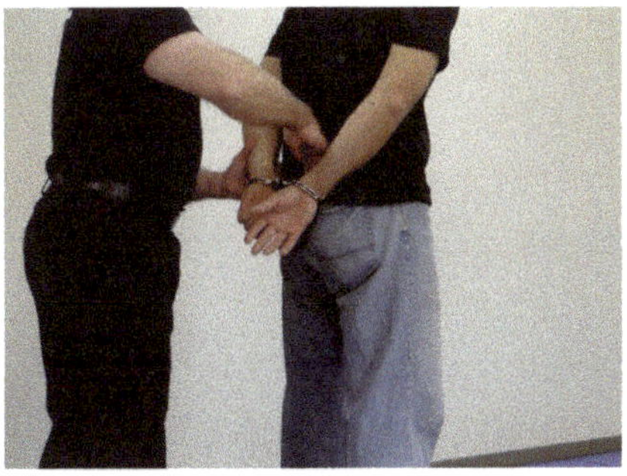
36L

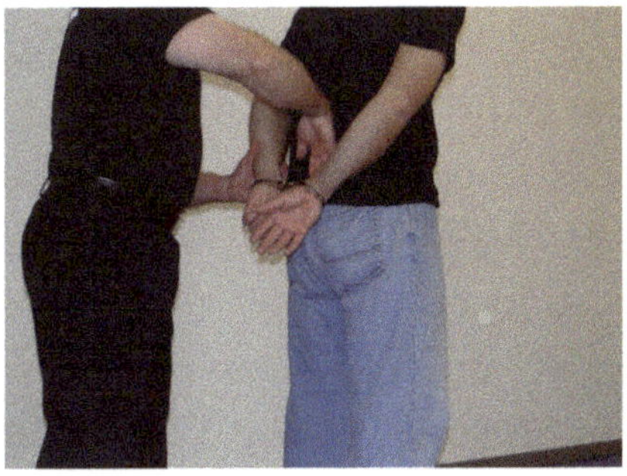
37L

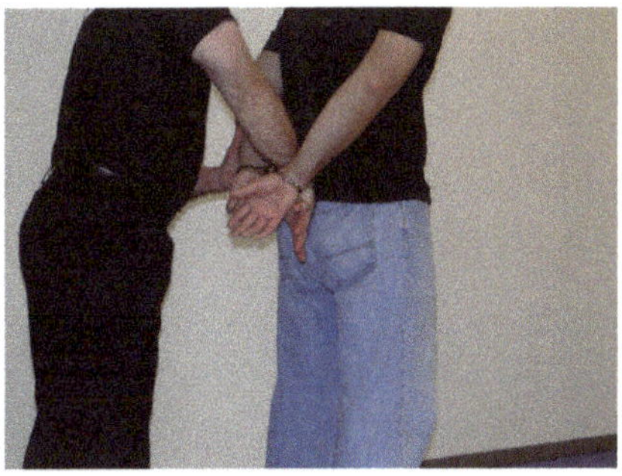
38L

Figures 36L, 37L, and 38L. When reaching inside the handcuffs to grip his fingers, use your left hand to pull his wrist back to allow you enough room to slide your right hand between the cuffs and his back. The back of your hand will be against your prisoner's back as you reach through.

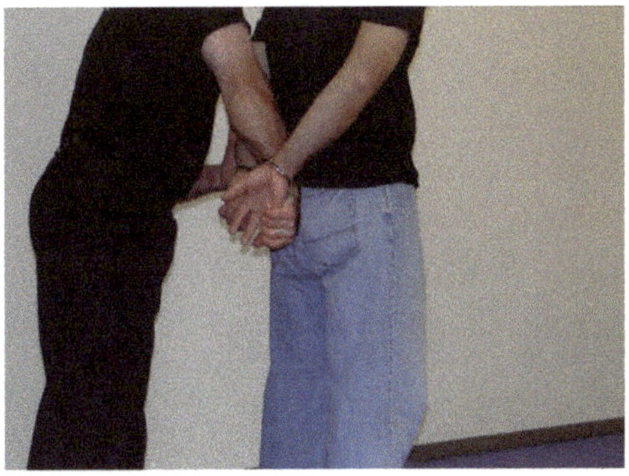
39L

Figures 39L and 40L. Your grip will be on the little finger and the ring finger. The action to get your grip should be smooth and quick, to prevent him from closing his fist.

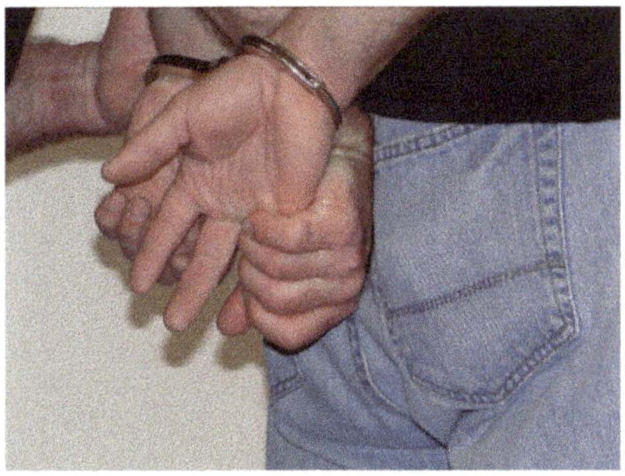
40L

41L

42L

Figure 41L. Once your grip is secure on your prisoner's fingers, pressure is applied to the prisoner's hand by pulling his hand back up through the handcuffs.

NOTE: Your grip on the prisoner's hand should be close to his hand not just on the ends of the fingers.

Figure 42L. When applying the pressure to his hand, move your left hand back to his shoulder. When the pressure is applied and he starts to experience pain, he will want to lean forward to relieve the pressure. Keep him erect for compliance while moving him. Remember to keep your left hand on the front of his left

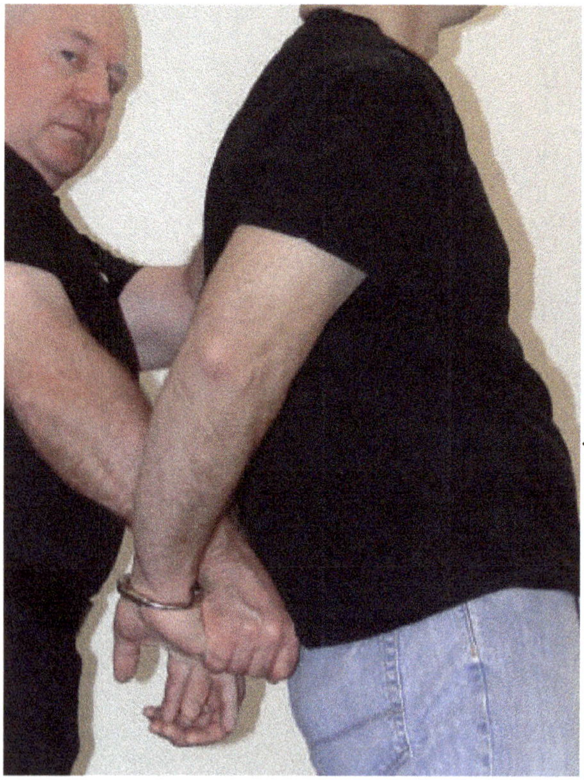

43L

Figure 43L. Look close at the angle of which the prisoner's fingers and hand is being pulled. The prisoner's wrist is also being pulled up against the cuffs. Remember the handcuffs used here are hinge cuffs, so they do not twist like chain cuffs. But the technique still will work. You will find that he will be compliant in moving him. You will know how much pressure to apply judging on his reactions.

NOTE: Caution should always be used to prevent injury to your prisoners. BUT,

PAIN
DOES BREED
CONTROL !!!

CHAPTER 7

Hug Traps and Yoke Traps

HUG TRAP

TO HITCHHIKER I CONTROL
RIGHT HANDED OVERHEAD BLOW

1M

2M

Figure 1M. Standing in a neutral position, an attacker swings from an overhead blow.

Figure 2M. Your first reaction is to step inside the line of danger. This was explained in the first chapter of the book. Step toward the attacker with your left foot just about 6 to 8 inches to the outside of his right foot. The left foot is used because this is the side the attack is coming from, and the inches outside the attacker's foot is to take you off the line of attack. At the same time, you are stepping forward, your left arm is being brought up as a guide to redirect the blow.

3M

Figure 3M. Watching the attacker's arm as it is coming down, your left arm is coming up to meet the attacker's arm on the outside. Your foot will step forward just to the outside of the attacker's right foot. The step you make should remain the same, even if his right foot is forward while he is attempting to strike you. Guide the strike always to the outside of the striking side, since this is the side that you have to control.

4M

5M

Figure 4M. When your left arm make contact with the attacking arm your weight is shifted forward on to the left foot. Your body will start to turn back to your right side, as you guide the attacker's right arm to his left. This will take you even more off line from his attack.

Figure 5M. As your left arm guides his arm down and past your face, there is no need to pull your head back. If you should pull your head back your balance would be off. Your right arm comes up from the bottom to catch his arm.

6M

7M

Figure 6M. Your left arm should be matching the speed of the attacker's arm coming down, but redirecting it past your face and body. Your right arm comes with palm up to catch his arm at your forearm.

Figure 7M. When the attackers arm makes contact with your right arm it is trapped by bending your right arm tightly back to you. The left arm continues to guide the attackers arm into the trapping motion of your right arm. Your left arm comes down over the top of his arm, and in front of your right arm as it is being trapped.

8M 9M

Figure 8M. When the attacker's arm meets your bent right arm, it is trapped back tightly. Your left arm comes over the top tightly as you now grip the inside of the forearm.

Figure 9M When both of your arms are tight, you should start turning your right shoulder back. This will keep his body in motion.

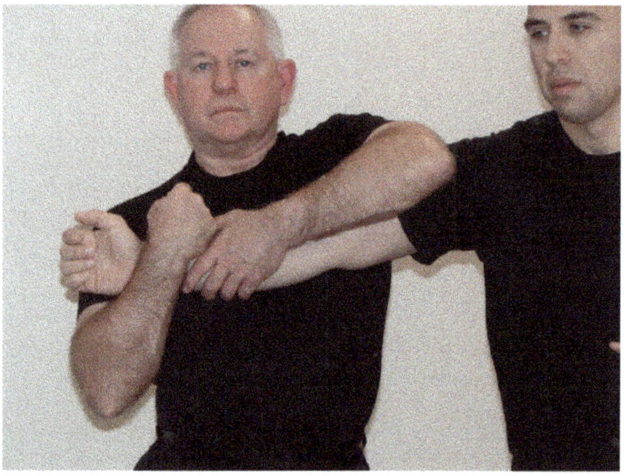

10M 11M

Figure 10M. When the attacker's arm is trapped, it is important that you keep his forearm forward away from your body but tight. By doing this, it will keep his arm from bending.

Figure 11M. This is the point that your grip will change. Slide your left hand down to the attacker's wrist closest to his hand. Adjust your right hand to move down to the bottom of his wrist behind your left hand. When your hands have moved, push the attacker's arm to your right across your body so that his elbow is against your chest. By pushing his arm forward, this prevents you from being struck with his left hand and will give you great leverage on his arm by hyperextension.

12M

13M

Figure 12M. After you have extended the attacker's arm across your chest in front of you, a change again in your hands happens. Slide your right hand back to the inside of his elbow keeping his forearm forward, hugging the arm tight against you. Planting the left foot on the floor with your back straight, start pulling back to your right.

Figure 13M. Step back to the right with your right foot and keep his arm tight to your chest. This movement will put pressure on his elbow, and he will be directed by the hyperextension of his elbow to follow you as you turn.

14M

15M

Figures 14M and 15M. As you take your first step back, you will feel the tension on the attacker's arm. A strong smooth gradual movement is the best control to get him moving around you. If you are dealing with a suspect that may be taller than you, like my attacker in the picture, you will find that they have to bend forward as you turn. If your attacker is shorter, you will find that he will stick his chest forward and arch his back to keep up with you. ***CAUTION: DO NOT*** MAKE YOUR FIRST STEP LARGE BY TAKING A 180 DEGREE STEP AND TURNING FAST BACK TO YOUR RIGHT! THIS WILL BREAK HIS ELBO.

16m

17m

Figures 16M and 17M. Now take the second step back with your right foot, pivoting on your left foot. This will start him in a faster motion to keep up with you. The object in this turning, like most things we do, has more that one purpose. The turning will keep him off balance giving you all the control over him. This also will allow you all the time you need to place your hands in the correct position, ready for the hitchhiker technique to be performed.

18M

19M

20M

Figure 18M, 19M and 20M. Take another step back with your right leg, keeping the tension on the attacker's arm, and his arm always tight to your chest. Keep the attacker in motion. ***DON'T GIVE HIM A CHANCE TO STOP UNTIL YOU ARE READY.*** Observe that my back is straight throughout the turn and that the left foot moves very little only to be a pivot point as you step back with your right foot. Each step back is about a 90 degree step. Remember that this process of turning the suspect around in circles is to allow you the time you need to adjust your hands and prepare you. There is nothing wrong with turning him as many times as you need to get prepared for the technique you are about to do. Also, there is no specific spot that you have to start your technique. Turning at a fast pace may be too fast for the suspect to keep up. Remember you are at the center of the circle, and he is about three feet away from you trying to keep up. **Turning at a fast speed will make him fly**! **Keep him on his feet**, that's where you want him.

21M

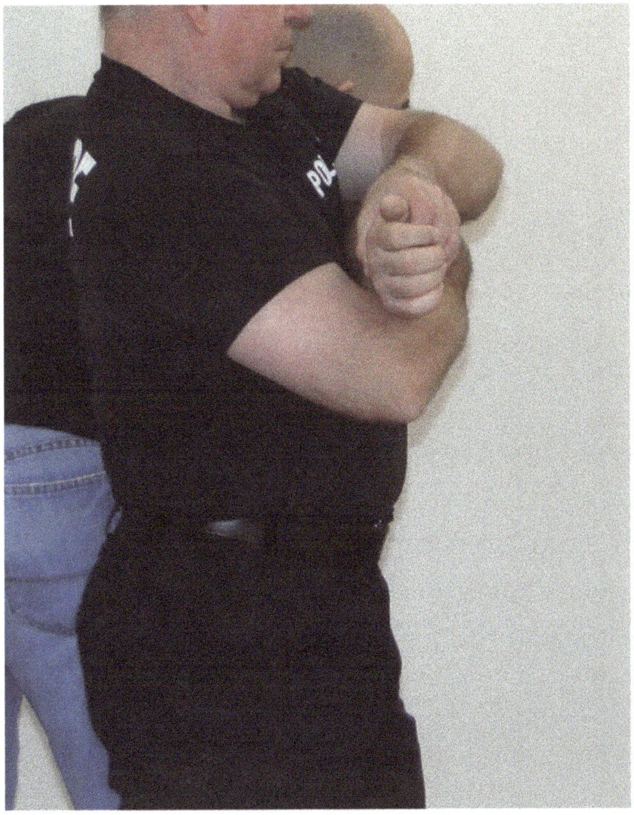

22M

Figures 21M and 22M. Taking another step back with your right foot, keeping him in motion, start the left hand to move to the attacker's right hand. His arm still needs to be forward making his palm also forward and his thumb is up.

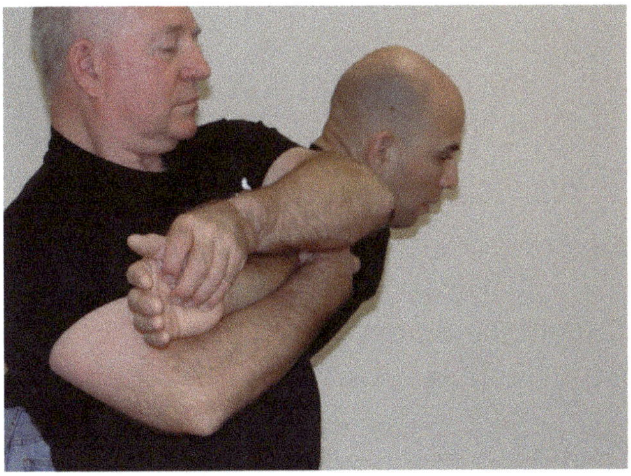

23M

24M

Figures 23M and 24M. As your hand has worked it's way to the hand positioning of the hitchhiker, everything else remains the same. It's is not the time to let up yet. Keep his arm tight, your back straight, and keep him moving in your circle not allowing him to catch up.

25M

26M

Figures 25M and 26M. When your left hand has his hand secure in the hitchhiker position, you are ready to execute the hitchhiker. Now take your last step back to the right, and pull his arm at the wrist area tight back to your right shoulder.

27M

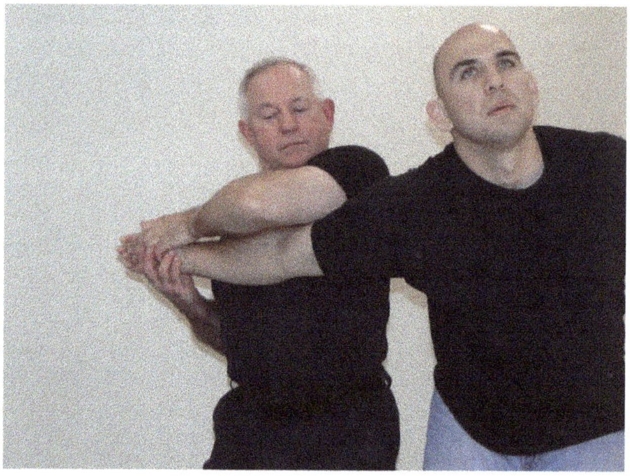
28M

Figures 27M and 28M. When the attacker's wrist is tight to your shoulder, your left elbow pushes forward faster and your armpit swings him a little faster to continue his momentum around you. Your left hand then moves from his forearm to the heel of his hand, preparing to reinforce the hitchhiker hand position as he goes by.

The push forward with your armpit area is the last motion that you do in this direction. Here's where the last step back with the right foot should be a little wider than the other steps in your circle to create a wider base for balance. The harder you are able to push him forward will increase his speed, so the left hand has to move faster to support the other hand. This increase in speed also determines how high his feet will go in the air once you reverse directions.

29M

30M

Figures 29m and 30M. Once the attacker's body goes past you, step back with the left foot now. This is in the reverse direction of which the attacker is moving. His arm will come away from your chest as he goes by. You now start your turn back with your body in the left direction.

31M

32M

Figure 31M. When turning back to your left side, make sure that your grip is as tight and secure as possible. When the attacker reaches a point that his body can not go any further, there is going to be a hard pull on your hands.

Figure 32M. When the attacker has reached the point that his body stops moving forward, and his arm is extended back, there will be almost a 180 degrees pull back. Notice that my arms appear to be extended in the picture. What is happening is that my arms are moving in a circular motion back, starting with the heel of his right hand to start the hitchhiker in a throwing position. With his body moving forward and you pulling back at this great of an angle, this will cause his feet to come off the ground. It appears that this is a great jolt on the attacker, but in reality it is more of a sweeping motion than it is a jerking motion.

33M 34M

Figures 33M and 34M. When your hands start the hitchhiker movement, first locking his wrist forward then back, his body will break down fast due to his momentum forward. Right away his elbow will turn in, and the shoulder will drop locking his right hip, because his balance point has been broken.

35M 36M

Figures 35M and 36M. When his balance has been broken, his momentum is still moving away from you. The reverse in the direction will pull his feet out from under him.

Understand in order to get good clear pictures of this portion of the throw, and to take it easy on my uki, this was done at a slow speed. In real life, this throw will cause your opponent to have his feet swept shoulder high or higher.

NOTE: A reminder of safety when working with your partner again.
This is the most critical part of this move and the most dangerous. You need to take it slow and be easy on your Uke. When practicing in a dojo, with experienced players who know how to fall without getting hurt, you will be able to do this technique at full speed but for beginners or inexperienced Uke's, be careful!

37M

38M

Figure 37M. After you pull back on the hand of the attacker in the hitchhiker position, he will fall back to his right hip before his feet hit the ground.

Figure 38M. After his landing, you need to pull up on his arm right away. When someone lands from a fall, they always try to put their arms down. You need to prevent this, so by pulling up on his arm, you will be able to keep it straight and maintain control.

39M

40M

Figures 39m and 40M. When straightening the attacker's arm step close to his body, and spread your feet wider then shoulder width. Pull up to keep his arm straight, and to pull him onto his back.

This should be a familiar position for you by now. Now do your fallow foot around him, placing him onto his stomach, step under his right shoulder with your left foot back, and evaluate and calm down and observe. Now take him to the hand cuffing position remembering to lock your knee behind the elbow and in front of it. Place him in cuffs.

YOKE TRAP
TO **HITCHHIKER I CONTROL**
OVERHEAD BLOW

The Yoke Trap to the Hitchhiker is similar to the Hug Trap. The differences are that it is a faster movement, and when catching the attackers arm, it is done with your hands. This will give you a greater margin for error; meaning that this takes a little more practice to perfect.

1N

2N

Figure 1N. When standing and the attacker attacks you with a right handed overhead blow, your response is to step inside the line of danger, which in this right handed attack would be stepping forward with your left foot to the outside of his right foot. Both right and left hands move up toward the striking arm at the same time as you are stepping inside the line of danger. Your hands will be positioned so your palms of each hand are facing the attacker's arm. Your hands are open so you will be able to grip the attacker's arm.

Figure 2N. After you have stepped inside the line of danger, your body will be bladed to the left side. This will allow your left hand to reach the attacking arm first. The object of grabbing the back of the attacker's wrist first is first to blend in with the speed of the attacker's arm from behind, not to block the arm and stop the movement. **Keep the energy of the swing in motion**. The second reason is to be able to guide the strike past you enough so you don't get struck, and also into the right hand. As soon as the right hand makes contact, it starts the redirection of his arm. I mentioned blending your speed with his; this is trying to match your hand speed with his to keep his energy in motion.

3N

4N

Figures 3N and 4N. Once you have made contact with both hands, your grip is tightened around his wrist, at the same time, as you guide the attacker's arm to the front of you.

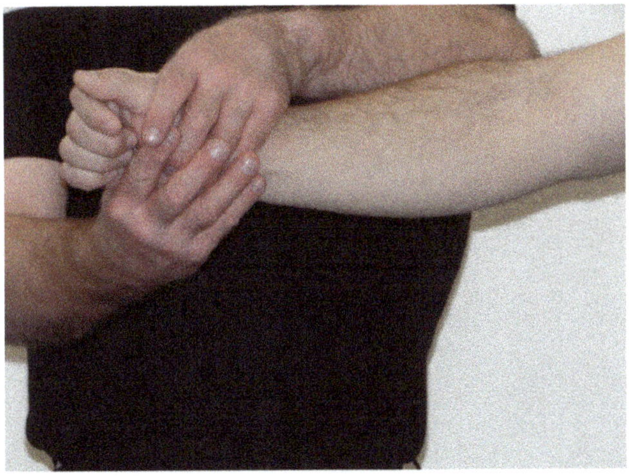
5N

6N

Figure 5N. Your hands slide down the attacker's wrist as you guide his arm in front of you. As his arm comes in front of you, the speed of your hands have caught up with the speed of his arm. When your hands gets to his wrist, you need to place his hand in the hitchhiker position. With the right hand overhead strike, you will be grabbing the thumb side of his hand with your left hand. Your fingers of that hand will grip around the meaty portion of his thumb. The right hand, positioned under the attacker's hand, assists by gripping the heel of his right hand.

Figure 6N. The attacker's arm is guided in front of you, and your hand placement is being put in the hitchhiker position. Here is where a small tug on the attacker's hand is done to cause a jerk to his arm, helping keep him off balance and keeping his momentum moving. The jerking of his hand past you will stop the down motion and cause the redirection of his balance to move forward.

7N

8N

9N

Figure 7N. Once the arm passes in front of you, and you have given the pull on his arm, you will see his balance come forward.

Figure 8N. The attacker's hand is placed in the hitchhiker position, turning it back toward him, as it is brought back in front of you and across your chest. Lock his hand back as it is coming across the chest.

Figure 9N. The wrist is locked back and forward, as you bring it back to your left side. When it is brought across, about the time his hand reaches your left shoulder, your torso will assist by turning toward the left side.

10N

11N

Figure 10N. When the hand and wrist are locked out as far as it can go, his elbow will turn in, and his shoulder will drop causing his balance to shift to his right foot, locking out his right hip.

Figure 11N. The attacker's hand will continue to be pushed toward your left side, as your torso turns and your right arm extends forward. The attacker's hand is taken down and to his right, away from his body. At this point, he will lose his balance. Your grip on the attacker's hand should be tight as he starts to fall. When bringing his hand back to his right side, try to keep from pushing his hand up against his shoulder. By keeping his hand away from the shoulder, you will be able to control his fall easier. If his hand is brought back to his shoulder, his elbow will come to his side, and his bicep and shoulder will be able to pull back against you.

12N

13N

Figures 12N and 13N. Once he is past the balance point, your grip needs to be tight as he goes down to the ground. You extend your arms as he goes to the ground, but still keeping tension on his wrist. Notice that the attacker is falling onto his hip first. In this first control, I allow his shoulder to touch the floor by stepping forward toward him. If the Hitchhiker Spin would have been used, you would have pulled back toward his feet as soon as his hip touched the ground.

14N

Figure 14N. After the attacker's shoulder has hit the ground, you pull up to your center, straightening his arm, and keeping his wrist bent forward and bent; both your hands still gripping tightly on his hand. You are now in first control. This is right before you Follow Foot around his head and turn him over doing Hitchhiker I.

HUG TRAP

OVERHEAD BLOW WITH WEAPON
RIGHT HAND TO HITCHHIKER I
TO FIRST CONTROL

1O

2O

Figure 1O. When a swing from overhead comes from the right side, first thing is step inside the line of danger with your left foot. Your foot will step to the outside of his right foot. Your left arm is brought up at the same time that your are making your step forward, to the outside of the attacker's arm.

Figure 2O. By the time your arm makes contact with the attacker's arm, your body has turned sideways off the line of the attack. Now that you are in contact with his arm, you control his arm by **guiding it** with your forearm. Your right arm is now starting to coming upward to catch the attacker's swinging arm.

3O

Figure 3O. Your left forearm should guide his arm away from your head area and past your face. The right arm comes up to make contact with the attacking arm at the forearm area. It comes up to make contact, and as soon as contact is made, it slows the force of the attacking arm down, as your arm comes down with it at a slower pace. If it did not come up to meet the attacking arm, it would receive a hard blow at the bottom.

4O

5O

Figures 4O and 5O. The attacker's arm is swept down in front of you and caught between the forearm and your bicep. The attacker's arm is pulled against the chest with your right arm. Even when catching the swinging arm, your right arm is bent at the elbow so that your palm is facing you during the entire movement. When the arm is caught, it is pulled back against the chest, as it absorbs and catches the blow, trapping it between your forearm and bicep of your arm.

6O

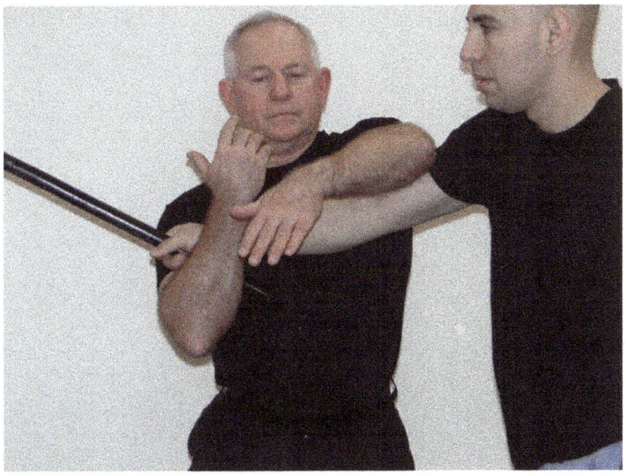

7O

Figures 6O and 7O. By the time the attacking arm has reached your chest area, it is being pulled in **tightly** to your chest. The left arm has done its job if the attacker's swing has not made any contact with any part of your body. The right arm comes up from below absorbing some of the energy as it is brought back to your chest with your palm facing you, as both arms meet at your chest area working together at the same time. With the left arm coming down over the top of his arm, and the right arm coming from below, the attacker's arm is trapped and hugged into the chest stopping the blow to your body, and the redirection of his force and energy will start.

8O

9O

Figure 8O. Slide your hands down the attacker's arm to his hand, as you pull the arm tight against your chest, positioning his arm so that his palm and the inside of his forearm are facing forward. When your hands reach the attacker's wrist, you push the attacker's arm forward until his elbow is against your chest, preventing him from bending the elbow and coming forward to face you.

Figure 9O. Once the attacker's elbow is across the chest, you step back with your outside leg, using the inside leg as a pivot point. When stepping back and starting the turn, continue to push his arm in front of you, keeping him as close as you can next to your left side. Continue hugging tightly on his arm and keep your back straight.

10O

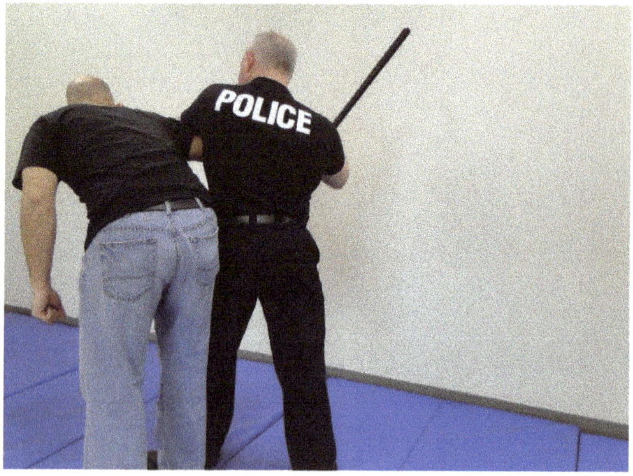

11O

Figures 10O and 11O. Keeping your back as straight as you can, take another step back with your right foot, leaving your left foot in place. If your attacker is taller than you, you will find that he will bend over as he follows you as you turn. If he is shorter, he will arch his back and have a tendency to drag behind you.

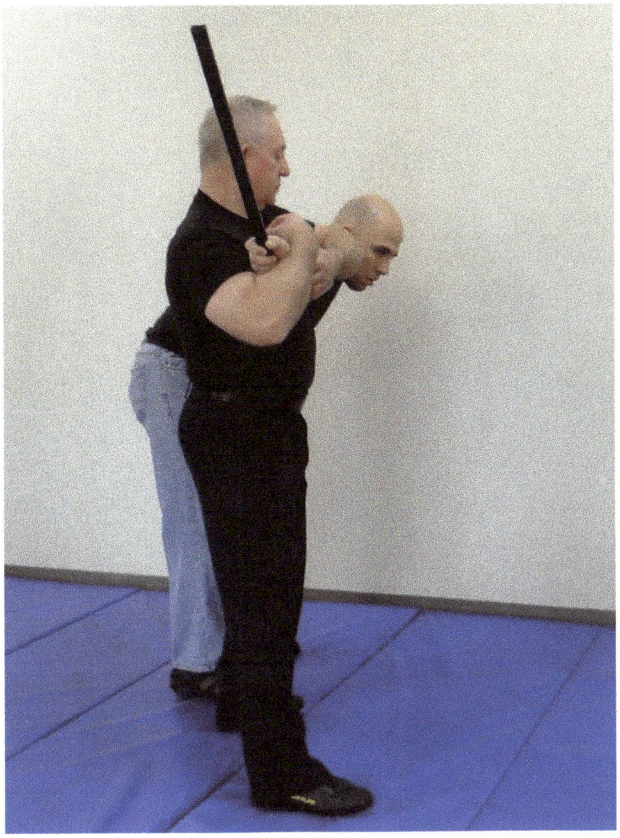

12O

13O

Figures 12O and 13O. Take another step back with your right foot, working yourself in a circle, leaving your left leg in the center as you pivot around it. The attacker will have a hard time catching up with you. Allow your left hand to work it's way to the actor's hand, and position it in the hitchhiker grip. **BUT DON'T STOP TURNING.** The actor's arm is still held tight against your chest.

14O

Figure 14O. When your hand is set in the correct position, you are ready to take one final step back with your right foot.

Figure 15O. Once your step has been made, lean forward against his arm and turn hard back to the right side with your torso. This will launch him forward faster at that last second preparing you for the next step.

15O

16O

17O

Figure 16O. After launching him forward, your weight will have to shift back to your right leg, allowing his momentum to carry him forward. Your right hand has now shifted to the hand he has the weapon in to assist in the hitchhiker grip on his hand.

Figure 17O. Step back with your left foot as he continues to move forward, reversing the direction of the energy flow.

18O

Figures 18O and 19O. When your step back has been completed, his momentum will continue forward for several more steps. You should allow the momentum to carry him past you by almost arms length. This distance will give you almost a complete 180 degree pull back in the opposite direction.

19O

20O 21O 22O

Figures 20O, 21O, and 22O. The motion back to your left starts with you extending your arms, and bringing his right hand back, locking his wrist down and back. Notice that my arms lock his wrist down first, and as I turn back to the left, his wrist is locked back, as I turn and my arms extend. His balance will break down quickly because his momentum is carrying him forward, and you are taking his hand in the opposite direction. This allows the breakdown relay to occur very quickly.

23O

Figure 23O. This is a reverse angle on how he breaks down when your hitchhiker position is brought back. In real life speed, at this point, his feet would be in the air. But to save on my Uke in this case, it is done in slow motion. The hand is locked back, and the breakdown is in order. The elbow turns in as the shoulder drops, and his weight has shifted over his right hip, locking it out. The balance has been broken at this point. This is where your arms pull back controlling his fall and the weapon. Notice my stance; it is wide for my balance as he is being brought around in front of me. Your grip needs to be tight, and the locking of his wrist needs to continue to pull him forward.

24O 25O 26O

Figures 24O, 25O, and 26O. Breaking at the balance point you need to keep your grip tight to maintain control through the pull of the actor falling to the ground. The control of his hand keeps him falling so that he makes his first contact with the ground his right hip. The pulling of his arm takes the arm and his shoulder out of play, giving you the best setup here for the Hitchhiker Spin later in this book. The Hug Trap will be taken to the first control in this case.

27O

Figure 27O. If by chance the actor should maintain in possession of his weapon, it is not a major concern. He may have possession, but you have the control. You control the hand that he has the weapon in. There is no need to try to pull the weapon from his hand, it will come loose easily as soon as you follow foot around, and lock his arm out in second control.

HUG TRAP
TO **HITCHHIKER I** CONTROL
OVERHEAD BLOW WITH WEAPON
LEFT HAND

Many techniques in the Cane-Albrecht Method do not use a mirror image due to faster learning by the officers, and many officers have problems working with their weaker hand. The Hug Trap unfortunately is one that we require you to learn as a mirror image. By doing "centering circle" exercises, this will make this technique easier for you.

1P

2P

Figure 1P. When your attacker is left handed, the response is mirrored from the right handed response. As soon as the attacker swings, your first response is to step inside the line of danger with your right foot outside the attacker's left foot. At the same time, bring your right arm up to the outside of the attacking arm.

Figure 2P. When your right arm makes contact with the outside of the attacker's arm, your palm should be forward. Your right arm starts right away to **guide the attacking arm and weapon** past its target in front of you by pushing his arm forward with your forearm. You will do a partial "centering circle" back with your left foot, which will position you off to the attacker's left side, out of the line of danger. Your left arm response is to reach up in the direction that the attack is coming from. Your left arm will reach inside trapping the attacking arm with your palm toward you.

3P

4P

Figure 3P. When the attacking arm has been guided in front of you by the right arm, it then comes over the top of the swinging arm. The left arm comes up to catch the down swinging arm, in a bent position, palm facing you.

Figure 4P. The left arm comes up around the wrist's forearm area, and the right arm comes down over the top. Both of your arms trap the attackers arm up against your chest.

5P

6P

Figure 5P. The attackers arm will slide down your forearm slowing it's force and power to the bend in your left elbow, assist the attackers arm with your right arm making it tight against your chest.

Figure 6P. When the attacker's arm comes to a stop, it should be extended immediately to your left, your right hand should grab the attacker's arm at the wrist or lower forearm, and push it to your left also. As the left arm tightens as it pulls back against your chest and to the left side. The attacker's arm has to be brought in front of you far enough so his elbow is against the side of your chest, and his forearm is facing forward. Notice that your right elbow should be putting pressure between the actor's elbow and his shoulder, which will keep it hyper-extended.

7P

8P

Figure 7P. Keeping his arm tight against your chest, step back with your left foot. Remember to keep you back straight as you step back, and turn back to your left. If you should bend forward, the attacker will also bend forward, making it hard for you to turn him. If you are shorter than the attacker, he will have to bend some because your armpit is over the top of his arm.

Figure 8P. When he starts to move with you, as you turn back to the left, take another step back to your left, always keeping ahead of him so he has to almost run to catch up. Keep in mind that you are in the center of this turning circle, mainly pivoting on your right leg. Consequently if you turn at a moderate speed, the actor will almost be flying around the outside. So turn at your own speed so that you will be able to control him throughout the movement. If you go too fast, he may fall and this will ruin you Hug Trap move.

9P

10P

11P

Figures 9P, 10P, and 11P. Keep control by hugging his arm tight to your chest, staying behind his elbow to keep his arm hyper extended as you pull back to your left. Keep his forearm forward throughout the turning, and your back straight, you should always stay in front of the actor as you are turning, and ***<u>DO NOT</u>*** let him catch up with you. As you are turning bring your hands down to his hand preparing for the Hitchhiker move. Turn him until you and your hands are ready.

12P

13P

Figure 12P. When you are ready and your hands are in place, take one more step back with your left leg getting a good base. When your last step is down and firmly planted, add an extra twist with your torso back to the left. This will launch the attacker forward with an extra thrust.

Figure 13P. When the actor is launched pass you, allow his body to go past, and bring your right elbow back over his arm, allowing his arm to come away from your chest to extend his arm back, as his weight pulls him forward. Start to turn your shoulders back to the right side.

14P

15P

Figure 14P. Having your hands in place for the Hitchhiker on the attacker's hand, lock the wrist down as you turn back to the right.

Figure 15P. Take the attacker's wrist back in the Hitchhiker movement, locking it back. This will cause the actor's body to break down. His elbow will come forward, and his left shoulder will dip down, as his body bends back at his waist to the left side.

Timing and speed at this point vary depending how hard you launch the actor forward, which will exaggerate the extension of his arm, and the way he will fall.

16P 17P

Figures 16P and 17P. Look at both sides of the Hitchhiker position when the attacker's hand is locked back, and the elbow has turned in. His balance is lost as soon as his torso has shifted over the hip, locking it out.

In a real life situation, when this is done quickly, 90 percent of the time the attacker will lose his weapon as you bring back his arm quickly. So you need to **be conscious of a possible loose weapon** if someone else is present when the technique is being done.

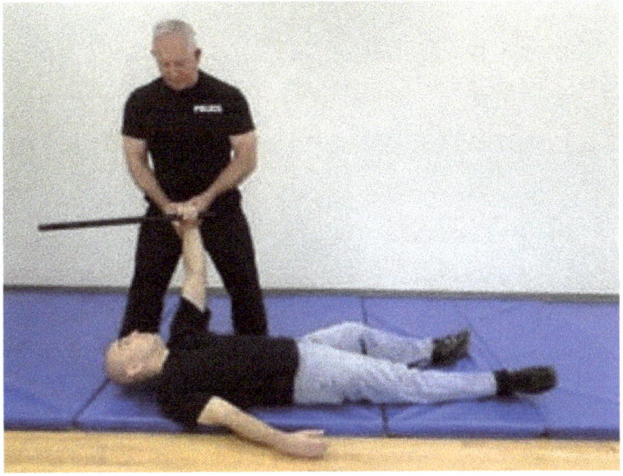

18P 19P

Figure 18P. When his balance is lost and he is falling to the ground maintain control left hand and the weapon. As he is falling bring your hands back toward your center. This will cause his left shoulder to come forward and stay in the air until he automatically bends at the hip allowing the left hip to be the first to touch the ground.

Figure 19P. When his body comes to a rest on the ground, remember to keep pulling up on his arm to your center, to keep his arm straight. Spread your feet to allow you better balance by widening your base stance and keeping his wrist locked forward.

YOKE TRAP

TO HITCHHIKER I CONTROL

KNIFE THRUST TO THROAT

RIGHT HAND

1Q

2Q

Figure 1Q. When responding to a knife thrust to the throat, a fast response time is crucial. If the knife come at chest height or higher, your response should be with a Yoke Trap.

Figure 2Q. Your first movement is to step forward with your left foot, at the same time, your hands are preparing to be raised to catch and redirect the right hand of the actor.

3Q

Figure 3Q. The faster hand to respond, as both of your hands come up to this attack, is your left hand to the back of the attacker's hand. In a knife attack, do not take your eyes off the weapon. Moving with the attacker and his weapon will help you gain control over the weapon before the attacker can complete his attack. The object of this response is to **guide the weapon** by you, as you keep the energy flow of the hand with the knife in motion.

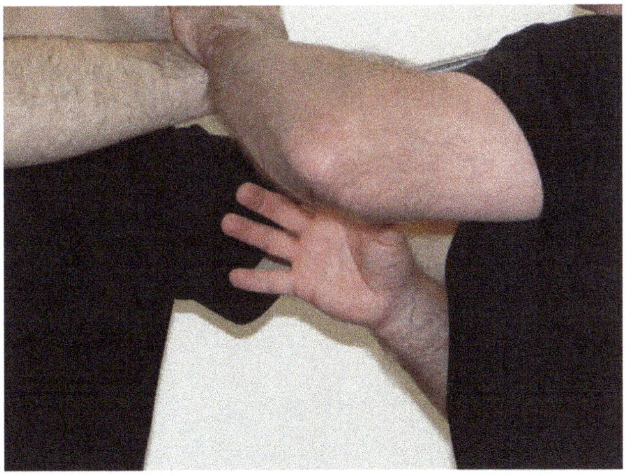

4Q 5Q

Figures 4Q and 5Q. Your left hand makes first contact with the side and back of the attacker's weapon hand, with your fingers on top of his hand, redirecting his thrust to the right side, toward your right hand. Your right hand should be coming up to catch the attacker's hand as it is redirected.

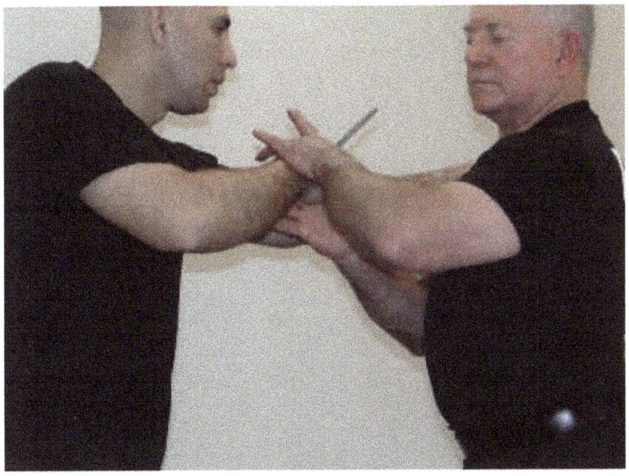

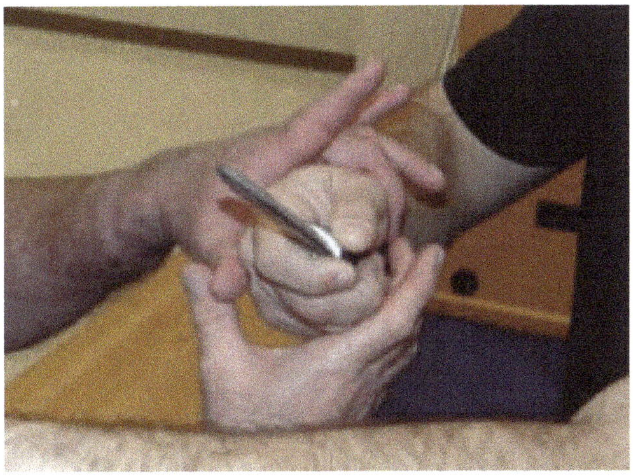

6Q 7Q

Figure 6Q. When redirecting the knife hand of the attacker, the left shoulder of your redirecting hand is also moved toward your right side to angle your body slightly. In the redirection of the attacker's hand, it is moved to your right and back toward him. Your right hand should make contact with the attacker's hand by this time.

Figure 7Q. When the right hand makes contact, your fingers should be grabbing the heel portion of his hand, as well as, the last two fingers of his hand that are gripping the knife. Your thumb should come to the back of his hand with your left thumb. With both of your hands around the attacking hand, you are again in the Hitchhiker hand position and ready to perform the Hitchhiker Technique for the takedown.

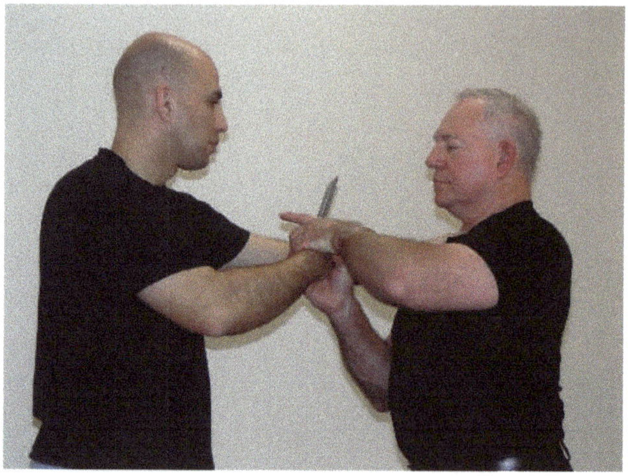

8Q

9Q

Figure 8Q. When your grip is secure on the attacking hand, it is brought back toward the attacker.

Figure 9Q. Lock the attacker's wrist back toward him in the down and back position. Your right shoulder turns back to the left side to increase the pressure and power of your hand positioning in the Hitchhiker position.

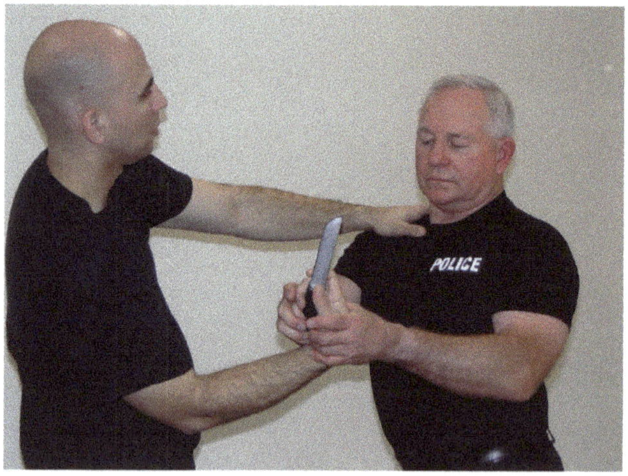

10Q

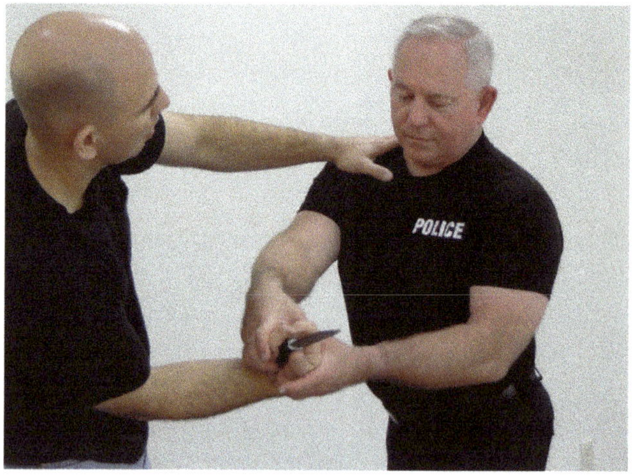

11Q

Figure 10Q. Take the attacker's hand and weapon back to his right side, keeping it locked back and turned to his right side to where it will lock. Remember the **turning of your torso and right shoulder** back toward the attacker will assist you in the power you will need to overcome the thrust of the knife hand.

Figure 11Q. Continuing the Hitchhiker position past the locking positions will now start the breakdown of his posture. First, his elbow will turn into his body and his shoulder will drop, causing his weight to shift to his right side. The **weight shift of the torso over the right hip** will lock out his hip. All of these shifts in his body cause him to become unbalanced to the right side, as you continue to lock his hand back and to the side.

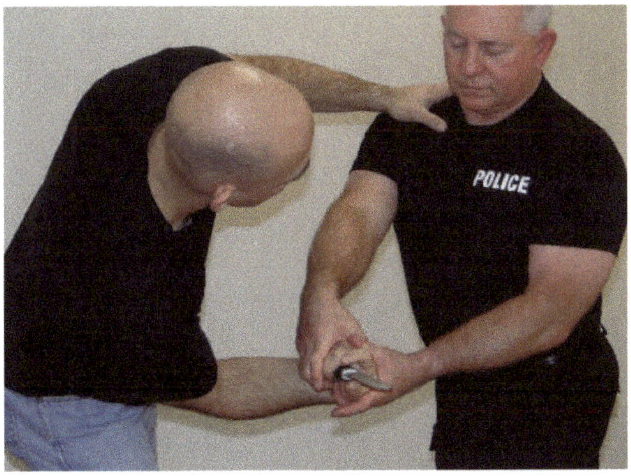

12Q 13Q

Figure 12Q and 13Q. Continue to lock the attacker's wrist back and to the side as you follow through. When his balance breaks and his right hip is locked out, his left foot will lift off the ground. This will leave him nowhere to go but to the ground on his right side.

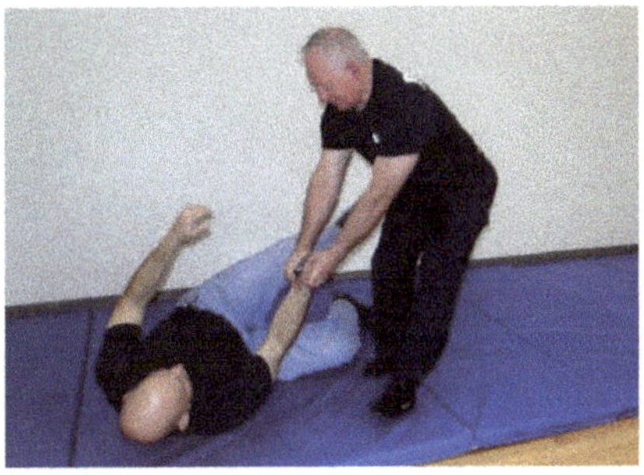

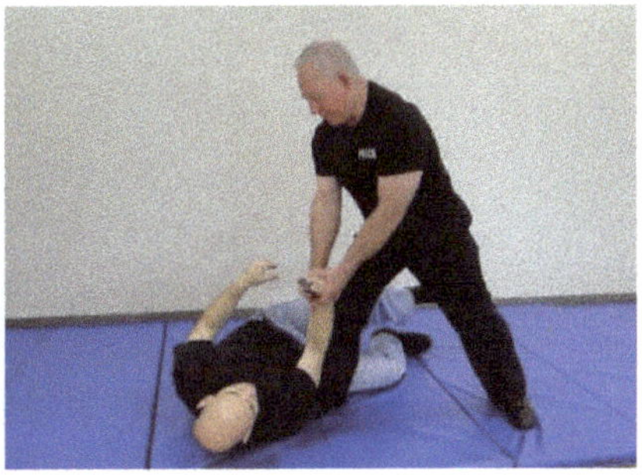

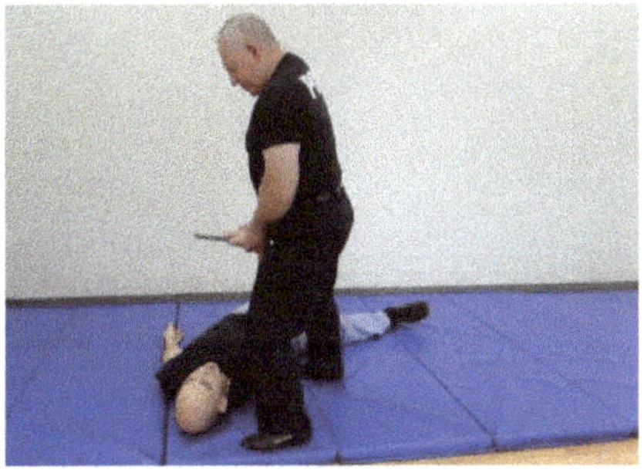

14Q 15Q 16Q

Figure 14Q. When his right hip touches the ground, pull back on his arm, which will pull his shoulder forward, preventing him from landing directly on his shoulder. This also forces his body to roll onto his back.

Figure 15Q. Step in with your right foot, as soon and as you can and as close as you can, to his body at his waistline. Continue to keep pulling up on his arm to prevent it from bending.

***CAUTION**: If the arm is allowed to bend and his elbow touches the ground, there are several things that may occur. First, this will give him a base to push off of, and he will be able to roll away or come up at you. Second, if his elbow comes low enough to touch the ground that means you would have to bend over which will give you a balance problem and possibly give him a chance to take a swing at you with his left hand.*

Figure 16Q. Step in with your left foot to establish a wide base and continue pulling up on his arm, preventing it from bending. Pull his hand to your center, keeping it bent down and forward. You are again ready to Follow Foot to control.

CHAPTER 8

Hitchhiker Spin

HITCHHIKER SPIN
RIGHT HAND TO CONTROL IN SQUATTING POSITION

The Hitchhiker Spin is a faster and less tedious way to get your attacker into the handcuff ready position. This technique is learned with practice and a little element of timing. When the Hitchhiker is able to be used in a situation, and you have adequate space, it has its benefits. As I had mentioned before, it is faster. When the technique is performed on an attacker, it becomes confusing to him. The main reason for this confusion is the semi-circular cannels in the ear. When the Hitchhiker Spin is performed, the attacker starts falling to the side first, then when his hip touches the ground, he is spun on his side. As he is spinning his body is being turned over which changes the direction in the ear which causes the momentary confusion. When his body stops spinning, you have not moved but he is in the handcuffing position, as if you had taken the time and Follow Footed around him like you have previously done. If he had never had this done to him before, he will be confused and have a hard time explaining what had happened during this takedown.

1R

2R

Figures 1R and 2R. In this practice with your Uki or partner, position your hands in the Hitchhiker position on his right hand, your fingers on the inside of his hand and your thumbs on the back of his hand, locking his wrist down and back. Start your partner in a squatting position. As you press back and to the right side of your partner's wrist, it will start the chain reaction of losing his balance.

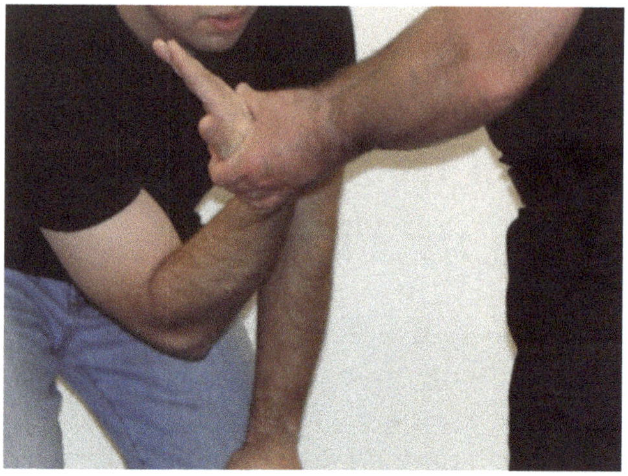

3R

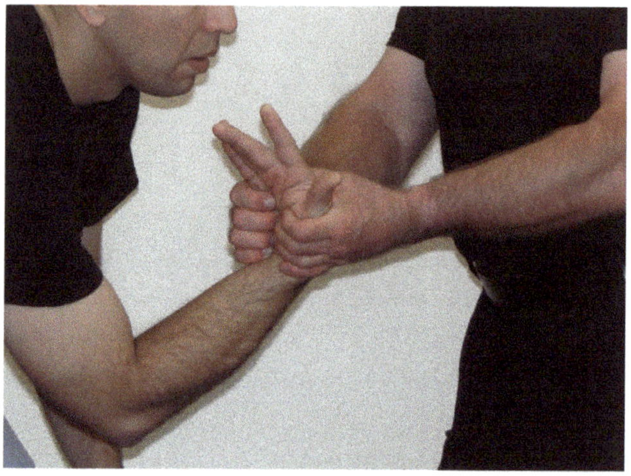

4R

Figure 3R. Place the thumbs on the back of his hand near the first knuckle between the middle finger and the ring finger. Keep pressure forward on his wrist and turned to your partner's right side or back to your left side.

Figure 4R. The fingers of your left hand are gripping around the meaty portion of his thumb, and the fingers of your right hand are gripping around the heel of his hand.

5R

6R

7R

Figures 5R,6R, and 7R. Apply the pressure to the wrist of your partner by locking the wrist back and to his right side. Do this slow so you are able to watch when the wrist action stops. His elbow will turn into his body, dropping his shoulder. He will then lean to his right side. With you pulling his arm toward you, his shoulder comes forward, and his right hip will lock. When his weight leans over his hip to the right side, this will lockout this hip, and he will not be able to move his right foot. His left foot will start to come off the ground as his weight continues to shift to the right side. Doing this in this slow motion will allow you to observe the reactions in how his body breaks down until his balance is lost. Continue to keep a tight grip on your partner's hand because he will still have an automatic response to want to place his hand on the ground to break his fall even if he is going slow and squatting down.

8R 9R

Figure 8R. Once his balance is lost his body will fall to the right side. Make sure to keep tension on his right arm by pulling it toward you, keeping it out of play in his fall.

Figure 9R. ***THIS IS THE MOST IMPORTANT PART IN TIMING WHEN IT COMES TO THE HITCHHIKER SPIN.*** Watch for the split second that his right hip touches the ground. This point is before his back comes to the floor and when his feet are still in the air. This is the point at which his body just touches the ground with his hip ***ONLY***.

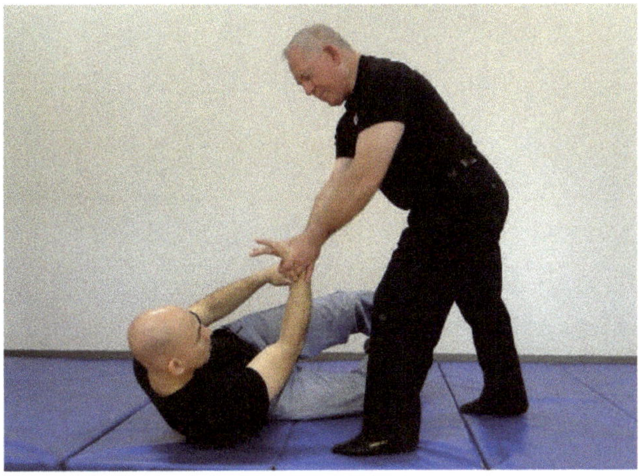

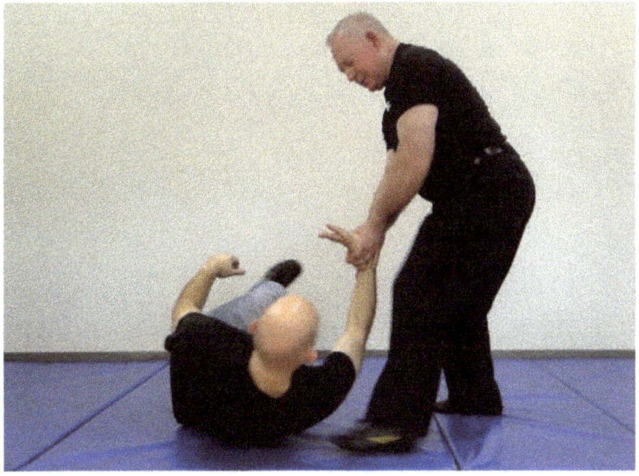

10R 11R

Figure 10R. As soon as his hip touches the ground you need to make a step back toward his feet, ***NOT BACK AWAY FROM HIM***.

Figure 11R. Pull his arm back hard in the direction of his feet, where you had just stepped, before his weight has a chance to settle into the floor. This will keep his body at a pivoting point on his right hip, launching him into a spin. His feet will spin back as his head and torso come forward toward you. You will find that the spin will be much faster done on a hard surface, such as asphalt or concrete.

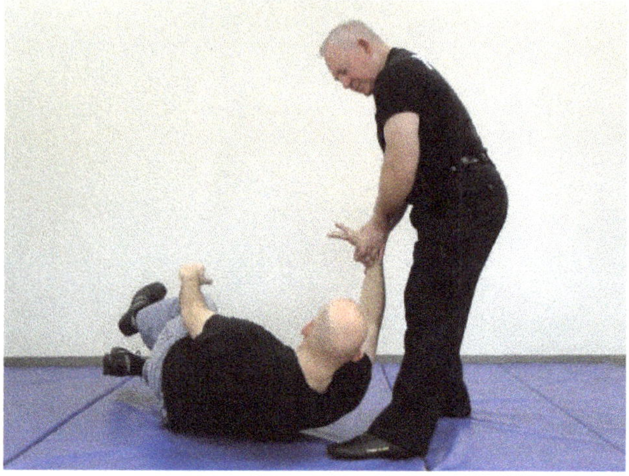

12R

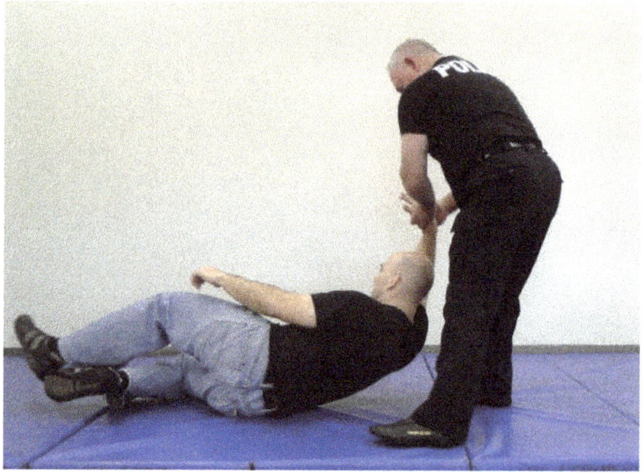

13R

Figure 12R and 13R. Follow through with the pull on his arm spinning his head and torso in front of you.

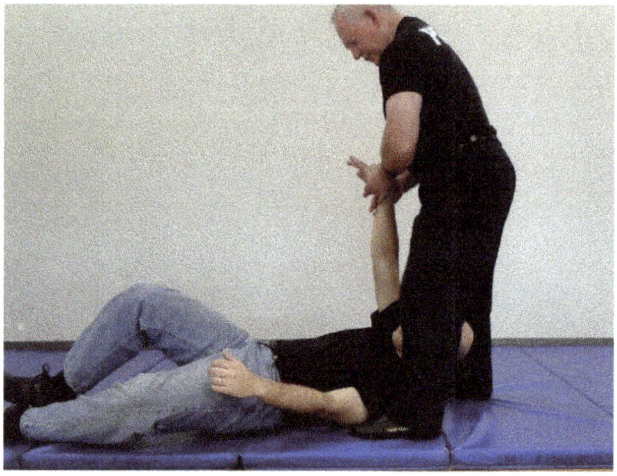

14R

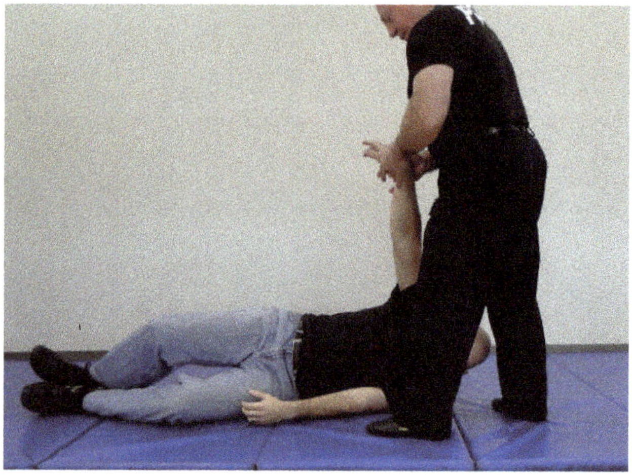

15R

Figure 14R and 15R. After the follow through on the pull to spin your partner, as he is still moving, come back to your center keeping a wide stance for a good base. You will see that as his body continues to spin, as you come back to your center, his body will start to turn over toward you. His right arm will extend as he rolls over his shoulder. His body will turn as well. Keep his arm straight and do not bend over.

NOTE: This is the portion of the spin that needs to be addressed. After the hard pull towards his feet, there is a follow through that needs to come directly back to your center. A problem that arises is what we call stirring. This is when you follow through with your pull and continue to move your arms in a circular manner to make your partner continue to spin, instead of coming back to your center. If this is done, it will cause you to have a momentary loss of balance that may cause you to fall forward onto your partner.

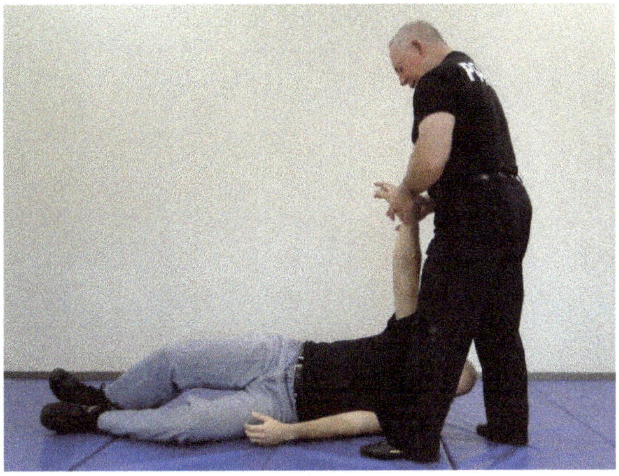

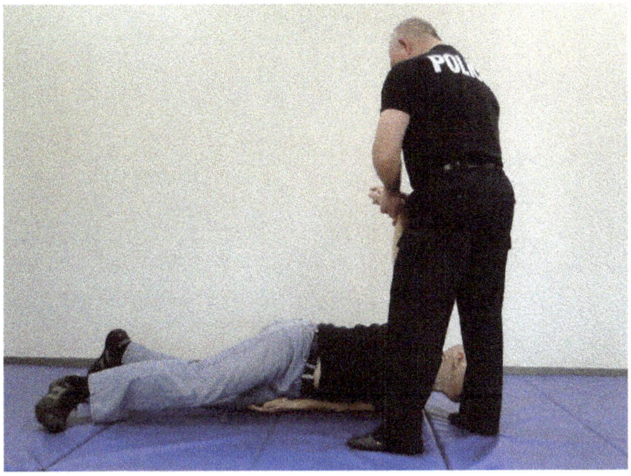

16R 17R

Figure 16R and 17R. Control over your partner's arm at this point starts with keeping his arm straight first. The second part of this control comes from the wrist. Keep your partner's wrist locked down and his fingers straight out from your waist at a 90 degree angle.

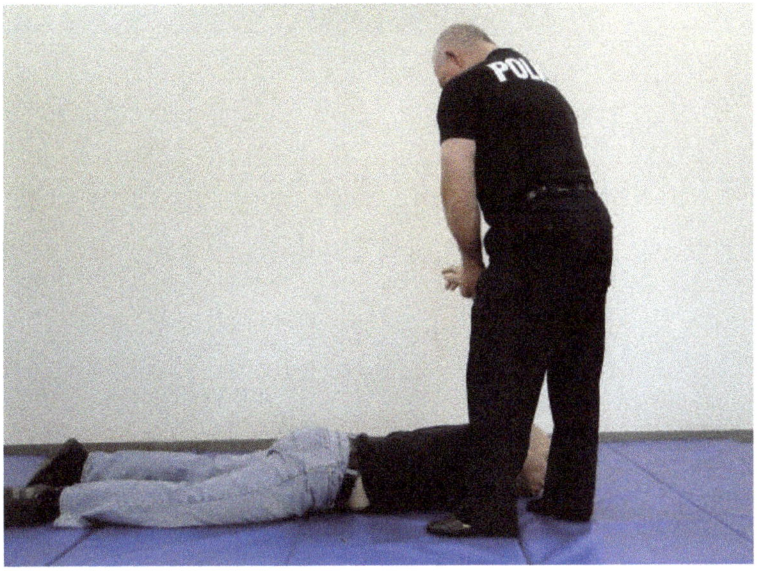

18R

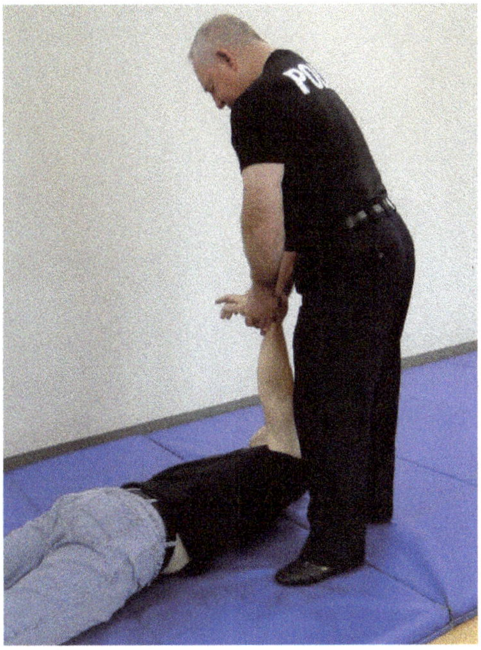

19R

Figure 18R and19R. Locking your partner out in the control position requires that his arm be straight up, and his wrist be locked forward. Pressure is applied to the wrist which pushes his shoulder into the ground.

NOTE: If the actor's shoulder does not go to the ground when he turns onto his stomach, the control is not complete. To lower the shoulder to the ground, you do not have to push down on the wrist. The trick is to turn the wrist toward his head which will rotate the shoulder, and it will go to the ground.

HITCHHIKER SPIN
LEFT HAND TO CONTROL IN STANDING POSITION

1S

2S

Figure 1S. Position your right hand to grab the actor's left hand. Your fingers grip around the actor's meaty portion of his thumb, and your thumb is placed on the back of his hand between the knuckles of the middle finger and the ring finger. Bend his wrist forward until it stops.

Figure 2S. Your left hand is brought up to reinforce the grip and to assist. The left hand grips the heel of the actor's left hand with the fingers to the inside of his palm. Your thumb should be placed on the back of his hand between the knuckles of his ring finger and middle finger.

3S

Figure 3S. Turn the actor's wrist to his left side while keeping it locked forward. The elbow will turn in when it locks his shoulder will drop, shifting his weight to his left side locking the left hip.

4S

Figure 4S. When his torso weight shifts over his hip, his balance is lost.

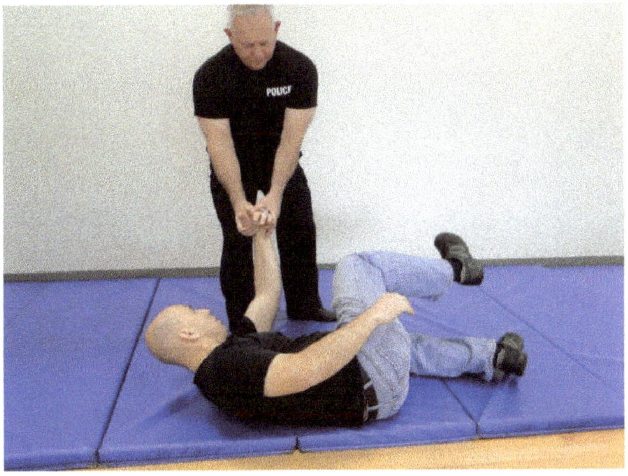

5S 6S

Figure 5S. When the actor loses his balance, he will fall to the left side. As he is falling, keep tension on the actor's arm by pulling forward. The tension that you apply by pulling will cause his left shoulder to go forward.

Figure 6S. When the actor falls to the ground to his left side, timing again is very important. When he is falling, you need to step back with your left foot toward the attacker's feet.

7S 8S

Figure 7S. This is where the timing comes into play. The moment that the actor's hip touches the ground, you need to pull hard back toward his feet. The pull has to happen before all of his weight settles onto the ground.

Figure 8S. When you pull back toward his feet, follow through with your pull. The pull will start the actor spinning on his hip. The attacker's torso will come toward you as his feet will swing away. Remember that the speed of the spin does have to do with the surface that you are spinning him on. The harder the surface the faster the spin. When the Hitchhiker Spin is performed on the street in real life, it is very fast.

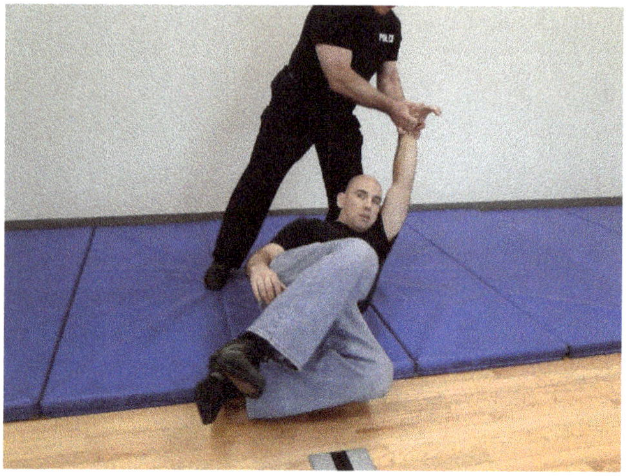

9S 10S

Figure 9S. At the top of your follow through pull, the actor is at the fastest part of the spin.

Figure 10S. When you finish the follow through pull, come back to your center, keeping your legs apart for a good base for balance.

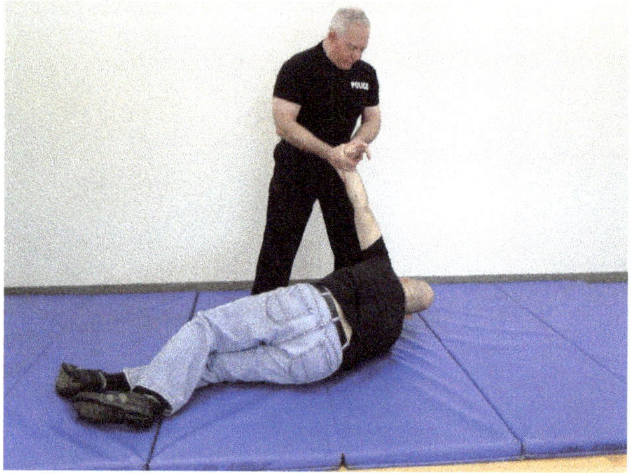

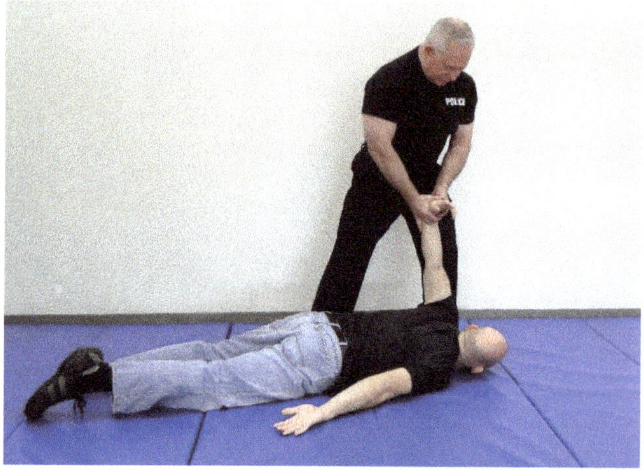

11S 12S

Figure 11S. When the actor is about three quarters the way through the spin, his left shoulder will come off the ground as he turns. This creates the extension of his left arm as he rolls over his right shoulder. Keep his hand at your center and the tension on the left arm, not allowing it to bend.

Figure 12S. When the attacker's body stops spinning, keep his hand at your center. The attacker should be laying directly in front of you. Apply pressure down on the attacker's wrist to drop the shoulder onto the ground to the control position.

Remember when an attacker only turns part way over, or does not put his shoulder down to the ground, keep the his hand at your center with his fingers pointing away from you. Turn the attacker's wrist toward his head which will rotate his his shoulder and it will drop to the ground.

HITCHHIKER SPIN ATTACKS

CROSS-WRIST GRAB TO CONTROL

1T

2T

Figure 1T. The attacke comes from a cross-wrist grab to your right wrist by an attacker.

Figure 2T. When you are grabbed, your first response is to cover. Cover is placing your hand over the attacker's grip on your wrist. In this case, your cover will be using your left hand to cover the attacker's right hand. The cover is used to secure the attacker's grip so he does not pull it back from your wrist. Also, to

3T

Figure 3T. The distract is very important. In this case, I use a front snap kick to his left shin. Maintain a good grasp on the back of the attacker's hand so it is not pulled away before you are ready to start your technique.

NOTE: Remember that a distract does not have to be painful. Just something that will take the attacker's mind off of his focal point for that split second. This will give you time to start your technique.

4T

5T

Figure 4T. The distract with the right snap kick is withdrawn as fast as it is performed to bring back stability for yourself. Both feet are about shoulder width apart for balance. The attacker's wrist is locked back and to his right side. The attacker's balance is already broken. His elbow is turned in, the shoulder has dropped, and his weight has shifted to the right side.

Figure 5T. The attacker is falling to his right side, and I am watching for the hip to touch as he falls. Your grip on the attacker's hand is tight, and the right shoulder is being controlled and brought forward by the tension that is being placed on his arm as he falls.

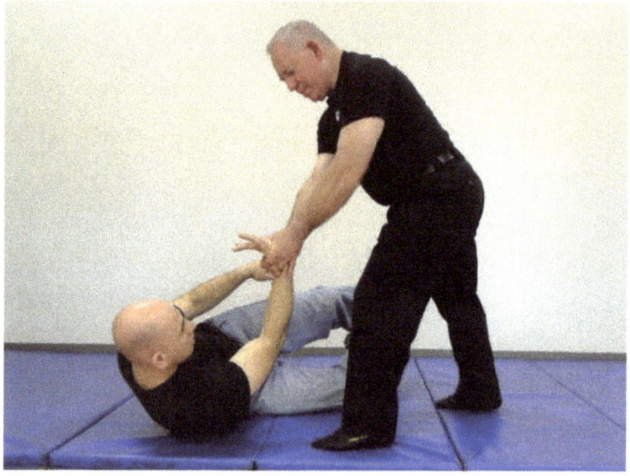

6T

7T

Figure 6T. Take a step back toward the attacker's feet with your left foot, and allow the right hip of the attacker to just touch the ground as you prepare to give a hard pull back toward his feet.

Figure 7T. Pull hard back toward his feet right away before his body weight has a chance to settle onto the ground. This will start him into a spinning motion counterclockwise.

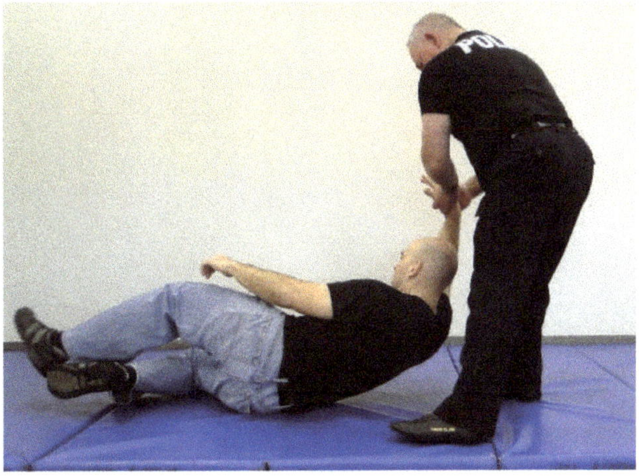

8T

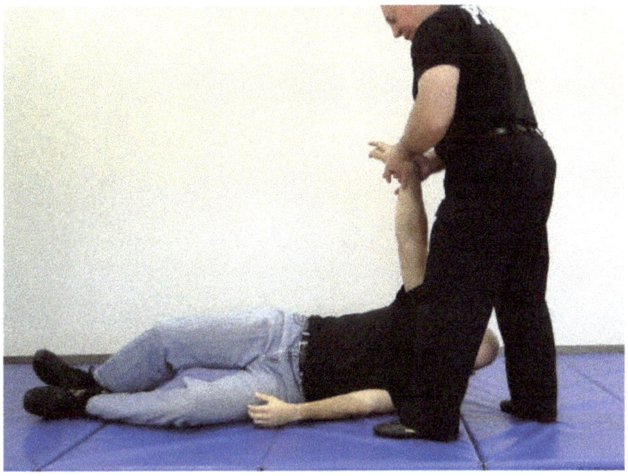

9T

Figure 8T. The hard pull is followed through to get the maximum spin on the attacker's body to allow the attacker's head to pass in front of you.

Figure 9T. As soon as his head passes in front of you, bring his hand back to your center. This will cause him to turn back toward you with his right shoulder, rolling over his left shoulder as he is still in motion.

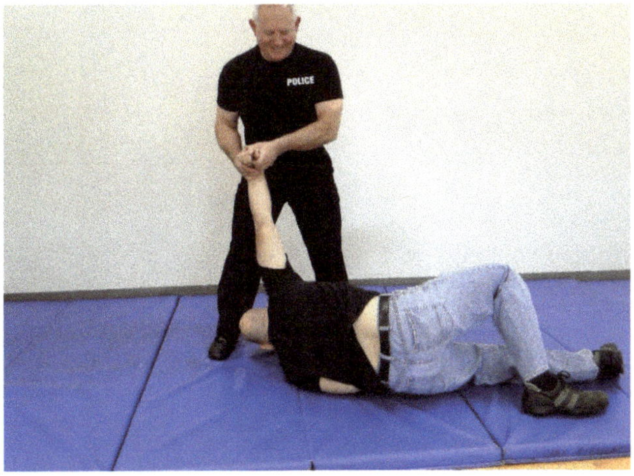

10T

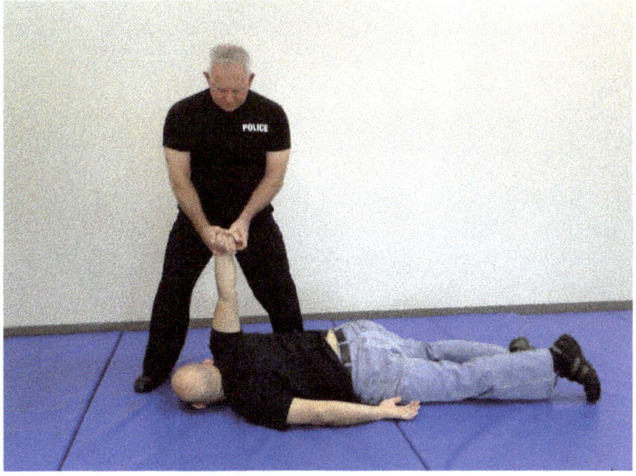

11T

Figure 10T. When the attacker rolls back toward you and rolls over his left shoulder, the right arm will extend upward for a short period of time. You need to make sure that your back is straight and pull up so as not to allow his right arm to bend.

Figure 11T. When he rolls over onto his stomach, keep his hand locked down and keep pressure on the back of his right wrist. Keep your stance wide for a good base and make sure that the attacker's shoulder is on the ground. He will be locked out at the first control. Remember this is not the stopping point yet, just a control point for the purpose of training.

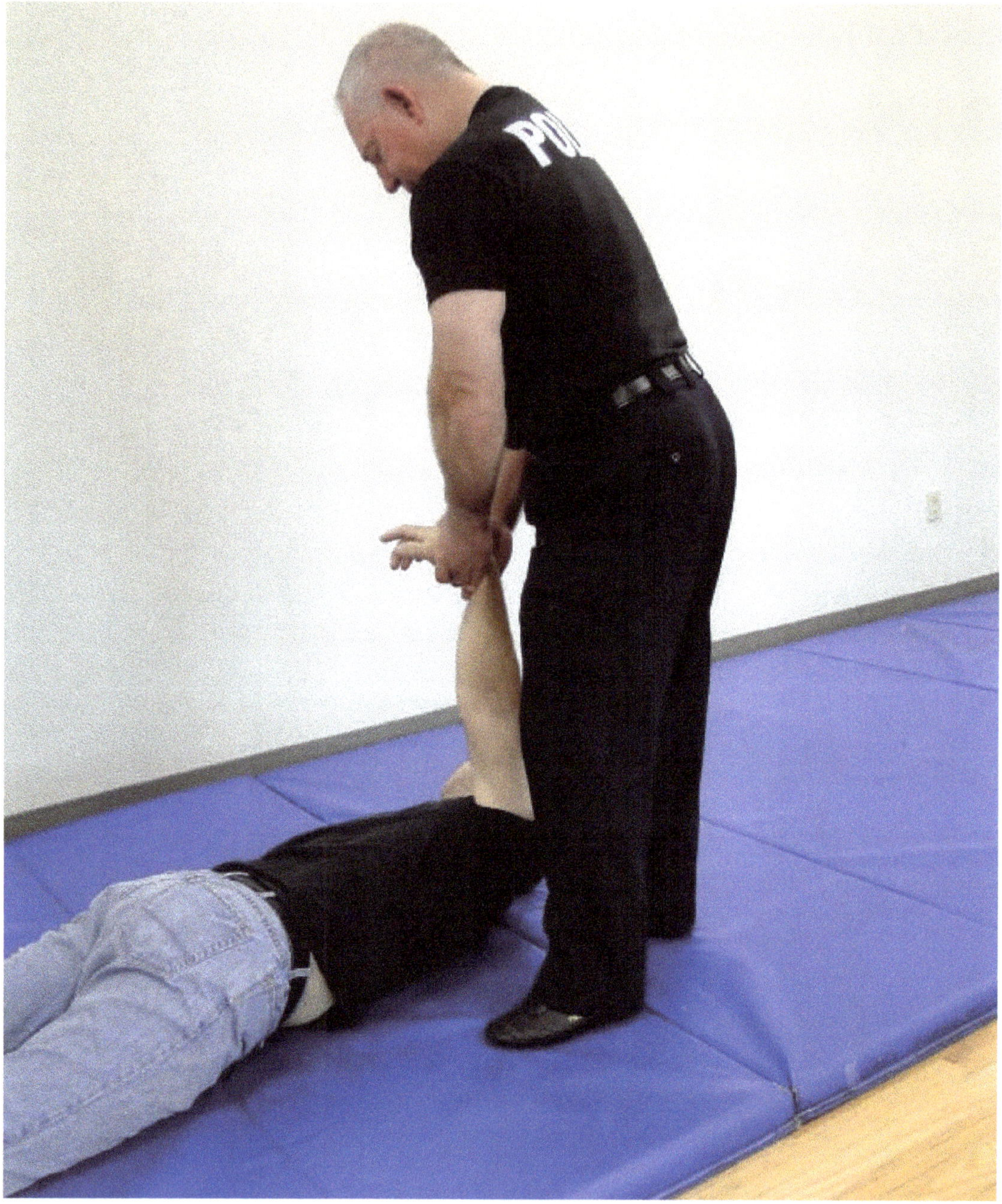

12T

Figure 12T. Take a close look and remember that the attacker's arm should be straight up from the ground to have maximum control. As mentioned previously, the shoulder needs to go to the ground and if it doesn't go all the way to the ground, there is a simple solution to this minor problem. There is no need to press down with undo pressure, just keep the pressure on the locked out wrist and turn it toward his head. This will rotate the shoulder in its socket, and he will put his shoulder down. **Do not over rotate the hand in this counterclockwise direction to prevent injury to your prisoner.**

CHAPTER 9

Yoke Spin

YOKE TRAP into the HITCHHIKER SPIN

RIGHT HAND OVERHEAD BLOW WITH WEAPON TO HANDCUFFING POSITION

The Yoke Trap is used to get a faster earlier control at a distance. The object of the yoke position is to get the arm or wrist of your attacker in the web of your hand to redirect the movement from you. Taking your attacker off his line of attack will assist you in gaining control. The Yoke Trap is using both of your hands open with your palms down. The thumbs are placed one on top of the other and in an open position, to allow the hand to maneuver around the wrist or arm whichever is trapped.

1U

2U

Figure 1U. When an actor swings with an overhead strike, your first move is to step inside the line of danger to the side of the actor that the object is being swung. This will get you inside the most dangerous part of the swing by decreasing the angle and distance. Also, reducing the speed and power of the blow. Both hands reach up to trap his arm as it comes down. The hands are open, one thumb is over the top of the other. Either thumb will work for being on top of the other.

Figure 2U. When contact with the attacker's arm is made with your hands, guide it down in front of you, as you turn your body inward behind the swinging arm. Redirect the swing in front of you, causing the redirection to take him off line.

3U

4U

Figure 3U. Continue to turn your body to your right with your torso. At the same time, bend your left elbow to allow his extended right arm to go in front of you. Slide your hands down to his wrist as you are turning, and keep his forearm and palm forward.

Figure 4U. When his arm gets in front of you, your left elbow should be over the top of his arm, and your hands should have slid to his wrist. You now start turning back by stepping back with the right foot which is the outside foot. Continue his motion by pulling his arm across in front of you.

5U

6U

Figure 5U. Continue to extend the attacker's arm to your right side in front of you as you take another step back with your left foot. At this point, your body should come into contact with the shoulder or arm of the attacker under your left arm. Your hands now have to be in the Hitchhiker position around the attacker's hand.

Figure 6U. When the contact is made under your arm, **turn your torso to your right fast,** as you now push his hand forward. This will launch him forward past you. Your hands need to be ready to do the Hitchiker technique.

7U

8U

Figure 7U and 8U. When you have launched him by, you continue to push his hand and arm passed you. When his entire body gets in front of you, you should now be fully extended to your right side with both of your hands.

9U

10U

Figure 9U and 10U. As the attacker's body is still moving forward passed you and you have reached your full extension to your left side, now start the Hitch-hiker. Bring the attacker's hand and weapon back to your left, locking his wrist forward and back. With his body still moving forward and you, now going in the opposite direction, this will cause his body to break down very fast.

NOTE: When this movement is done at a fast speed, you will find that the attacker's feet will leave the ground. You need to be prepared to watch for the right hip touching the ground to make your pull ready for the spin.

Another action that may be done at this point is to extend your arms forward and across the attacker. This will cause him to strike himself across the face or neck with his own weapon.

11U

12U

Figure 11U and 12U. The Hitchhiker Technique starts to breakdown his body as he is brought back in the opposite direction. The elbow then turns in and the shoulder drops quickly. As said in the notes previously, if done quickly, his feet will come off the ground. For training and demonstration purposes, the move is done slower to allow you to get your timing. Remember that when he starts to fall, there is some tension put on his right arm to allow his hip to touch the ground first and keep the shoulder forward.

13U

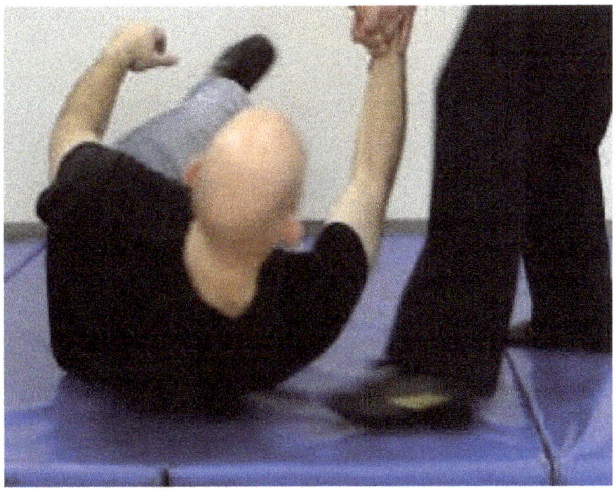

14U

Figure 13U. Watch for his hip to make contact with the ground. Keep tension on his arm, and at that split second, when his hip touches and his body is balanced on that tip of the hip, that is when you give a hard pull back toward his feet.

Figure 14U. The attacker will feel that he is falling onto his right side first. Pull back to your right side, toward his feet. The actor's body will spin on his hip, turning him onto his back, bringing his head and torso forward toward you, and his feet and legs away from you.

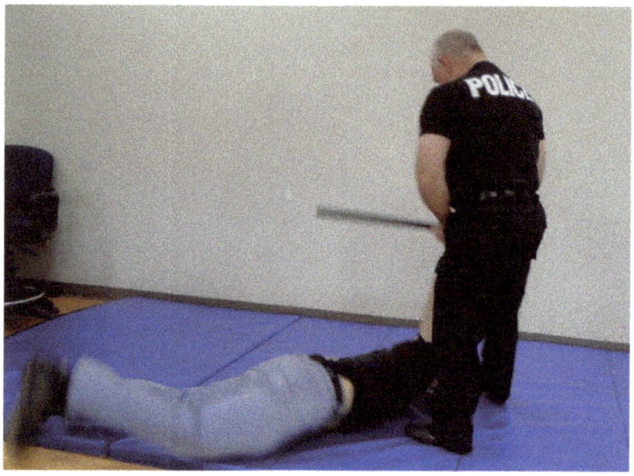

15U

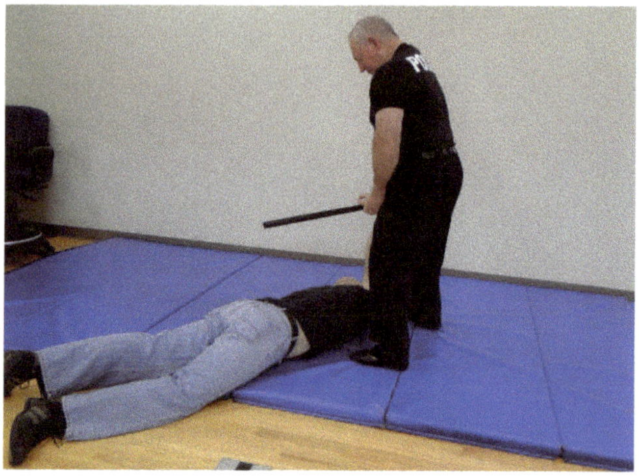

16U

Figure 15U. His body continues to spin as hid head comes in front of you and his feet extended off to your left side. During this spinning action he has gone from falling to his right side onto his back the rolling over his left shoulder onto his stomach while spinning counter clockwise.

Figure 16U. When his spin come to a stop he should be laying in front of you with his arm straight up to your enter and locked out. Turn your body square with the actor keeping your feet wide for balance. The actor's shoulder should be on the ground. You should be putting pressure down on the back of his wrist for control.

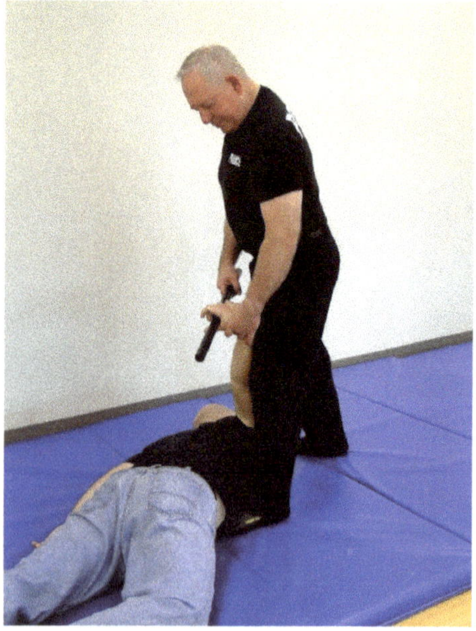

17U

Figure 17U. Release your right hand and take hold of the baton, controlling the attacker's arm by keeping pressure down on his wrist with your left hand.

Figure 18U. Place your right foot at the top of the attacker's right shoulder, between his head and shoulder, with your toes forward under him. Turn your body to face the length of his body.

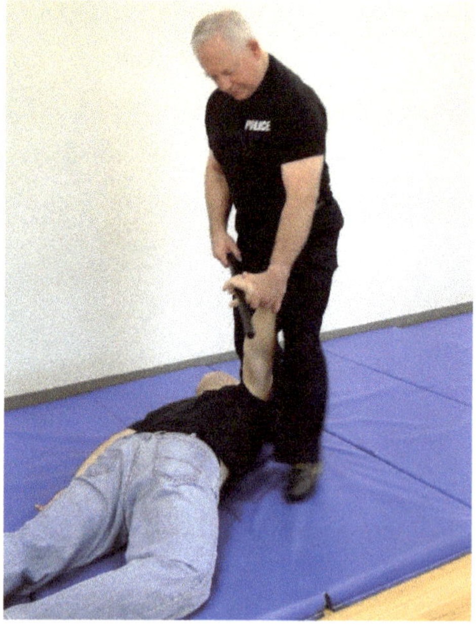

18U

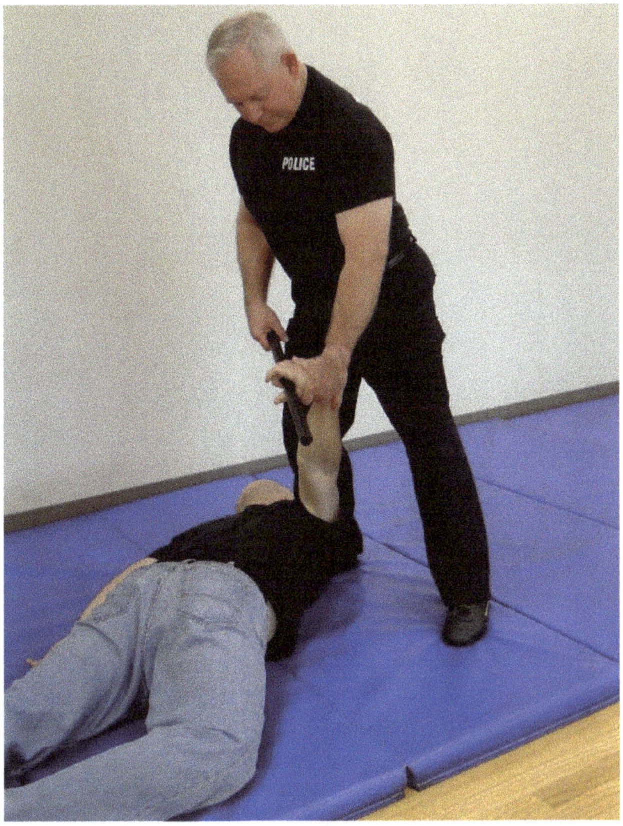

19U

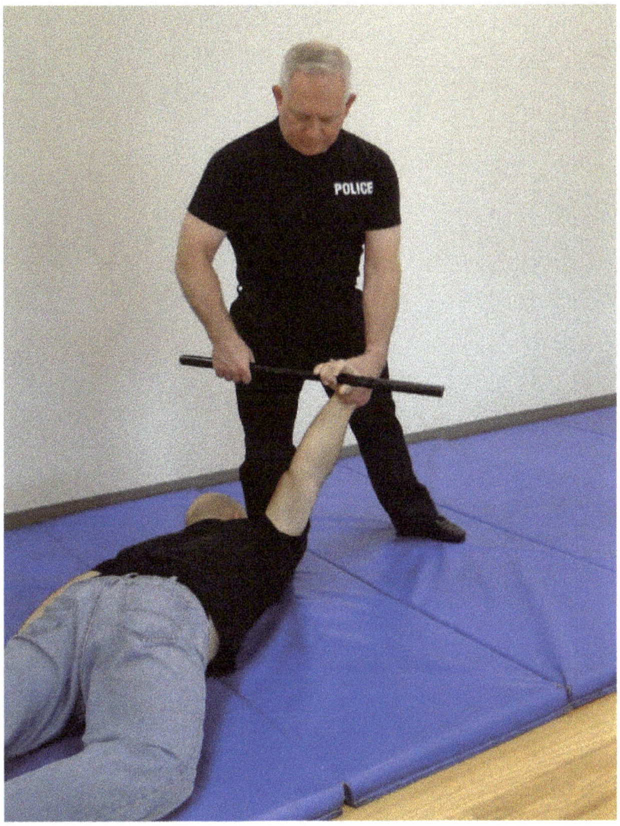

20U

Figure 19u and 20U. Swing your left foot back behind you, allowing the attacker's arm to come to the side, as you bend forward with your right knee. The right knee will bend slightly across the triceps just below the elbow, as you pull the arm back with your left hand. Still control the baton with your right hand, if he is still trying to hang onto it.

21U

Figure 21U. If the actor is still trying to hang onto the baton, pull his arm back to increase the tension as you bend your knee forward. The baton will come loose easily at this time.

Figure 22U. Keeping the tension on his arm, take the baton and place it under your arm for control of the weapon. Don't take the chance of putting it on the ground.

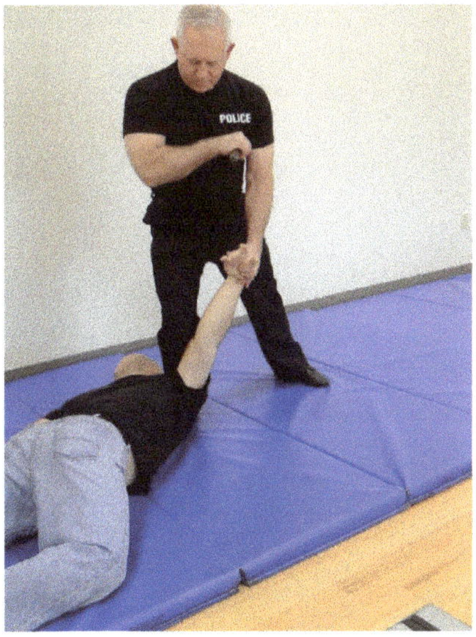

22U

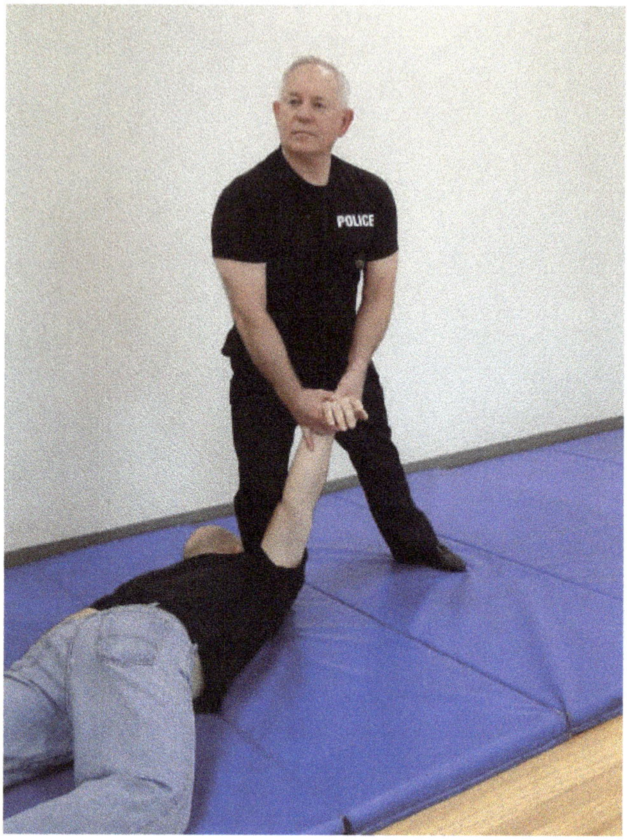

23U

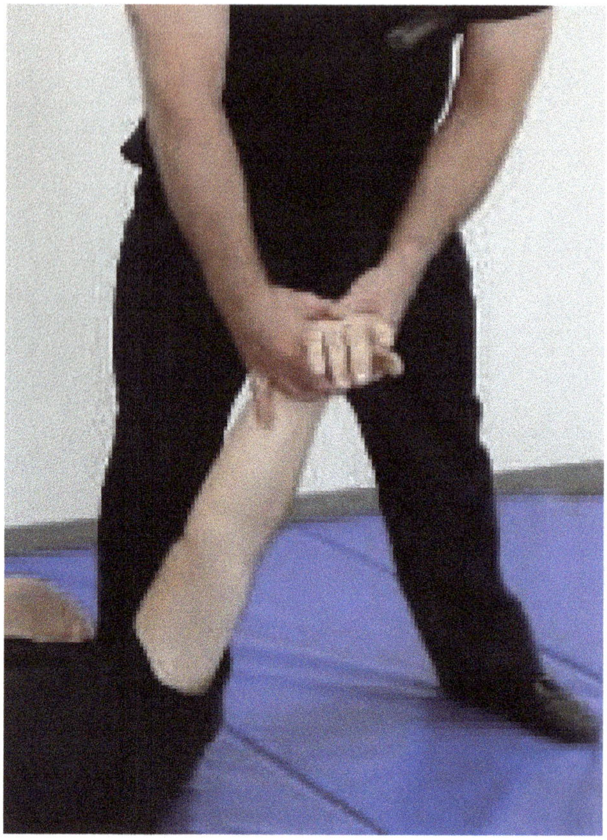

24U

Figures 23U and 24U. After securing the baton, regain control over the attacker's arm with both hands. Keep the tension on his arm by pulling back with your hands and bending forward with your right knee. This is the time to evaluate your situation and give yourself a few seconds to come down from the adrenaline rush.

Take three deep breaths and look up and around you at this time. Make sure there

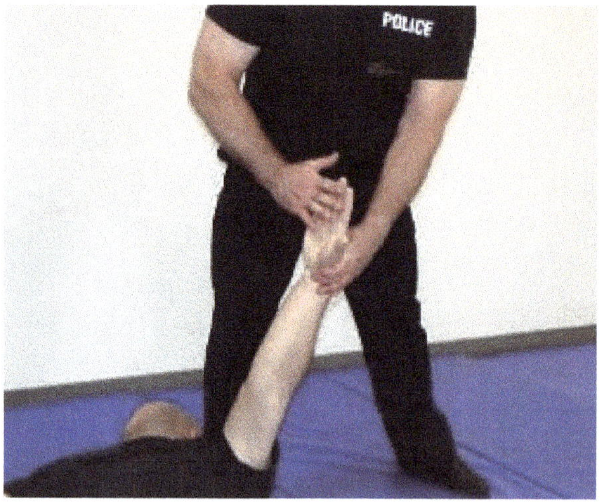

25U

Figure 25U. Keep the control over the attacker's arm by keeping the tension on his elbow and pulling back with your left hand. Release your grip on his wrist with your right hand. Now, open his hand by using your fingers and extending his fingers straight up. Your left hand stays at his wrist with your index finger at the bend of his wrist, and your thumb is still on the back of his hand. Keep you stance wide and your left leg back behind you.

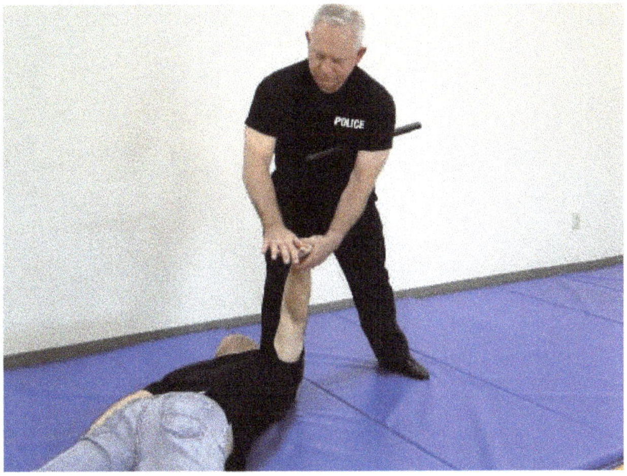

26U 27U

Figure 26U. Keep the attacker's fingers extended and push his finger's back and clockwise, keeping your left hand at his wrist.

Figure 27U. Bring his fingers around in the clockwise direction until they point at the attacker's feet. Now place your left thumb on the attacker's palm, for better control.

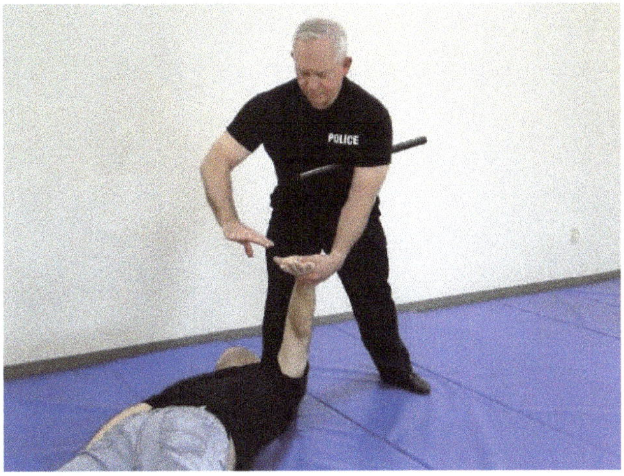

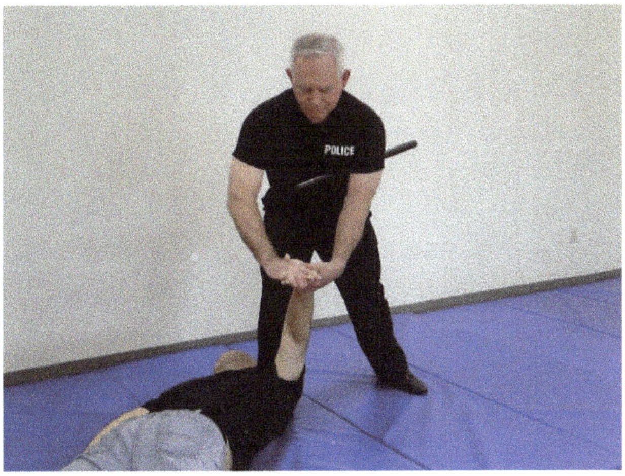

28U 29U

Figure 28U. Bring your right hand away, turning it inward. Reach across the attacker's hand as if you were going to shake his hand. Make sure that your hand is wide open when taking your grip on the attacker's hand.

Figure 29U. Grip the attacker's hand by pushing the web portion between your thumb and index finger against the same portion of his hand. Your grip size will be determined by the size of your hand and the size of his. In this case, I am able to get a good grip on three of the attacker's fingers. Gripping two fingers works just as well or if you have large hands, taking all four fingers in your hand. After the grip is secure, turn your gripping hand clockwise slowly.

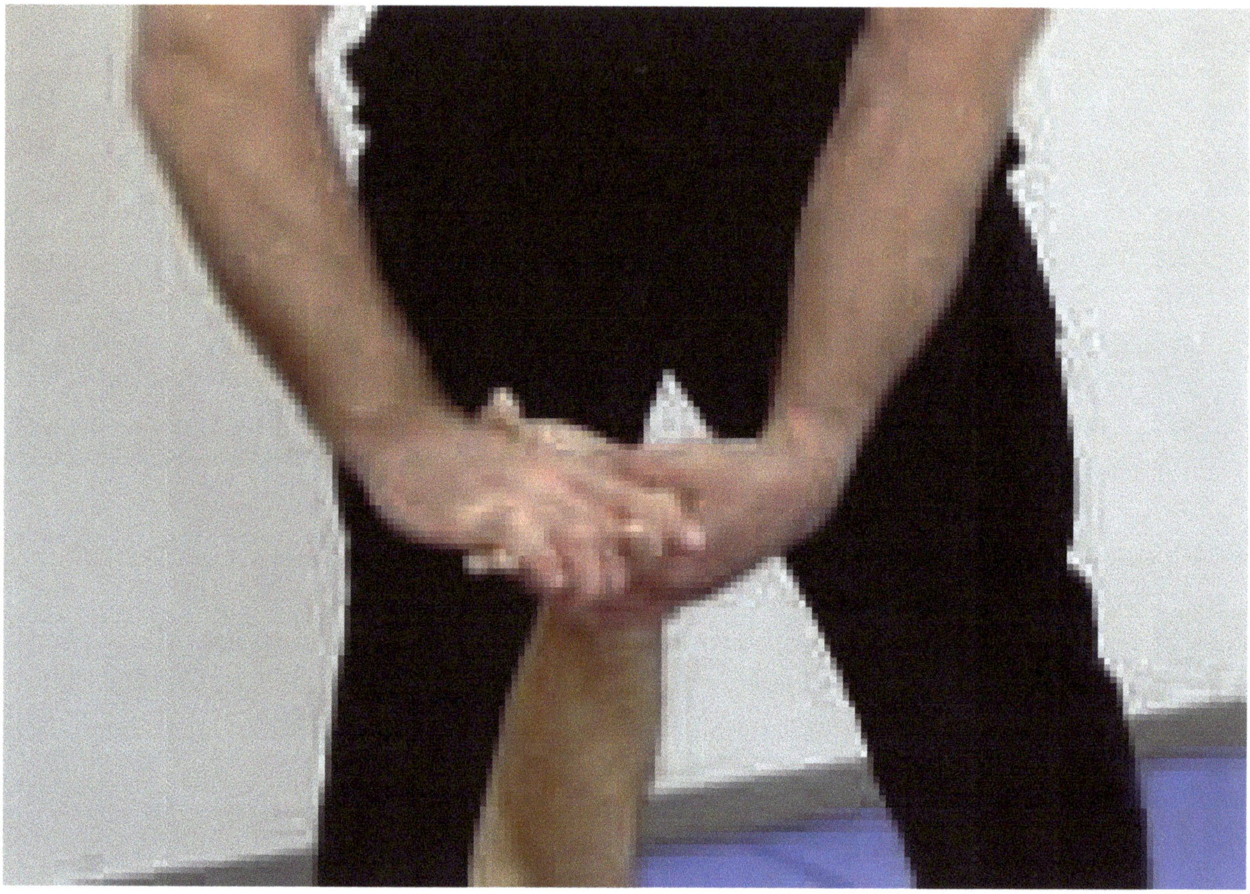

30U

Figure 30U. This is a close up of the grip of three fingers of the attacker's hand. Notice that the attacker's wrist remains bent back and controlled by your left hand. **Remember the attacker's feet will come up when your grip is correct.**

31U

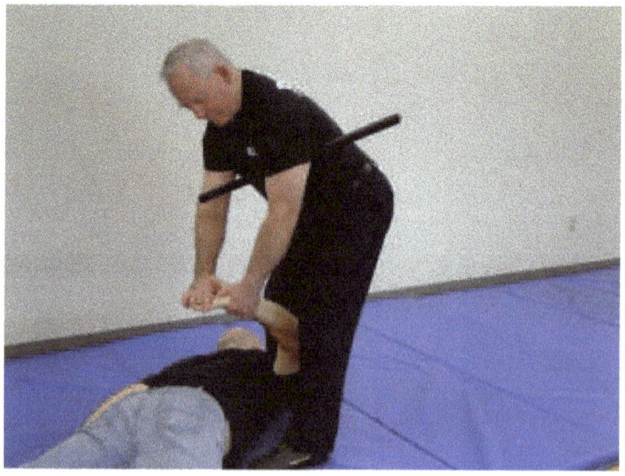

32U

Figures 31U and 32U. When you start to bring the actor's hand down to his back turn his hand with your right hand. Lift your left foot off the ground, and with one large step, step around to the actor's waist, allowing his arm to come down to his back.

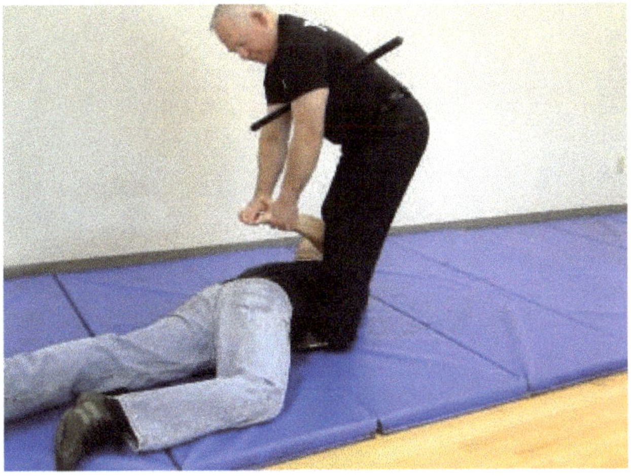

33U

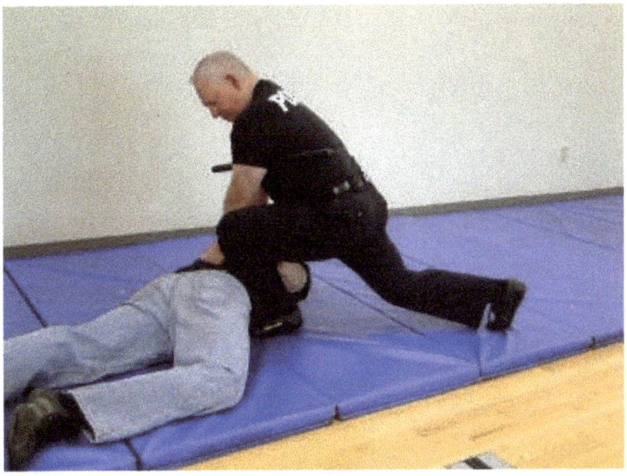

34U

Figure 33U. Make sure your left foot is at his waist under his stomach as you come down with his arm.

Figure 34U. When the attacker's arm is laid across his back, your left knee bends and kneels on the attacker's back below his elbow and arm to prevent the arm from being pushed down. At the same time, your right leg is extended back.

35U

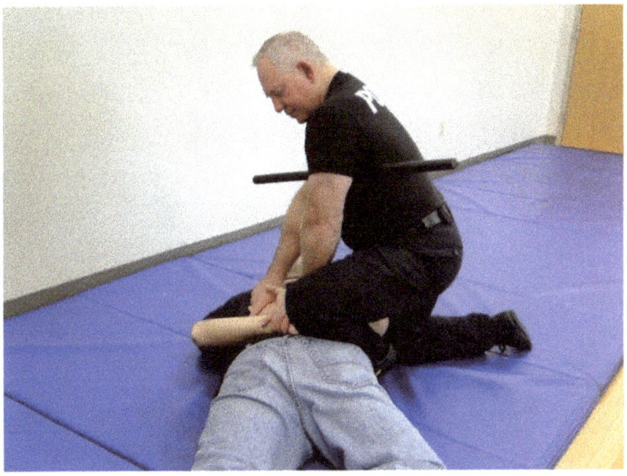

35U

Figure 35U. The right knee is brought forward striking the back of the attacker's right arm. This will secure the arm from being pulled out. The other reason for the strike to the back of his arm is to push the attacker's arm further across the back, giving you extra room to handcuff the other arm when it is brought back. With the attacker's arm in the position where both of your knees are blocking his arm from moving down and out, this will actually give you freedom to move both hands.

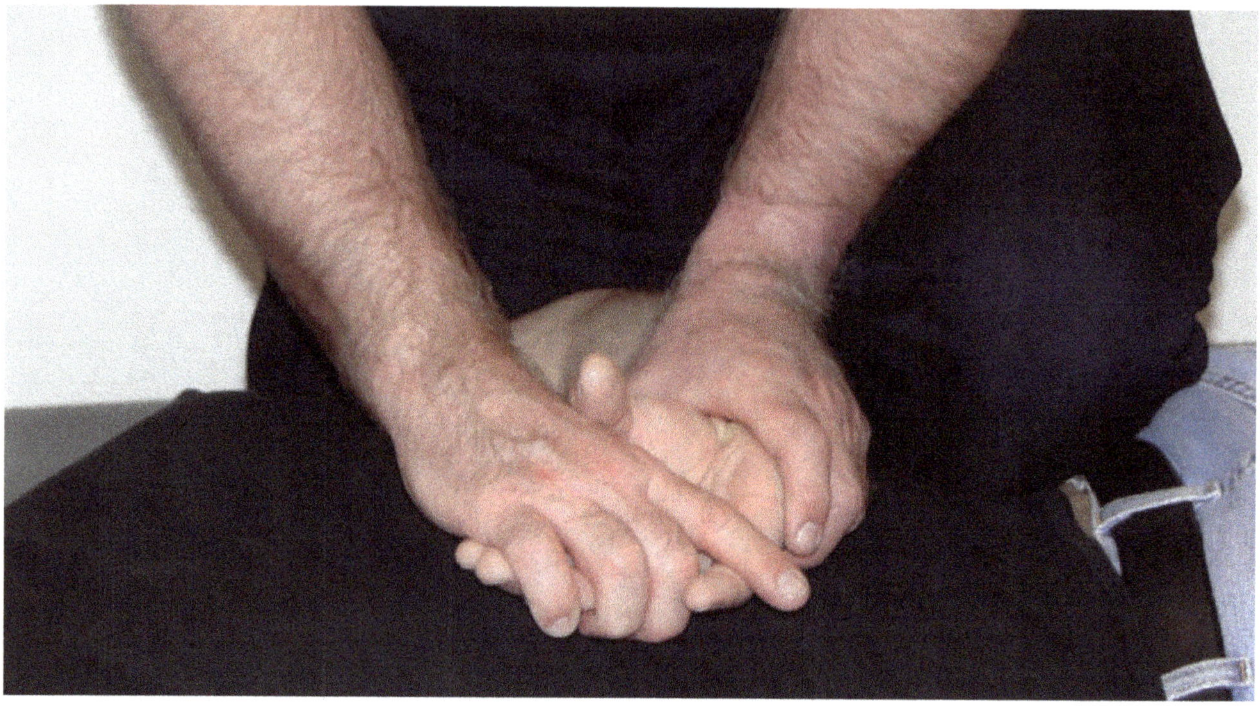

36U

Figure 36U. This is a close up of the grip while the actor's hand is on his back. When asking the attacker for his other hand to handcuff, keep the back of his wrist flat. Your grip on his fingers now turns to the side for compliance of your prisoner. This will make him willing to give you his other hand whether or not he may be laying on it. **He will find a way to get it to you**.

37U

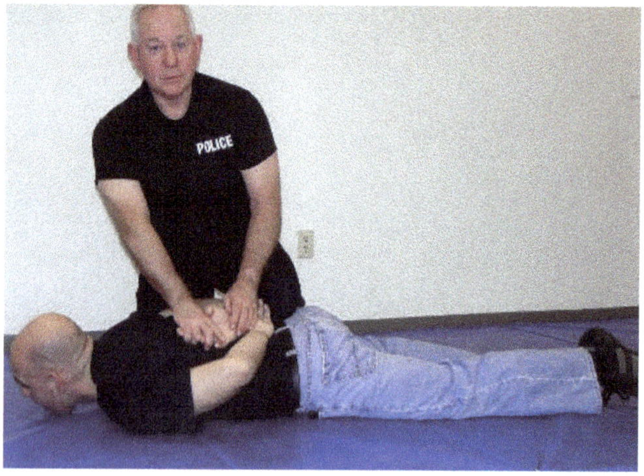

38U

Figures 37U and 38U. Keeping the attacker's wrist flat on his back and turning the fingers to your right side, will make your attacker cooperate right away when you ask for his left hand to be placed on his back.

YOKE TRAP
HITCHHIKER SPIN
LEFT HAND OVERHEAD BLOW

1V

2V

Figure 1V. Standing at a right natural stance, the attacker swings with a left handed overhead blow with a baton.

Figure 2V. First step inside the line of danger with your right foot. This will decrease the distance, the angle of the swing, and the power of the blow with the weapon. Extend your arms upward to get control of the swinging arm. Your right arm reaches to the outside of the swinging arm and your left hand to the inside.

3V

Figure 3V. The right hand makes contact with the attacker's arm first. Redirect the swing to the inside, and into your left hand. This first contact with the attacker's arm is the most important to take the attacker off the line in his attack. Your left hand is in a short waiting stage, but still extended until your right hand and left hand meet. As the right hand is directing the swing to a position in front of you, it is also positioning its grip around his wrist.

4V

5V

Figure 4V. When your hands meet around the attacker's wrist in front of you, keep the momentum of the swing moving. Take a step back with your left foot as you pull forward with both hands. This will extend his swing forward pulling him slightly off balance as well as off target.

Figure 5V. When you have pulled his arm into a fully extended position, take a large step in front of him. Both of your hands should have positioned themselves to the Hitchhiker position on the attacker's hand with the weapon.

6V

7V

Figure 6V. After taking the step with your left foot in front of the attacker, your hand position on the attacker's hand should push his wrist forward locking it down.

Figure 7V. Now, bring the attacker's hand back to your right, keeping the wrist locked down and forward. As you bring his hand back to your right, turn your body back to the right side as you step back with your right foot. Your step back needs to be a step of 160 to 180 degree back. Turning your body as you step back, allows your body to turn his wrist without having to use just arm strength.

8V

9V

Figure 8V. Bringing the attacker's wrist back to the locked position starts to break the attacker down. When the his wrist stops, the attacker's elbow turns into his body, and the shoulder will drop as his body weight will shift to his left side over his left hip and locking it out.

Figure 9V. When the attacker's body breaks down he will fall to his left side. Remember keeping the tension on his arm will keep his shoulder forward as he falls to his side.

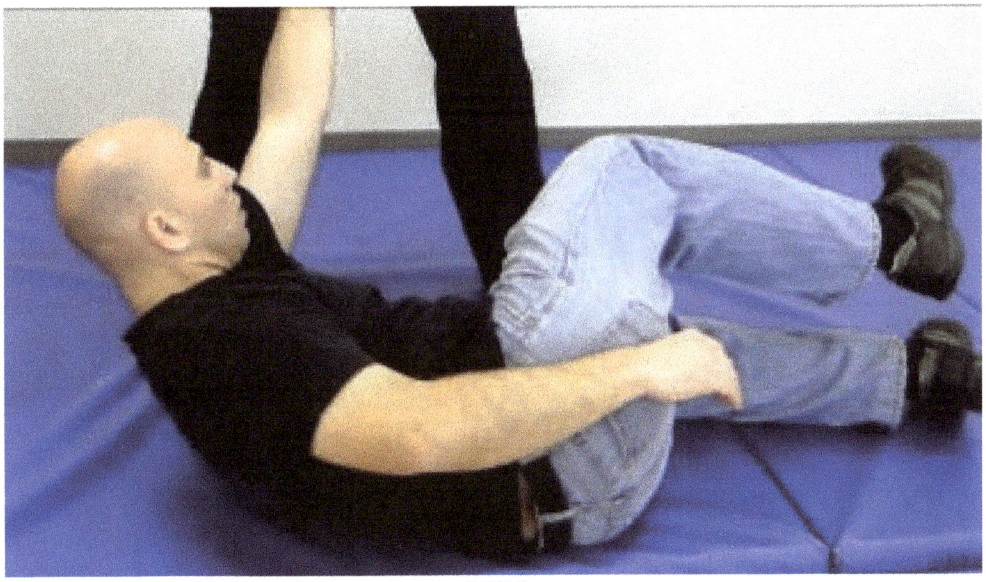

10V

Figure 10V. When the attacker's hip touches the ground, as said before, it is the most crucial point of the spin. This is the point where the attacker's weight has come off his feet and shifted to his hip. At this point, there is a pivot point that need to be taken advantage of at that second. The pull comes as you take a step toward the attacker's feet. This will allow you a good base to have a hard pull on the attacker's arm in the direction of his feet.

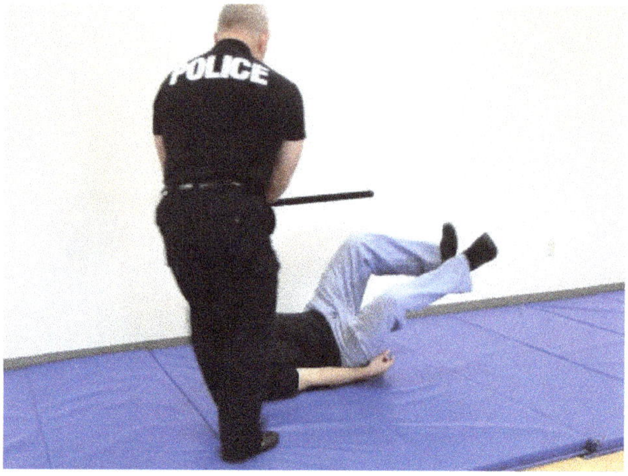

11V 12V

Figure 11V. With the hard pull toward the attacker's feet, this will send him into a spin from his hip which gives him a feeling of confusion. The confusion comes from the semicircular canals in the ear. The first reaction that he feels is the falling to the side. Then, as you pull on his arm, he spins clockwise and halfway through the spin, his body turns over as he is still spinning. His body turns completely around and completely over.

Figure 12V. At the end of the spin, his body will come to a rest in front of you, with his left arm extended up behind him. At this point, you still have control with the wrist locked and the arm locked up behind him.

13V 14V

Figure 13V. To lock out the attacker's shoulder, step in with your left foot, placing your toes under the attacker's shoulder while keeping the his arm straight and extended up behind him. Your left knee is bent slightly, and the attacker's arm is pulled back tightly for control. The wrist with the weapon is locked forward.

Figure 14V. Keep control over his arm while removing the baton from his hand. Use the right hand on his wrist and remove the baton with your left hand, and place it under your right arm for control.

15V 16V

Figure 15V. Regain control over the attacker's arm with both hands. Place your left hand just below the wrist while continuing the pressure on his elbow, by pushing you knee forward keeping the elbow tight.

Figure 16V. Release the right hand grip and slide it over the palm of his hand. This will open his hand so that the fingers will be pointing toward his feet. Your left hand will reposition so that your index finger will be right at the bend of his wrist. Your thumb of your left hand will move over the top of his thumb to the palm of the attacker's hand.

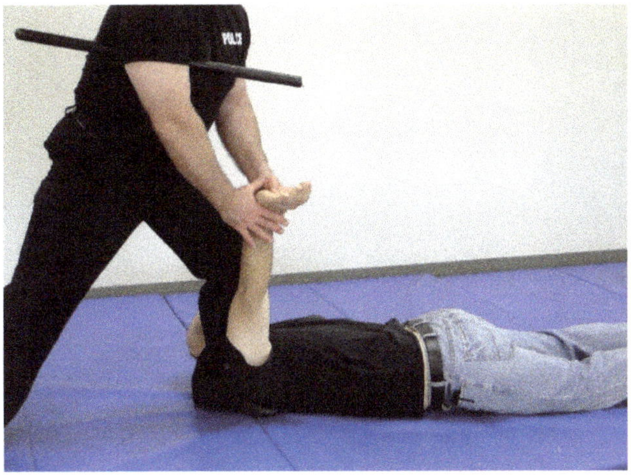

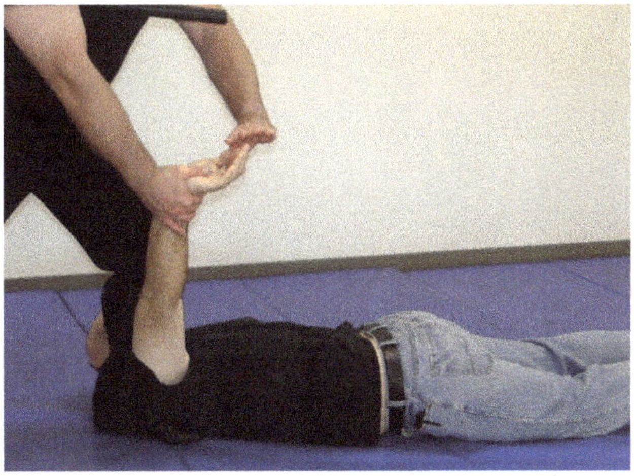

17V 18V

Figure 17V. Bring your right hand back to the attacker's wrist. Grip it so the index finger is at the bend of the wrist, and the thumb is across the heel portion of his hand onto the palm area.

Figure 18V. The left hand is released and turned inward with the palm down. This will allow you to position your hand to reach your fingers across the palm of the attacker's hand while his hand is in the open position. The grip with your right hand is tight. Keep the tension pulled back on his arm and, also, keep the attacker's palm open by applying pressure down with your thumb.

19V

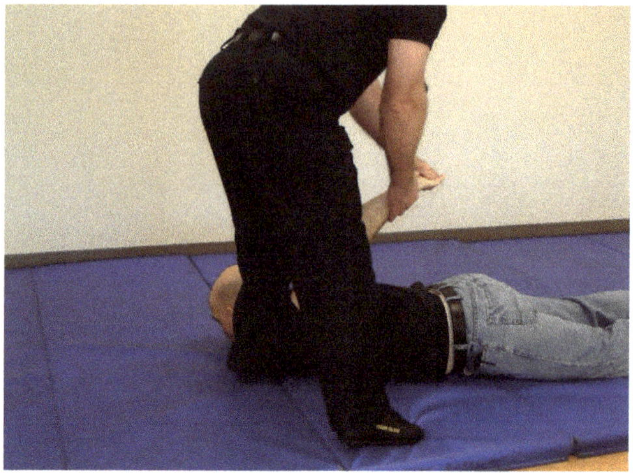

20V

Figure 19V. Reach across the attacker's hand pressing the web portion of your hand tightly against the web portion of his hand. Your grip may be three or four fingers depending on the size of your hand or his.

Figure 20V. Turn your left hand in a circular motion down and across the attacker's back, giving support with your right hand under his wrist as you go down. At the same time, you are moving the his arm down to his back, you need to step around with your right foot toward his waistline.

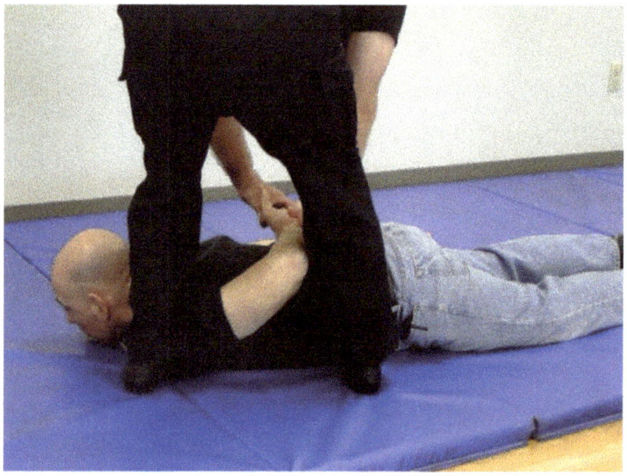

21V

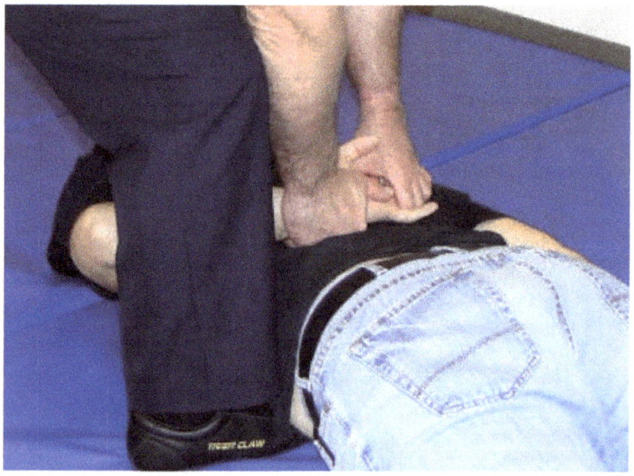

22V

Figure 21V. Allow the attacker's arm to bend at the elbow until it comes to a rest on his back. By this time, your right foot should be at his waist and your toes pushed under his body.

Figure 22V. When the attacker's arm is placed on his back, press down to keep it on his back as you are moving. Keep his hand and wrist in a flat position on his back, not allowing him to bend his wrist back. Your right hand will assist in keeping it flat by lifting up slightly on his wrist, as you press on the finger area.

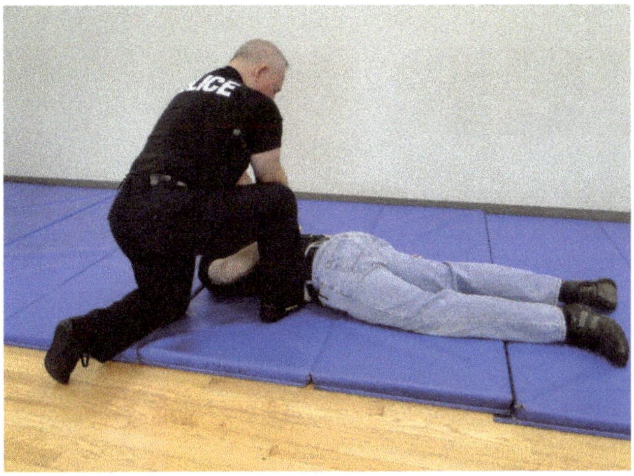

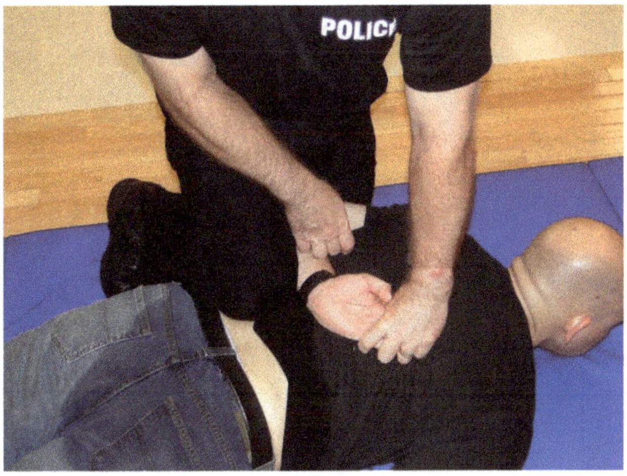

23V 24V

Figure 23V. Bring your left leg back as your squat down along side of him.

Figure 24V. Bring your right knee down across the attacker's lower back below his arm, to secure it from being pushed down toward his feet. Then bring your left leg forward against the his elbow, which will push his arm across his back. This will allow the attacker's arm to be as tight as it can be, giving you less distance to handcuff his other arm when it is brought up.

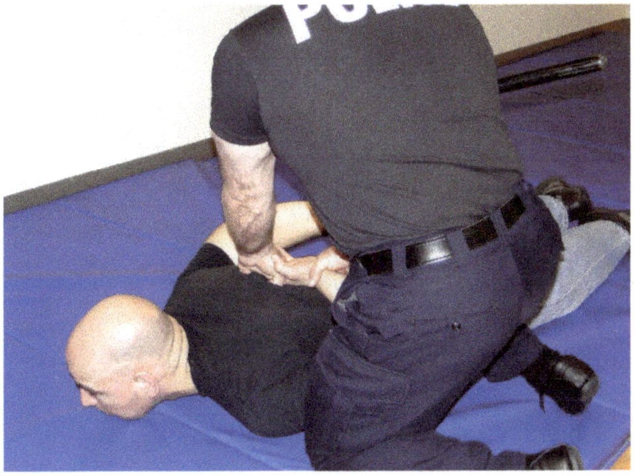

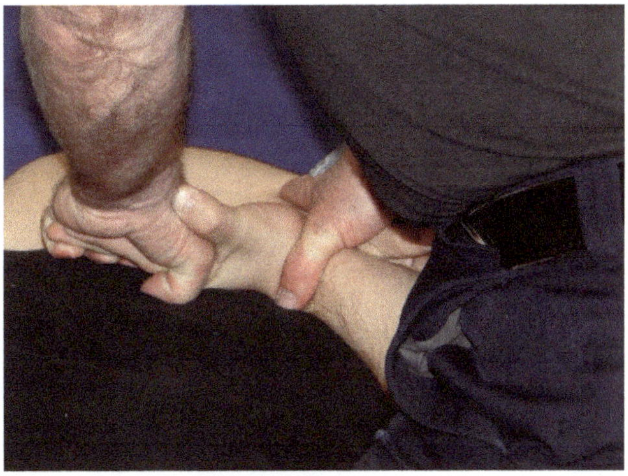

25V 26V

Figure 25V. The attacker's arm is secured with your knees, at the bottom and at the elbow area. The his wrist needs to be flat on his back so as to not bend the wrist back. Your grip is tight and deep into his hand on his fingers. The fingers of your right hand support his wrist from underneath, keeping it from bending.

Figure 26V. If the attacker does not comply when telling him you want the other arm, the need to apply some pressure may be needed. The pressure is applied with your left hand by turning the his fingers to the side. Remember not much pressure will be needed to make him comply, so **be careful when applying the turning motion so as not to injure your prisoner.**

CHAPTER 10

Yoke Trap to Hitchhiker Spin

YOKE TRAP into the HITCHHIKER SPIN

From Right Punch to the Face

1W

2W

Figure 1W. Using a Yoke Trap is a fast reaction move to what could have been a "sucker punch" by an attacker. Stand in a left natural stance or as an officer, an interview stance, when the attacker makes a move to punch you in the face.

Figure 2W. Your response requires several things to react at the same time. Once you have recognized the attacker's movement to swing, your hands need to be brought up in the yoke position. This is bringing your hands together one over the top of the other. Opening your hands so the thumbs cross over each other, one hand inside and the other on top of it. The tips of your thumbs are placed so they are at the base of the index finger on each side. This should allow the web portion of the hand, between the thumb and the index finger, to match, forming one "v" shape web between your hands. The hands are brought up to catch the attacker's arm and redirect the punch past you without stopping the momentum. As the hands are being brought up, you should make a small step inside the line of danger with your left foot. This step will be to the outside of the attacker's right foot slightly, and also will be turning your body back to your right side. Going back to the first part of the basic movements that need to be practiced, the centering circles are one of the most important. The movement of stepping with one foot and turning your body should almost be instinctive by now, and that is exactly what is done at this time.

3W

4W

Figure 3W. When your hands make contact with the attacker's arm, your hands guide the momentum of the punch, as they slide down his arm to the Hitchhiker position on the attacker's hand. When your hands get to the attacker's wrist, they should add an extra push to the his swing which will bring him forward and off balance. This is such a fast response, there is no need to continue the centering circle with your right foot.

Figure 4W. Now bring his hand back toward him in the Hitchhiker position by turning your torso back to the left. Place pressure forward on his wrist as it is brought back around.

5W

6W

Figure 5W. Pressing the actor's wrist down and forward, by the time you have brought his hand in front of you he will be locked out and his balance will start breaking down.

Figure 6W. To continue with the Hitchhiker movement your left foot is brought back, as his shoulder drops and his weight shifts over his right hip to lock it out.

7W

8W

Figures 7W and 8W. Continue pressing his wrist back and down to break his balance as it is brought across to your left side. Once his weight has shifted over his right hip, the hip will lockout, and he will have no choice but to turn to his right side. With you still controlling his hand and arm, he will turn his hip to the ground just before he falls.

9W

10W

Figure 9W. Be prepared for his weight to shift and the "pulling forward" with his right arm. The "pulling forward" with his arm is an automatic reflex for him to fall to his side. Keep the tension on his arm to keep his shoulder out of play and watch for his hip to touch the ground.

Figure 10W. Watch for the attacker's hip to touch the ground. Keep his arm forward and a good tight grip on the attacker's hand. Shift your weight toward your right, stepping toward his feet, and give the attacker's arm a hard pull back in the direction of his own feet. At that precise second, his weight is balanced on his right hip. This pull will start the attacker to spin back toward you.

11W 12W

Figures 11W and 12W. When you make your hard pull, the spin will turn him counterclockwise, and also start his body rolling back to his left side as soon as his head gets in front of you. **Remember in practice, on a mat, your partner turns slow compared to an attacker on a hard surface such as the hard ground, asphalt, or concrete.**

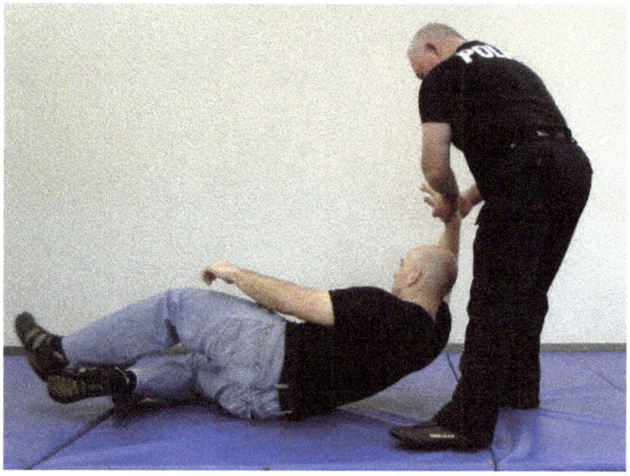

13W 14W

Figure 13W. Follow through with your pull back, to your right side, so you are able to get the spin necessary for his body to make it all the way around. Your stance throughout the pull remains wide for your balance.

Figure 14W. When his head reaches the point that it is in front of you, you need to regain your center by bringing his hand back to your centerline. Shift your weight back to the center as well. This shift will not stop the spin of his body in the direction his feet are moving. By only bringing his arm up to your center and stopping there at this time, this will cause the action for him to turn over his left shoulder onto his stomach. The fall to his right side in the takedown, the spin of his body, and the turning of him over onto his stomach, causes a him confusion.

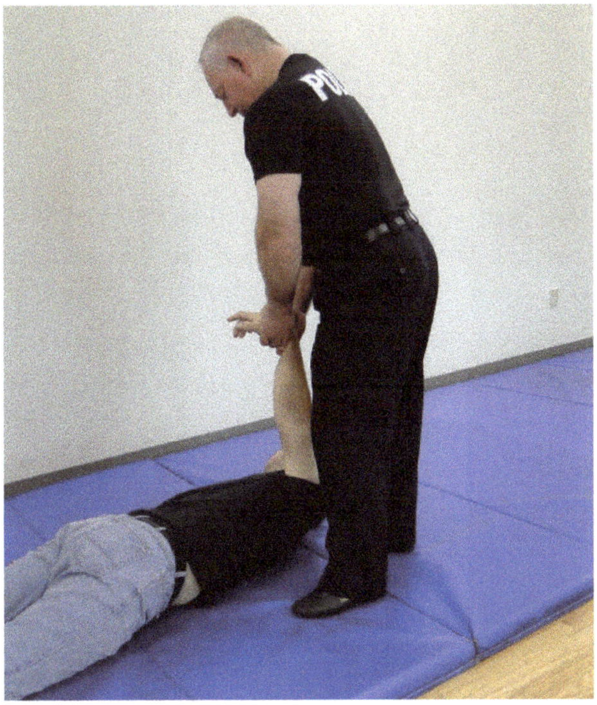

15W

Figure 15W. As the spin comes to a stop, the attacker should have stopped right in front of you on his stomach in a controlled position face down. The attacker's arm is locked at the wrist, as well as, elbow and shoulder.

The control of the attacker in this position is based on you placing his shoulder on the ground. If his shoulder is up and **not flat on the ground**, the control is not complete. The attacker may have an opportunity to pull down with his arm if it has any bend in it at all. If by chance, he was unable to bring his left arm out from under him during the spin, and you do not have his shoulder to the ground, there is a possibility he could roll back and reach your foot with his left hand. So complete the move all the way to handcuffing position.

DON'T STOP UNTILL YOU HAVE WON

BE SAFE OUT THERE
GOD BLESS YOU ALL

CLOSING

Take care of each other out there. Your brother officer is the one you should be able to depend on, to back you, and to cover you. Our police agencies should coincide with each other. We are the few that people depend upon in a crisis. Some people have lost sight of our value on the streets. Despite this, it is our duty to be honorable, ethical, and forthcoming in the public eye. It goes a long way in our communities.

With this job, there comes constant scrutiny for every word you say and every action you do. In the age of video technology and watchful communities, doing our job has become more stressful. Do not be part of the few that can give the perception of police as the "bad guy". Be the one that stands out in his/her field and that can never be swayed. Be the one to go to for police officers and civilians alike. Remember, we are doing a job that a majority of people would not want to do. You are in an honored profession, and it is your duty to do it proudly.

It has been a real pleasure to write this book, as well as, to teach these classes for the many police agencies out there. I would be honored to provide this course to any police agency interested in learning these techniques.

Sincere thanks and God Speed.

Gary G. Albrecht

www.ingramcontent.com/pod-product-compliance
Lightning Source LLC
Chambersburg PA
CBHW040311240426
43666CB00025B/2931
* 9 7 8 0 9 8 6 1 0 7 1 1 5 *